Sunset

YOU CAN BUILD

Masonry

by Steve Cory
and the Editors of
Sunset Books

© 2010 by Sunset Publishing Corporation
80 Willow Road, Menlo Park, CA 94025

ISBN-13: 978-0-376-01598-3
ISBN-10: 0-376-01598-5
Library of Congress Control Number: 2008932439

10 9 8 7 6 5 4 3 2 1
First Printing January 2010
Printed in the United States of America

Oxmoor House, Inc.
VP, Publishing Director: Jim Childs
Editorial Director: Susan Payne Dobbs
Brand Manager: Fonda Hitchcock
Managing Editor: L. Amanda Owens
Project Editors: Emily Chappell, Vanessa Lynn Rusch

You Can Build: Masonry
Contributors
Author: Steve Cory
Managing Editor: Bob Doyle
Editor: Ben Marks
Design & Production: Hespenheide Design—
    Gary Hespenheide, Randy Miyake
Prepress Coordinator: Eligio Hernández
Copy Editor: John Edmonds
Proofreader: Jennifer Block Martin
Interns: Natalie Heard, Allison Sperando,
    Christine Taylor
Indexer: Marjorie Joy
Series Designer: Vasken Guiragossian
Front cover photography by Mark Rutherford,
    styling by JoAnn Masaoka Van Atta

To order additional publications, call 1-800-765-6400
For more books to enrich your life,
    visit **oxmoorhouse.com**
Visit Sunset online at **sunset.com**
For the most comprehensive selection of Sunset books,
    visit **sunsetbooks.com**
For more exciting home and garden ideas, visit
    myhomeideas.com

Note to readers: Almost any do-it-yourself project
involves risk of some sort. Your tools, materials, and
skills will vary, as will conditions at your project site.
Sunset Publishing Corporation and the editors of this
book have made every effort to be complete and accurate in the instructions. We will, however, assume no
responsibility or liability for injuries, damages, or losses
incurred in the course of your home improvement or
repair projects. Always follow the manufacturer's oper-
ating instructions in the use of tools, check and follow
your local building codes, and observe all standard
safety precautions.

How to Use This Book

You Can Build: Masonry is organized by chapters, of course, but we have also created a number of repeating features designed to help you successfully and safely complete your masonry project.

 ### Skill Level Required

Many masonry projects are Easy, but some are Moderate and a few are downright Challenging. The actual Degree of Difficulty will depend on your experience and skills.

 ### Shopping Guides

In some cases, you can use the information in these boxes as the basis for your shopping list before you head off to the home improvement center. In other cases we offer tips and advice to help you shop smart.

 ### What It Will Take

As with the Degree of Difficulty, the time it takes to complete a masonry project will vary with your skill level and experience, but this should help you plan for a quick masonry project that can be completed in under an hour or a weekend-long one.

 ### Preparation Help

Having the tools you need on hand before you begin a project saves multiple trips to the home improvement center, so give this box a quick glance before you begin your project.

 ### For More Info

To save you a trip to the Index, we've placed Related Topics boxes on many pages in *You Can Build: Masonry*. You may want to consult these pages before you begin a project, just in case your masonry job is a bit of a hybrid.

Contents

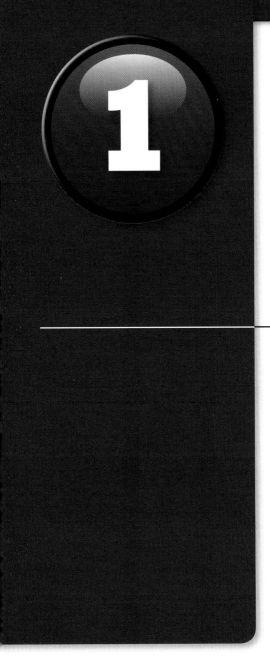

1

Designing & Prepping

In this chapter, you'll learn how to get ready for your home masonry project, whether It's a path, patlo, or wall. We show you how to choose materials such as brick, flagstone, ashlar, tile, and concrete, from pavers to blocks. You'll also find out the differences between pebbles and gravel, and we'll give you the basic dimensions for some of the most common patio configurations.

Chapter Contents

Tile
page 22

**Other
Materials**
page 24

**Landscape
Design**
page 26

**Drawing
a Plan**
page 30

**Planning
Drainage**
page 32

**Working with
Professionals**
page 36

Imagining the Possibilities

When designing your outdoor space, consider a range of possibilities. You can always narrow down your ideas later. Even if you can't do all the work now, form a complete plan, which may include patios, paths, walls, raised beds, and perhaps an outdoor kitchen.

Layouts that Work

An outdoor setting should not only look great, it should also suit your needs and be comfortable to live in. A good layout avoids bottlenecks and offers ample space for the activities that are most important to you. Plan comfortably sized spaces for dining, cooking, entertaining, and lounging. Allow for pathways at least 3 feet wide that connect the various activity centers. Even gardening can be made more convenient with planters positioned at a comfortable working height. A functional layout is often an attractive layout, because it exudes a comfortable, lived-in ambience.

Floors & Walkways

A patio is a masonry surface that provides a smooth and natural transition between house and yard. Patios and masonry paths made of natural or natural-looking materials will harmonize with most foliage. Outdoor floors are not expected to be pristine, so it's fine to use rough materials with loose joints—for example, flagstone with irregular joints filled with soil and crevice plants. For a stately look, install bricks, concrete pavers, or tiles.

Going Vertical

Even if only a few feet tall, a structure that projects upward can catch the eye more than a patio or path. A short section of wall, a raised bed, or several planters can create an appealing frame for your yard and help define various activity centers. A retaining wall usually leans back, or "batters," into the soil it retains, while a garden wall rises straight up.

Most any masonry material—concrete blocks, bricks, natural stone, and even broken chunks of used concrete—can be either mortared together or stacked dry. When designing a vertical element, include plants in the plan, both nearby shrubs and flowers, as well as smaller crevice plants that thrive in nooks and crannies. A masonry wall often looks better when partially covered with foliage.

Focal Points

Often it's not the main patio or the walls that make a yard memorable; it's the little creative touches. Small decorative elements can have a large visual impact. For instance, add a touch of whimsy by making your own steppingstones, planters, or birdbaths. It may take only a trip to an outdoor supply center or resale shop and an hour or less of easy labor to add just the right touch.

Shopping for Materials

The success of a home improvement project often hinges on your choosing the right materials, and this is especially true with masonry projects. Don't just pick the type of brick or stone; examine the pieces to be sure you get the colors and shapes you want.

Finding Good Sources

Your local home center probably carries a selection of blocks, pavers, gravel, and mortar. You may also be able to order bricks and flagstones from the same store. For a better selection of paving and building materials, excluding tile, visit a dedicated masonry supply yard, sometimes called a stone yard or brickyard. There you will likely find both indoor and outdoor displays and large outdoor bins containing masonry materials in many colors, sizes, shapes, and prices. A masonry supply yard may also be the best place for buying substrate materials such as mortar, compactible gravel, and stone screenings (sand).

While masonry supply yards cater mostly to professional masons, their employees should be able to work with homeowners. If a salesperson does not give you the information you need, speak to another salesperson or go to another yard. You should feel free to wander around the yard and look at all the possibilities.

Buying Natural Stone

Getting the right number of stones is a matter of estimating. Even pros often end up with too few or too many. For a flagstone patio, figure the square footage you want to cover and then choose the type of stone you want. For a wall, measure the length and height. A salesperson will use your figures to estimate how many pounds or tons of material you will need. Poundage varies greatly depending on the thickness and type of stone you choose.

Flagstones, cobblestones, rubble, and ashlar (see pages 14–15) are often sold in large pallets weighing a ton or so. The stones on the pallet may be wrapped in plastic sheets, wire mesh, or both. Take a good look at the stones in a pallet so you get the color and sizes, and the variation in color and sizes, that you desire. Often two pallets of the same type of stone can vary greatly in appearance and size.

Small stones are usually displayed for sale on pallets.

Buying Bricks, Pavers & Blocks

Natural bricks, concrete pavers, and concrete blocks are sold by the unit rather than by weight. See pages 16–19 for the types. Consult a salesperson to be sure the units you choose will be durable in your area and for your purposes. For example, some bricks may be durable when used for a wall but are prone to cracking if used on a patio.

Delivery Methods

If you need only a small amount of stone, you can carry it into the store and weigh it on a scale. For medium-sized loads that you can haul in your vehicle, the store's staff will weigh your van or truck when it's empty, then again after you load it with stone, and charge you for the difference. For purchases of half a ton or more, browse through the yard and choose a pallet or two full of stones for the yard to deliver.

Ask the staff detailed questions about delivery methods and arrange for the delivery truck to drop heavy materials as close to your site as possible, without damaging your lawn or property. Keep these considerations in mind:

Large stones that are meant to be focal points in a landscape are sold individually.

- If possible, have any gravel and/or screenings (sand) dropped directly into the excavated site. If you need to have it unloaded on a nearby lawn or driveway, first spread heavy-gauge plastic, then lay sheets of plywood for the materials to rest on. Make sure the material does not stay on a lawn for more than a few days, or the grass may die.
- Be sure a load of stones or bricks is not dropped onto your driveway. A one-ton pallet can safely rest on a driveway as long as it is set down gently. If it is dropped from the truck, as often happens, the driveway will likely crack.
- If you need several types of material—for instance, gravel, screenings, and pavers for a dry-laid patio—plan the deliveries carefully. It is probably worthwhile to pay for separate deliveries if having all the materials delivered at once means the pavers will end up inconveniently far from the site.

Natural Stone

For walks, walls, and patio floors, no material is more beautiful than natural stone. Limestone, marble, sandstone, granite, and bluestone are available in a large array of colors and textures, and all look great next to foliage or a wooden structure.

Flagstone

Flagstone is not a specific type of stone but rather a general term for large, flat stones that are 1 to 4 inches thick. Most flagstone is sedimentary rock, which formed in layers and therefore splits into relatively flat pieces. Common types include sandstone, slate, quartzite, and limestone. Porous stone, especially sandstone, is likely to become covered with slippery moss if you use it in a shady spot in a damp climate. Flagstone is usually sold as paving and has a split surface that provides good traction. The relatively uniform thickness also makes it useful for short walls, capstones, and veneer.

Flagstones

Cobblestone

Often made of granite, cobblestones (or cobbles) are roughly cut into squares or rectangles. Some are cubes 4 or 5 inches on each side, while others are more like jumbo bricks up to 12 inches long. Though they are not as regular in shape as tile or even ashlar, they can be wedged together to form stable paving or edging.

Cobblestones

Stone for Walls

A supplier may list a large variety of wall-stone categories, but basically three types of stone are available: rubble, semidressed stone, and ashlar.

RUBBLE

Also called fieldstone, boulders, or river rock, rubble is uncut stone, usually with rounded rather than sharp edges. It is inexpensive but difficult to stack into a stable structure. Use rubble for accents or for a low retaining wall. Building a freestanding rubble wall is painstaking work and calls for plenty of skill.

Rubble (fieldstone)

SEMIDRESSED STONE

Semidressed stone is roughly shaped, at least on two sides. It can be stacked to form a stable wall, though you will need to spend lots of time experimenting and testing various arrangements as you stack. This can be difficult work, especially if the stones are heavy.

Semidressed Stone

ASHLAR

Ashlar is fully trimmed, so it is nearly as easy to lay as brick. The ashlar shown below left is all the same thickness. Some ashlar comes in varying thicknesses. In a coursed ashlar design, each course is composed of stones that are the same thickness. A random or combination ashlar wall (below) combines stones of various thicknesses in patterns that resemble a patchwork quilt.

Ashlar

Veneer Stone

Most veneer stone is actually a manufactured product, typically made of portland cement and a lightweight aggregate such as pumice. These materials have a surprisingly natural look and are easy to work with and reliable in color. Less commonly, natural stone is sometimes cut to make veneer stone. Veneer is usually 1 inch thick or less, making it light enough to be mortared directly onto a block wall, much like tile. Thicker stones may need a separate foundation and/or metal angle irons for support. Many types have special corner pieces, which produce the illusion of much thicker stones.

Veneers

Brick

Brick has a timeless beauty, with baked-in color that will never fade. Many patterns are possible, and building with brick is not physically taxing, as each piece fits comfortably in one hand. Brickyards offer a wide variety of wall and paving bricks.

Brick Strengths

Bricks are formed from clay or shale and then heated in a kiln. The higher the temperature, the less porous the bricks become. In a cold climate, freezing and expanding water can cause bricks to crack or crumble, so the less porous a brick is, the greater its resistance to cracking. You can use bricks rated SX or SW (for severe weathering) anywhere. Use MX or MW bricks (for moderate weathering) only in warm climates or possibly for walls in areas where temperatures dip below freezing only occasionally. Bricks rated NW (negligible weathering) are for interior use only. There is no downside to using SW bricks for all applications, so many manufacturers simplify by selling only these. Your local building inspector can tell you what's required in your area.

Paving Bricks

Bricks used for paving are always solid. Standard-size bricks are sold by their actual dimensions, usually 4 × 8 × 2¼ inches. Use them for paving where pieces have only about ⅛ inch of sand between joints. They're also good edging pieces for paths or patios. If you intend to use mortar between joints, buy modular-size bricks, which are typically 3⅝ × 7⅝ inches, so you can have ⅜-inch-wide mortar joints and still get patterns to line up correctly. These bricks feature slightly rounded, or chamfered, edges, which add slip resistance and allow water to drain better. The one pictured has a white surface coating. Most traditional patterns are based on the assumption that a brick's width, or effective width including mortar, is half its length.

Standard and modular paving bricks

Concrete bricks

Faux used brick

Thin faux bricks

Used Bricks

Used bricks, which often have bits of mortar stuck to the surface, add a pleasant rustic look to garden projects. But be careful, as some used bricks weren't made to be out in the weather, particularly as paving. Mortar bits on all faces are clues that bricks were inside a wall and are probably not strong enough to be used for paving. But if the bricks served as paving in your part of the country and stayed intact, they will work well. You can also find new brick that's been tumbled and splashed with white and black paint to resemble used brick. This type comes with a weather rating.

Concrete Bricks

These are made of durable concrete but are tinted and molded to look like clay bricks. They cost less and can be used in the same ways as clay-based bricks. You can also buy concrete bricks colored to look like used common bricks, as well as thin faux bricks. However, clay bricks retain their color, while concrete bricks may fade in time.

3- and 10-hole bricks

Wall Bricks

Wall bricks may be solid or cored, with several holes in the center. The holes cut down on weight and raw materials, but their main purpose is to ensure stronger walls. The mortar between layers oozes up and down into the holes, helping to lock the pieces together. In walls, use solid bricks only for the top course, or for low garden walls or planters that don't need much strength. Wall bricks are sold only in modular dimensions, as walls always need mortar.

Wire-cut and facing brick

A wall brick's facing surface (the side you will see) may be smooth or decoratively rough. A wire-cut brick like the one at bottom center has closely spaced vertical lines.

Brick Veneer

Brick veneer is a type of thin brick designed to be added to walls built of concrete block, poured concrete, or even wood. Unlike the thin bricks made for paving, veneer pieces are cut to expose the side dimension so the finished wall looks as if it were built of solid brick. Some manufacturers make special corner pieces that hide the thin edge of the veneer.

Brick veneer

Concrete Pavers

Concrete pavers are modular units tinted in various colors. The manufacturing process results in concrete that's especially dense and frost-resistant, making concrete pavers suitable for any climate.

A Wide Variety

Some pavers are shaped and tinted to resemble brick (see page 17), but they come in many other sizes and shapes. Large pavers, which make attractive steppingstones, may be rectangular, round, or hexagonal. Some have an exposed-aggregate surface, while others are fairly smooth.

INTERLOCKING PAVERS

Interlocking pavers have special shapes designed to fit together like pieces of a jigsaw puzzle. However, simple rectangular pavers form a surface that is just as stable, so choose interlocking pavers only if you like the pattern.

Interlocking pavers

PAVER ENSEMBLES

Many pavers are available in collections that you can use to create circular or fan-shaped patterns reminiscent of European patios and walkways. Although it's possible to create these patterns with standard rectangular pavers or genuine cobblestones, using the ensembles saves you from cutting numerous pieces. You can also buy concrete cobblestones already attached to nylon mesh in circular, fanned, or straight patterns, making installation a breeze.

Concrete pavers are sold in many shapes and styles.

STONE-LOOK PAVERS

Some concrete pavers have rough textures and mottled colors to closely resemble natural stone. These can be used as steppingstones.

Stone-look paver

CONCRETE COBBLESTONES

These simulate the look of weathered stone. Manufacturers tumble the pieces to give them rounded edges, and they usually sell a mixture of shades, to produce a natural-looking surface.

Concrete Choices

Concrete blocks, usually but not always assembled with mortar, offer a quick way to build a wall. Inexpensive and long-lasting, poured concrete is one of the most popular options for patios and walkways.

Concrete Blocks

Concrete blocks are often wrongly referred to as cinder blocks. Most commonly, they are stacked with mortar joints between them, much like wall bricks. Manufacturers list standard blocks according to nominal dimensions—8 inches high by 8 inches wide by 16 inches long. Pieces are actually ⅜ inch smaller in each dimension to allow for mortar space. They can also be purchased as half blocks, corner pieces, and special shapes for use around windows and doors. These might come in handy for garden walls where you want to add a gate.

STANDARD BLOCKS

Standard stretcher blocks typically have two large holes, or cells, that you can leave open or fill with mortar for extra strength. The holes also make it easy to add metal reinforcement where needed. At corners, you can use a half block or cut a full stretcher yourself.

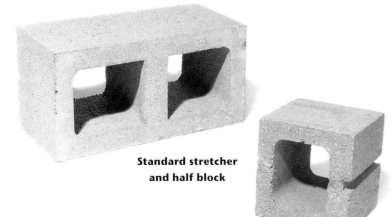

Standard stretcher and half block

DECORATIVE BLOCKS

Concrete building blocks are available with various decorative faces. Split-face blocks have a textured face with a vertical groove. You can also buy blocks with a stone-like face.

Split-face block

GRILLE BLOCKS

Screen or grille blocks form patterned walls that admit light and air while providing some privacy. They are only 3 inches thick and must be laid in a single wythe—meaning the wall can be only one block thick—so they should be reinforced with pillars at least every 8 feet.

Grille block

Stackable Retaining Blocks

These interlock without mortar to form a wall solid enough to keep a slope or a garden bed firmly in place. The blocks are easy to install and are widely available. They may be rectangular for straight walls or trapezoidal for curves. You don't need a poured foundation, just a gravel base and gravel backfill so any water behind the wall can drain out. Once you have excavated for the base, stacking the blocks will likely take only a few hours.

The blocks are designed to automatically batter, or slope, the retaining wall toward the soil it is retaining. Check with your building department, because there may be special rules for even low retaining walls. Also check the manufacturer's specifications. Some styles can be used for walls up to 4 feet high, but height limits vary. If you want to tuck plants into the wall, get blocks that are hollow in the center.

Another type of concrete block interlocks, so you can dry-stack the blocks on top of each other to form a firm wall. Then apply a stucco-like surface-bonding cement to both sides of the wall for extra strength.

Stackable retaining blocks

Poured Concrete

Concrete is a mixture of portland cement, water, and aggregate (usually a combination of sand and gravel, though sometimes only sand or only gravel). Cement, the smallest component, glues the stone bits together.

COLOR

Concrete can be tinted in several ways. When pigment is mixed in with the other ingredients, it's known as integral color. If an edge chips, you'll see that the underlying concrete is the same color as the surface. There's no extra labor involved, but you pay for the pigment. Broadcast color is tossed into and troweled into freshly poured concrete, so the color is only near the surface. You can use several colors and wind up with interesting mottled effects. It's also possible to combine the two approaches and wind up with concrete that is one basic color throughout but has streaks or swirls of another color on the surface. A third approach involves applying a decorative stain after the concrete hardens. One kind, known as acid stain, reacts with ingredients in the concrete and permanently changes the color of the material near the surface.

TEXTURE

A concrete slab can be smooth, or you can texturize it to add interest and make it less slippery. Although it's possible to cut patterns with a grinder or saw after concrete stiffens, textures are easier to create when the mix is still somewhat plastic. You can create a broomed surface, which has a series of straight or curved lines, by dragging bristles across the surface. With a brick jointer or other simple tool, you can outline flagstone shapes and simulate the look of grout lines between stones. And there are

Exposed-aggregate concrete

stamped designs, created with special textured mats or materials that you improvise. Stencil patterns used in combination with textured rollers are another option.

EXPOSED AGGREGATE

This is concrete with pebbles partially embedded on top. Most stones aren't as porous as concrete, so this surface resists stains better than standard concrete. The pebbles also provide better traction. Some people like exposed-aggregate finishes because they are decorative without mimicking something else. You can opt to expose gravel and sand that are already in the basic concrete mix, or scatter additional pebbles on top. If you want an expensive stone on the surface, broadcasting (tossing stones on the surface after the concrete has been poured) is more cost-effective because it uses a smaller amount.

Colored concrete

Tile

If you're looking for splashes of vibrant color or a patio surface as smooth as the floor of an indoor room, tile is your best choice. Most ceramic tile is very resistant to stains, while some stone tiles can stain easily.

Stone Tile

Natural stone cut into square or rectangular tiles creates a stately appearance. Some types (right) are cut as precisely as ceramic tiles, while others are hand-cut and vary in thickness and width. Many stone tiles must be laid in a bed of mortar atop a solid concrete slab to prevent them from cracking. Some very thick and strong tiles can be laid in a dry bed.

Certain stone tiles are not strong enough to withstand freezing winters, and others may be slippery when wet or frosty. Some may be porous and prone to staining, rendering them unsuitable for a patio eating area.

Bluestone (below) is quarried mostly in New York and Pennsylvania but is increasingly available nationwide. It has a rich blue-gray color, sometimes imbued

with tinges of green, rust, yellow, and purple. You can obtain bluestone tiles of various sizes for use as pavers. Because they are often thick, bluestone tiles may be referred to as pavers. Bluestone tread stock is thick and strong enough to be used as steps without extensive support.

Slate tiles come from all over the world (including India, Africa, and Mexico) and in a stunning array of colors. The texture is usually bumpy yet smooth. A single tile may be matte in some spots and shiny in others.

Ceramic Tile

Ceramic tile is made from clay and fired in a kiln. The tiles can be left unglazed, or they can be coated with a baked-on decorative layer. Some glazes have a slightly bumpy surface, which provides skid resistance. High-gloss glazes are generally too slippery for a patio.

In most cases, ceramic tile must be set in a bed of mortar (usually thinset mortar)

atop a solid concrete slab. You'll also need grout to fill spaces between tiles. Choose a contrasting grout color to emphasize individual tiles, or a grout color that blends in with the tiles to make the paving seem more like one solid surface. Latex-reinforced sanded grout is a good choice for most outdoor applications. Be sure to check labels for recommended joint widths.

QUARRY TILE
The name of this type of tile is misleading. Quarry tiles are not actually cut from quarry stone but are made of fired clay. Quarry tiles are unglazed and very hard, so they make for a surface that is skid-resistant and often strong enough to survive freezing winters. Colors are generally limited to earth tones and grays.

PORCELAIN TILES
These are made from dry-pressed porcelain clay fired at very high temperatures. Porcelain tiles are virtually impervious to water,

so they can be used even where winters are cold. They are also incredibly stain-resistant, making them a great choice for outdoor paving where you're worried about spills. Glazed porcelain tiles, like standard glazed ceramic tiles, have a design layer on top of the clay. Through-body porcelain tiles have the same color all the way through, which makes chips or scratches less noticeable. Porcelain tile is often textured and colored to resemble stone or other paving materials.

MEXICAN SALTILLOS & TERRA-COTTA TILES
These have a soft reddish glow that lends warmth to a patio, as shown above. However, most types are suitable only for warm climates. With one hard freeze, they could crack. If you like the look but need something more durable, consider porcelain tiles that have a similar appearance.

Other Materials

Pebbles and gravel are an economical option for patios and walkways. For a silent path, get crushed gravel. If you want a path that crunches underfoot, pea gravel is a great choice. Adobe is another good way to go, or you can mix and match materials to suit your space.

Pebble patio

Crushed gravel

San Simeon beach stone

Mexican pebbles

Red lava

White dolomite rock

Black lava

Crushed granite

Pea gravel

Navajo rock

Serpentine

Maintaining Loose Surfaces

Loose paving needs to be replenished occasionally, as it gets tracked away or breaks down. Home centers typically sell loose materials in bags suitable for small projects. At a stone yard, sand and gravel company, garden center, or building materials supplier, you may find bins of loose materials, which you can shovel into your pickup or have delivered.

To keep gravel paving from being tracked inside, buy pieces that are too large to be caught in the treads of shoes. Round pebbles $5/8$ inch in diameter will stay put, and they're difficult for pets to dig in.

Another potential problem with loose surfaces is keeping them clean. Leaves are a hassle to sweep off a gravel or pebble surface. A leaf blower works well, but only if you catch the leaves when they are dry.

Adobe Pavers & Blocks

Traditional adobe is made from a mix of sand, clay, water, and straw. The mixture is placed in molds and allowed to dry in the sun. If this adobe becomes damp, it can swell and soften. Today, you can also buy stabilized adobe, which incorporates cement or asphalt emulsion so that it holds up outdoors, even in wet climates.

Set adobe pavers in a dry bed, not in mortar on concrete. Because the blocks are large and heavy, they may not need edging. You can also build a wall using adobe blocks, which are massive, often 4 × 8 × 16 inches.

Mixed Materials

Paths, patios, and walls of mixed materials catch the eye with contrasting colors and textures, which can be bold and bright or subdued. Either way, the materials you combine will add your own creative stamp to the garden. Combining materials with colors and textures that are similar will create a restful look, while pairing unlike materials will yield a livelier result.

A few tricks keep projects from looking like a jumble of disconnected parts. Like plants in a perennial border, mixed materials look better when they are grouped or repeated, not used singly. If you arrange materials in a pattern, repeat the pattern along your wall or path. Or lay out paving in a geometric pattern and fill some spaces with one type of material and others with a contrasting material.

Plan how you will keep all the materials solidly in place. Gravel will need to be retained with solid edging materials. If tiles or pavers are set amid or next to gravel, you may need to first lay individual concrete slabs, then set the pavers in mortar on the slabs. Or you can use hidden edgings to keep the pavers in place.

Landscape Design

Chances are you're looking for more than just a simple patio surface or a wall to retain soil. Think of your yard in terms of a series of outdoor rooms—inviting and relaxing places to lounge, dine, visit, or cook.

The Dreaming Stage

Take time to envision the possibilities for your yard before settling down and making a serious plan. In addition to gathering ideas from this book, look at yards in your neighborhood and note materials, structures, and layouts that appeal to you.

Experiment with ideas by making rough sketches on paper, but also test your ideas at full scale. Use a hose, rope, or stakes and string to mark the outline of a future patio or path. Large cardboard boxes can stand in for walls. Then set out the patio furniture—table and chairs, grill, lounge furniture—to see how the layout feels.

If your plans are extensive or you are feeling out of your depth, consider hiring a landscape design pro for a consultation, or for a full-blown set of plans.

Related Topics

Working with pros, 34–35

Defining Areas & Paths

When planning a patio, think in terms of defined areas, or outdoor rooms, joined by paths. Here are some time-tested rules of thumb for dimensions.

- A dining area includes the table plus 3 feet or more for chair space on all sides. A typical round or square table requires an area 10 to 12 feet square.
- A rectangular table for eight diners calls for an area 10 to 12 feet × 16 to 18 feet.
- A lounge chair or hammock with a small end table will fit comfortably into an area about 4 × 8 feet.
- For a simple barbecue area, allow space for at least one small prep table. A space 6 × 8 feet will fit a cook and a couple of advisers.
- Be sure to leave room for paths, as they must be separate from the other defined areas. A 3-foot-wide path is sufficient for light traffic.

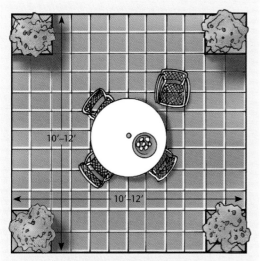

Round table with chairs

Capturing the Night

Well-placed lighting makes outdoor living space usable at all hours and accents attractive features of your landscape. Make sure any wiring that needs to go underground is in place before you build masonry projects. If you need a new electrical receptacle or want lights that operate on standard current, have an electrician run cable, or consult Sunset's *You Can Build: Wiring*. Take care not to damage the lines while you excavate and build.

Low-voltage lighting, available in convenient kits, can usually be installed after structures are built, but plan ahead so you won't wish later that you had put part of the system underground. Plug the adapter into a receptacle and run the thin lines in shallow trenches or staple them to the undersides of structures. The lights themselves can usually be simply poked into the ground or screwed to a wooden or masonry structure.

Lights for paths or security should be controlled by photocells that turn power off in the daytime, or by motion sensors. Use a standard switch for lights in a dining or lounging area.

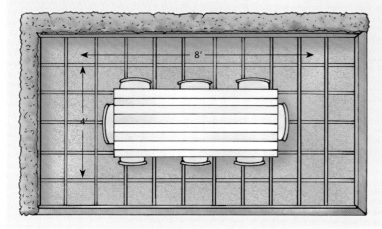

Rectangular table with chairs

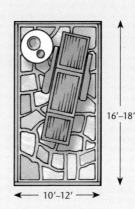

Lounge chair with small table

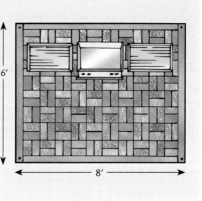

Barbecue area

Solving Problems & Finding Opportunities

Most people consider their yards to be less than perfect. Often, however, what seems like a drawback can offer exciting design possibilities. For example:

- A heavily sloped lawn may be uninviting, but it offers the possibility of two or more patios on different levels, or perhaps a wide stairway or series of terraced garden beds.

- If you have only enough room for one patio, consider it an opportunity to make it an extraordinary one. Because you need to buy and install fewer materials, you can more easily afford to use expensive and labor-intensive materials.

- A small yard with too-close neighbors can be transformed into a private retreat with the addition of masonry walls.

- If you need to hold back soil, consider it an opportunity to build an attractive retaining wall.

The Sun in Your Yard			
Seasonal sun angles	Sun's position/hours of daylight (see map on page 29)		
Hour / date	Area 1	Area 2	Area 3
A) Noon, December 21	21°/8 hrs	29°/9 hrs	37°/10 hrs
B) Noon, March 21 & September 21	45°/12 hrs	53°/12 hrs	60°/12 hrs
C) Noon, June 21	69°/16 hrs	76°/15 hrs	83°/14 hrs

Weather Considerations

Plan for outdoor rooms that you can enjoy over the longest possible season, and take advantage of the weather patterns on your property.

TRACK THE SUN

Your patio's exposure to the sun is usually the most important factor in your enjoyment of the space. Knowing the sun's path over your property may prompt you to adjust the position, size, and shape of your proposed patio in order to add weeks or even months of sun or shade each year. You may want to consider adding an overhead structure or an awning to create shade during the hottest times.

All other factors being equal, a patio that faces north receives less sun than one that faces south. A patio on the east side is relatively cool because it receives only morning sun. One that faces west receives sunlight in the afternoon, which could make it very hot, and late-afternoon sun often creates a harsh glare. In a hot region, you probably want a patio on the east and north sides, while in a cooler climate, south and west orientations may be preferable.

Also consider the sun's path during the year (see illustration above). The sun's arc is higher in summer and lower in winter, which will alter sun and shade patterns on your patio.

TAMING THE WIND

Observe wind patterns around your house and over your lot. Ideally, you want a gentle breeze blowing during the hottest times. Wind flows like water, spilling over obstacles, breaking into currents, eddying and twisting.

A solid fence will provide protection only for a small area — roughly the same distance as the height of the fence. Farther away, wind will swirl downward onto the patio. A barrier with openings, such as lattice or shrubbery, will diffuse rather than block the wind and provide protection for a larger area.

MICROCLIMATES

Nearby buildings, trees, shrubs, and overhead structures create microclimates, so conditions on your patio may be very different from those on a neighbor's patio. And one area of your patio may feel very different from another area.

Certain materials reflect sun and heat better than others. Light-colored paving and walls diffuse or spread sun and heat, but they can be uncomfortably bright. Beige pavers and siding are usually cooler.

Drawing a Plan

Take the time to make some fairly detailed drawings. This will help you think through the project and envision the finished look so you can avoid planning mistakes and anticipate challenges.

Map the Yard

You can work out ideas with a computer program or on paper. Either way, start by making a base map of your yard. If you have a surveyor's or deed map, photocopy it and use it as a base. Professionals often draw landscape plans with a 1:10 scale, meaning that 1 inch represents 10 feet. You may want to use a 1:4, 1:5, or 1:6 scale in order to show more detail.

If you will use paper and pencil to draft your plan, you'll need a pencil with a good eraser, a compass, a clear lined draftsman's ruler for drawing parallel lines, a calculator, and a curved-line guide, all of which are shown in the photo on the right.

Draw in all the trees, indicating measurements of their trunks and canopies. Then add shrubs, flower or vegetable beds, and other plantings. If you know where future plantings will go, include those as well. Indicate any downspouts and other drainage features. If the lawn slopes, indicate where and how steeply. Note areas that are shady or sunny.

Bubble Plan

Make five or six photocopies of the base plan, or save several copies of plans as you work onscreen. Some people go straight to the serious drawings, but many find it helpful to make a bubble plan, which indicates where you would generally like things to go.

To make a bubble plan, sketch rough circles or ovals on the base plan to indicate approximate locations and sizes of each use area. Concentrate on logical placement and juxtapositions. For instance, place children's play areas in full view of a living area and/or a kitchen window. Place a dining area about 8 feet from a cooking area—close enough for convenience but distant enough so smoke will not bother diners. And be sure to emphasize any attractive views.

A few simple tools enable you to calculate materials, draw straight and parallel lines, and make smooth curves.

Planning with bubbles

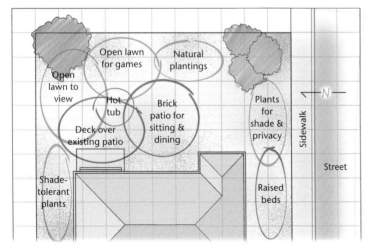

Triangulation Method

To precisely locate a tree or other feature, triangulate by measuring from two widely spaced fixed points to the feature. Working from scale, use a compass to draw two arcs. The intersection of the arcs marks the exact spot.

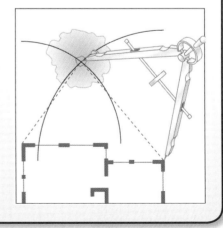

Related Topics

Landscaping design, 26–29
Planning drainage, 32–33
Working with pros, 36–37

Sketching with Graph Paper

Many people find it helpful to design in a modular way with graph paper. Using uniform design units enables you to be more exact in planning and gives a sense of order to a design. You'll also find modules helpful when estimating material. Figure the materials needed for one module, then tally the modules to arrive at a total.

The illustration at right shows how an outdoor room can be designed in 5-foot-square modules. The L-shaped patio is made up of two sections that are 30 × 20 feet and 25 × 15 feet. The overhead, the path, the privacy trellis, the flagstone patio, and the raised flower bed all have dimensions that are multiples of 5 feet as well.

The Final Drawings

Once you've worked through your ideas using a bubble plan and graph paper, you are ready to create a set of detailed and accurate plans to help you execute your design with fewer mistakes.

ELEVATION DRAWINGS

Also make elevation, or side-view, drawings. These should depict underlying structures as well as surface materials and show how things are put together. Be sure to detail the depth of the excavation, the depth of the gravel and sand beds, and the length of any reinforcement materials. Also include drainage solutions.

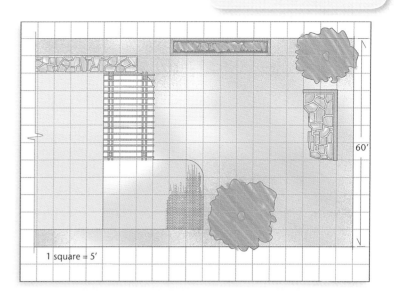

1 square = 5'

THE PLAN VIEW DRAWING

Draw a plan view, also called an overhead view, to scale. Include as many details as possible. This will give you a realistic idea of the available space and will help you estimate materials.

If you have a large sheet of paper and plenty of patience, or if you are using design software, you can draw individual pavers to scale. For flagstones, estimate sizes. To get a better idea of how the space will look and feel, sketch in accessories such as patio furniture and flowerpots.

THE MATERIALS LIST

As you draw, create a running list of all the materials you will need. An accurate list will save trips to your supplier. You don't need to figure how many pavers or how much sand and gravel you will need, but you should indicate how many square feet are to be covered. The masonry supplier can then calculate materials.

4 × 4 edging anchored with ⅜" rebar every 4'

1" sand
3" compactible gravel

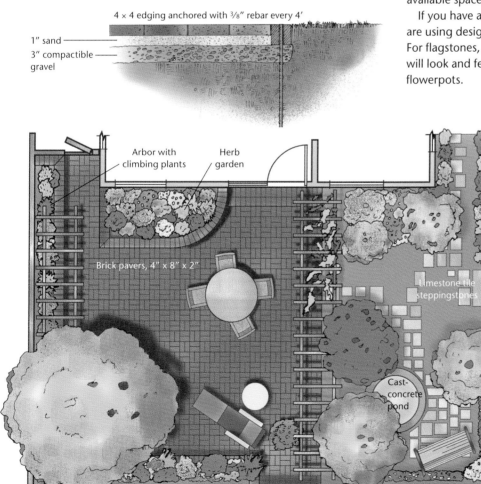

Arbor with climbing plants
Herb garden
Brick pavers, 4" x 8" x 2"
Limestone tile steppingstones

Cast-concrete pond

Tip

Design Software

Many landscaping and patio design programs are available, most of them for less than $100. Most will enable you to draw the outlines of a project and experiment with various materials and colors. Some have a 3-D feature so you can look at your project from various points of view.

Planning Drainage

Adding a patio or installing walls and moving soil around may cause puddles to form after rainfall, or cause more serious issues. While most problems can be addressed after a patio is built, a major complication on a large project may require a dry well and/or a drainage pipe that is installed before the patio is laid, so plan for drainage ahead of time.

Drainage Principles

If you follow the instructions in this book and install a patio that is consistently sloped away from the house at a rate of at least ¼ inch per running foot, the patio itself will not develop puddles. However, water will run to the edges of the patio, which can create wet spots there. If you cannot slope the patio away from the house, you must install a drainage system before laying the pavers.

If a patio has wide joints filled with sand or soil on a dry base (rather than on a concrete slab), some rainwater can seep through. However, a standard sand-laid patio with tight joints will let very little water seep through. Pervious concrete will allow water to run through freely.

Before installing drainage, consult a contractor or building inspector about local soil conditions. You may choose to have a contractor install a drainage system for you.

Perimeter Trenches

A simple gravel-filled trench at the downhill edge will handle an average puddle problem. Either before or after constructing the patio, dig a 12-inch-deep trench and fill it with stones or large gravel, perhaps topped off with decorative pebbles. Or dig the trench 16 inches deep and fill all but the top 4 inches with stones. Place a layer of landscaping fabric over the gravel, fill the rest of the trench with soil, and plant grass on top. Either way, use rounded gravel or stones, rather than compactible gravel, to allow for easy drainage.

Trench with exposed gravel

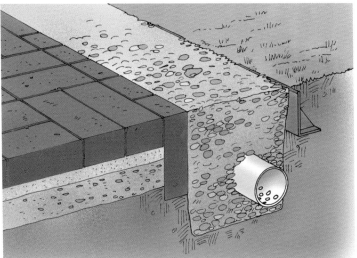

Hidden trench

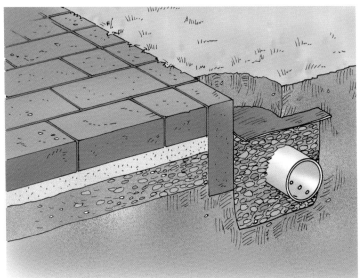

This drainpipe will be mostly covered with soil with its end exposed. A hinged metal gate prevents critters from crawling inside.

Drainpipes

For greater drainage, lay a perforated drainpipe in a trench, with the holes pointed down so gravel won't clog them. (If you want all the water to be carried away, use an unperforated pipe.) Line the trench with landscaping fabric, shovel in a couple of inches of gravel, and then lay the pipe on top. Cover it with more gravel. Some water will trickle down through the holes, and the remaining water will flow through to the end of the pipe.

Slope the pipe so it carries water away from the area during a severe rain. Run the pipe into a planting bed and let the water trickle out there. Or extend the pipe to a point where the water can flow down a hillside or into a dry well or rain garden.

How the Pros Do It

"The earth is the best cleanser of water. We basically do anything we can do to prevent water from running off and eventually carrying contaminants into a river, lake, or ocean. Allowing water to soak downward cleanses and replenishes the aquifer below."
Ken Coverdell, Blue Sky Design

Gravel Beds Aid Drainage

If you install pervious paving or pervious concrete, water will simply flow through the patio into a gravel bed below, solving most drainage problems.

For a small job, flexible perforated drainpipe is easy to lay.

Dry Well

A dry well is simply a large hole filled with rounded gravel. The spaces between the stones act as a reservoir so runoff water can flow in through a pipe during a heavy storm, then slowly percolate into the surrounding soil. A well about 3 feet wide and 3 feet deep will solve most problems, but consult a contractor to be sure. To make a dry well, dig a hole and run sloped drainpipe into it. Fill the hole with rounded gravel, cover it with three layers of landscaping fabric, and top that with soil and sod.

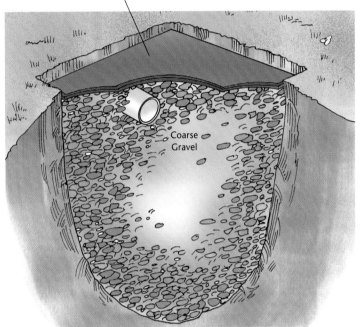

Three layers of landscaping fabric

Coarse Gravel

Where to Put a Catch Basin

If you cannot slope the patio away from the house, you may need a central catch basin. This must be installed before you lay pavers. Slope the excavation so water will run to a spot near the middle of the patio. At that spot, dig a hole and install a cylindrical or rectangular catch basin, available at masonry supply stores. (Some are made of concrete, while others are made of plastic.) Position the basin so the grate will be at the level of the pavers. From the catch basin, run solid (not perforated) drainpipe at a slope to carry water away from the patio. Once the pipe reaches the edge of the patio, perhaps switch to perforated pipe and run it around the yard or to a dry well or rain garden.

The grate will catch leaves and other large objects that could clog the pipe. Occasionally you may need to sweep the grate clean so water can flow through it.

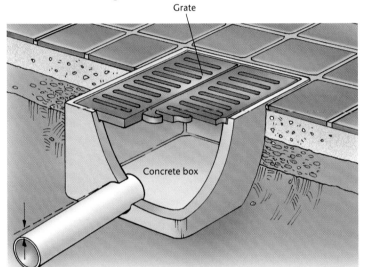

Grate

Concrete box

Retaining wall

Drainpipe

Catch basin

Here, a permeable band of stones ensures that the water seeping through this dry-laid retaining wall doesn't drown the lawn below it.

A retaining wall made of dry-laid stones allows water to seep through, preventing a buildup of water pressure on the wall.

This mortared retaining wall will be backfilled with soil that will cover the drainpipe. Drain water will seep into the soil.

Drainage for Retaining Walls

During a storm, plenty of water can seep into the soil and move toward a retaining wall. If a retaining wall is made of dry-stacked stones or pavers, the water can simply seep through the joints. But if the wall is made of mortared stone or other solid materials, a great deal of water pressure could build up, which could cause the wall to buckle and crack.

There are two solutions. One, as shown in the illustration at bottom left, is to run a sloped drainpipe sideways, along the wall, so it can carry water to another location. On a long wall, you may want to start in the middle and slope the pipe in both directions. Dig a trench, fill it with several inches of rounded gravel, and lay the pipe on top. Make sure the pipe slopes at a rate of ¼ inch or more per foot. Cover with more gravel, top with landscaping fabric, and cover with soil and sod.

The other solution is to make weep holes in the wall to allow water to seep through. If the weep holes will be exposed, they can be small and placed every 2 or 3 feet. Be sure not to cover these holes. If the holes will be covered, run pipes through the wall. Cover the pipe opening with a grate and/or gravel before backfilling with soil.

Working with Professionals

If you are considering an overhaul of your yard, consider hiring a landscape architect or designer. In addition to planning for paving, planting, and lighting, pros can design structures, solve site problems, secure permits, and be on hand during inspections.

Types of Pros

The best type of professional help depends on whether you have a large or small job and whether you want to do some of the work yourself.

LANDSCAPE ARCHITECT

A landscape architect typically gets involved at every stage of a project, from conceptual plans to construction drawings to supervision of the installations. He or she should have good working relationships with several contractors. Hiring a landscaping architect is pricey but may be worth it if you have little time to devote to the project. Be sure any landscape architect you hire is accustomed to working with residential customers; some are more comfortable with commercial clients.

LANDSCAPE DESIGNER

A landscape designer may not have the credentials, either academic or state-issued, of a landscape architect but will likely be less expensive. Designers often work only on the planning stages, allowing you to build the project or supervise masons yourself. They usually do most of their work with residential customers, so they should be attuned to your needs and budget.

MASONS & GENERAL CONTRACTORS

The men and women who do the actual work may be in close association with an architect or designer, or they may work for a general contractor who also builds non-masonry projects. If the job is small and you have a clear idea of how you want it built, you may have a mason work directly for you. If your project calls for many elements, a general contractor might be your best bet.

LANDSCAPE ENGINEER

If your yard has a severe slope, serious drainage problems, or unstable soil, you may need to call in a landscape engineer, who will perform calculations to make sure the installation will be stable and durable.

The sheer volume of heavy boulders and large pieces of stone, along with the engineering associated with the patio's slope into the pool, makes a project like this difficult for most do-it-yourselfers.

On a large project, an architect will produce a sheaf of drawings that tell the masons precisely what to install and where.

Hiring & Contracts

Interview several contractors if possible. You may need to pay a fee for an interview at your home, while an interview at the contractor's office may be free. Ask for references, such as other residential clients the contractors have done similar work for. Call former customers and ask whether they would hire a particular contractor again. You should feel a rapport with your contractor. Don't let him or her pressure you into a deal you're not comfortable with.

Be sure to get a clearly worded written contract. Read it carefully and negotiate any changes before you sign. It should be very specific about which materials will be used (even specifying manufacturers' names), and drawings should be attached so that the size and shape of the project are clear. Installation methods should be described in detail. There should also be assurances that your property will not be damaged while work is progressing. The timetable for the work must be laid out clearly. It's reasonable to pay a deposit before the work begins, but structure the remaining payments so that the contractor has plenty of incentive to do a good job and do it on time.

A landscape architect's office has plenty of room to spread out plans.

Basic Masonry Techniques

In this chapter, we introduce you to the tools you'll need—from excavating to finishing—to pull off a professional-looking masonry project. You'll learn how to lay out a patio, remove sod, and trim bricks and other pavers to size with both hand and power tools. Once your patio is laid out, we show you how to arrange flagstones to achieve a natural pattern.

Chapter Contents

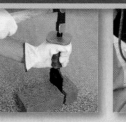

Transporting Heavy Stones
page 56

Forming & Pouring a Footing
page 58

Working with Rebar
page 60

Mixing Mortar
page 62

Crevice Planting
page 66

Masonry Tools

Compared with carpentry tools, masonry tools are inexpensive, so go ahead and buy professional-quality tools. They feel comfortable in your hand, are precisely milled to make your work accurate, and will last for years.

Tools for Laying Out

These tools enable you to quickly mark and check the perimeter of a patio or the contours of a wall. A framing square checks small layouts for square. Buy mason's line, which stays taut, unlike string or twine. A chalk line makes perfectly straight marks. Red chalk is permanent, while blue chalk washes away easily. You'll need at least a 30-foot tape measure, and you may need a 100-footer as well. Use a plumb bob to mark a spot on the ground directly below a spot above (you can also use a chalk line for this). To check a layout for level or correct slope, set a carpenter's level atop a long board or use a water level.

Tools for Excavating

To remove sod and excavate for a moderately sized patio or wall, hand tools may be all you need. Use a pointed shovel for basic digging and a square shovel to slice lines in the sod and to scrape the bottom of an excavation smooth. Shovels and spades should have sharp tips and straight blades and should be kept free of encrusted material like old concrete. If you run into large roots or rocks, pry them up or cut them with a digging bar. Use a garden rake to smooth excavated areas and to spread gravel and sand. Drive stakes with a hand sledge. To excavate a large area, consider renting a sod cutter or a small earth-moving machine.

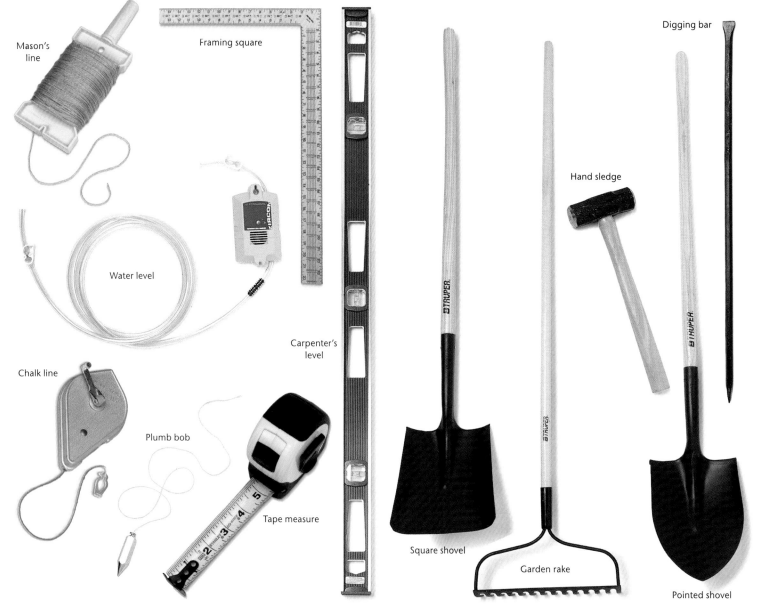

Mason's line

Framing square

Water level

Chalk line

Plumb bob

Tape measure

Carpenter's level

Digging bar

Hand sledge

Square shovel

Garden rake

Pointed shovel

General Carpentry Tools

You will likely need a basic set of carpentry tools. An angle square will help you mark pavers quickly for cutting. You will sometimes want to apply adhesives or caulks using a caulking gun. A basic hammer and a flat pry bar are useful for assembling and dismantling boards. Use a drill to bore holes and drive screws. Cut boards quickly with a circular saw.

Safety Gear

Though it may be a bit annoying and make you feel dorky, you really should wear protective gear and clothing when cutting and installing masonry. Wear long clothing and work gloves when handling bricks and stones. When cutting masonry units, always wear protective eyewear.

Circular saw

Angle square

Caulking gun

Claw hammer

Pry bar

Cordless drill

Tools for Cutting & Setting Pavers

If you need to cut only a few pavers or stones, use a brickset chisel for softer materials, such as brick, and a narrower cold chisel for harder materials. A mason's hammer lets you chip pavers roughly. Use a grinder equipped with a masonry blade or a diamond blade to partially cut through pavers or stones, then complete the cut with a hammer. When tapping pavers into place, use a rubber mallet so you won't damage them. Brick tongs enable you to pick up and carry six or more bricks.

Grinder with extra blade

Rubber mallet

Brickset chisel

Brick tongs

Mason's hammer

Cold chisel

Masonry Power Saws

Power saws make it easy to cut through the hardest masonry materials. A wet-cutting saw has a sliding tray and a smooth-cutting blade for making precise cuts. A masonry cutoff saw is less precise, but it can still make surprisingly accurate and straight cuts.

Cutoff saw

Wet saw

Tools for Setting in Mortar

You can mix small batches of mortar in a 5-gallon bucket, but it is easier in a wheelbarrow or in a plastic masonry trough. A mason's hoe mixes mortar and concrete quickly. Once mortar is mixed, either scoop it directly from the wheelbarrow or trough, or place a workable amount on a hawk. Throw a line of mortar using a brick trowel. A pointing trowel helps you slip mortar into tight spots. If you need to work mortar into joints after the masonry units have been installed, use a grout bag.

Use a torpedo level to check bricks for level. Hook a wooden or plastic corner block to a brick at each end of a wall and stretch mason's line between the blocks to align bricks quickly as you lay them. To finish joints in a brick or block wall, use a jointer. Brush joints with a mason's brush.

Tools for Concrete Projects

Use lineman's pliers to cut reinforcing wire mesh and to tie together pieces of rebar with wire. For the first round of concrete finishing, use a darby for a small slab or a bull float for a larger slab. For the next round, some people prefer a wooden float. However, most do-it-yourselfers find that a magnesium float is easier to use. To produce a very smooth surface, go over it with a steel trowel. Be aware, however, that it takes a good deal of practice before you can use a steel trowel successfully. Use an edger to round the edges of the slab, and a concrete jointer to make control joints in the middle.

Mason's hoe

Hawk

Grout bag

Concrete jointer

Magnesium float

Darby

Jointers

Bull float

Edger

Mason's brush

Torpedo level

Wooden float

Corner blocks

Steel trowel

Pointing trowel

Lineman's pliers

Notched trowel

Margin trowel

Brick trowel

Mortar tub

Grout float

Measuring & Laying Out

Once you have determined the outline of your patio or wall, mark the perimeter. Some projects call for only casual marking, while others require more precision.

Laying Out for Corners & Curves

Though a patio can be laid out quickly with lines attached to stakes, batterboards are the better way to go. They are not easily bumped out of position, and they make it easy to remove and reattach the lines as needed. Estimate the outline of your project, then pound two batterboards into the ground about 2 feet beyond the estimated location of each corner. To check for a square corner, use the 3-4-5 method depicted below or measure the diagonals. To lay out a curved corner, place a stake along a diagonal line, tie a string to the stake, and use a can of marking paint to draw the curve.

Simple Height Layout

For rough flagstones that vary in thickness, you may want to use string lines to roughly gauge the depth of the excavation at the same time as you generally mark the patio or path's perimeter.

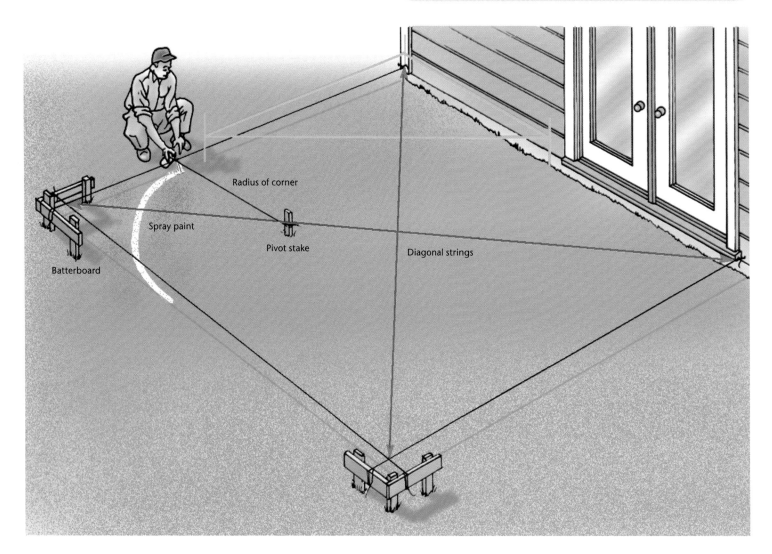

Radius of corner

Spray paint

Pivot stake

Diagonal strings

Batterboard

Related Topics

Arranging flagstones, 54–55
Designing stairs, 136–137
Excavating, 98–99
Pouring a concrete patio, 172–177

1 Build batterboards

- For each batterboard, cut two 2 × 2 stakes about 18 inches long, depending on the hardness of the soil. Cut a 1 × 4 to 2 feet long.
- Drive two screws into each joint.
- Drive two batterboards into the ground, about 2 feet beyond the corner.

2 Run the lines

- Take into account the thickness of any edging you will use.
- At the house, drive a single stake. Stretch lines low but not touching the ground between stakes and batterboards.
- Temporarily wrap lines around batterboards so you can shift positions.

3 Measure for square

- Mark a spot on the house 6 feet from the corner.
- Use tape to mark the adjacent string 8 feet from the corner.
- If the distance between marks is 10 feet, the corner is square.
- Adjust strings as needed.
- If your patio is large, use larger multiples of 3, 4, and 5, such as 12, 16, and 20, or 30, 40, and 50.
- Double-check for square by measuring diagonals, which should be equal lengths.

4 Mark corners

- Mark batterboards so you can remove and replace lines as needed.
- Dangle a plumb bob (or chalk line) so its string nearly touches the intersection of two lines.
- Lower the plumb bob to nearly touch the ground.
- Drive a stake at each corner.
- Stretch lines from the stakes to mark for excavating.

5 Mark for a curve

- To mark a simple radius, use a line and a can of spray paint, as shown in the illustration on page 44.
- To create a curve that is not a simple radius, lay a garden hose on the ground in the desired shape.
- Pour sand, flour, or lime over the hose.
- Pick up the hose to reveal a clear outline.

OPTION Easy marking for a casual project

- Where precision is not needed, simply mark the ground with spray paint.
- Cut the soil or sod along the sprayed line.

Excavating

Once you've outlined your project on the ground, it's time to excavate. This means removing any sod and plants, then digging down to the correct depth.

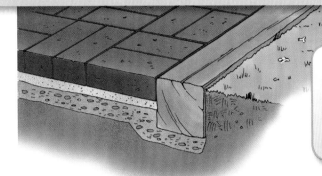

Got Leftovers?

Before you start digging, decide where to put the excavated sod and soil. You may be able to use soil to fill up a new raised planting bed or use sod to patch bare spots in your lawn. If it's just in the way, advertise locally for someone to haul it away for you.

Getting the Depth Right

The excavated site must be the correct depth so that the finished patio will be slightly above grade, a height that will let you run a lawn mower over it. The site must also slope away from the house at a rate of at least ¼ inch per running foot. Depending on the type of edging you choose, you may need to excavate the perimeter deeper than the rest of the patio (see the illustrations above).

If you use solid edging, like timbers or pavers set in concrete, you can first install the edging, then string lines from it to determine the correct depth of excavation. Another method is to first excavate the entire site and then use a long board with a level on top to check that the excavation is sloped correctly. The edging is then installed after the pavers.

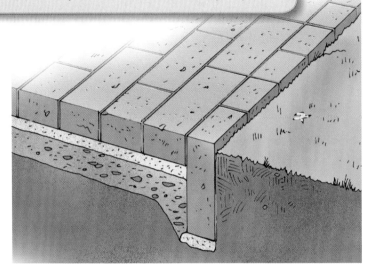

Cutting Sod

All sod, roots, and organic material must be removed or the patio will sink later when the plant material rots away.

Dig by hand

- For a small patio, dig up sod with a square shovel.
- Cut a perimeter line, holding the shovel straight up.
- Slice a parallel line about 18 inches inside the perimeter line.
- Undercut the sod between the lines while a helper rolls it up.

Foot sod cutter

- A kick-type sod cutter can remove uniform strips of sod.
- Press the cutter down and forward with your foot to slice off sod.
- The sod pieces can be replanted elsewhere.

Power sod cutter

- For a large area, rent a sod cutter.
- Slice through the sod.
- Roll up the sod after each slice.

Tools You'll Need

Digging Bar
Level
Shovels
Sod Cutter

Related Topics

Edgings, 100–107
Excavating, 98–99
Forming & pouring a footing, 58–59

Excavating to the Correct Depth

You may need to remove your guidelines at this point. Consider installing some or all of the edging to help establish the correct depth.

1 Establish the slope

- Starting at doorway, use level atop a board, or a water level, to check slope
- If yard is uneven, drive a stake at the end of patio and mark the stake for level
- Measure down from level line and mark a line ¼ inch per running foot lower; use this as a guide for excavating

2 Dig & scrape

- Use temporary boards to hold guidelines, or install permanent edging and stretch lines from it.
- Create a grid of guidelines.
- Dig away soil, taking care not to dig too deep.
- Use a shovel as a measuring device and scrape the bottom smooth.

3 Tamp

- Use a hand tamper or plate compactor to tamp the soil firm.
- Pour and spread gravel to the correct height, then tamp that as well.

Excavating by Machine

A rented earth-moving machine such as a front loader or skid loader can make quick work of excavation. Ask the rental company for detailed instructions on using the machine; you can probably get fairly proficient in an hour or so. Establish a route for the machine that will not damage your yard. You may want to make a temporary path using sheets of plywood.

Dig & scrape

- Position the loader's bucket fairly level so you do not dig too deep.
- To finish, point the bucket downward and scrape, moving backward.

Fill

- You can also use the loader to fill in other areas of the yard.
- Be aware that the filled soil will not be firm enough for a patio.

Trenching

- With some machines, you can exchange the bucket for a pair of pallet forks.
- Push the forks close to each other and use them to dig a trench.

Cutting Bricks, Pavers & Stone

Many methods are used to cut masonry units. The one you select will depend on the hardness of the material, the number of cuts you need to make, and how precise the cuts need to be.

Measuring for Cuts

As often as possible, install all the full-sized pavers or stones first, then measure for the ones that need to be cut.

1 Mark for a cut

- Hold the paver where it will go; this is more precise than using a tape measure.
- Mark both sides of the cut.
- Use a square to draw lines up to the face of the paver.

2 Capture the angle

- Set a T bevel in place, then tighten the wing nut to preserve the angle.
- Use the T bevel to draw the cut line between the two lines from step 1.

Marking flagstones

- On a casual project, you may just eyeball a cut line.
- For more precision, use a tape measure to mark a line that is parallel with the adjacent stone.

Cut by Hand

The is the low-tech way to cut bricks and blocks. Pros can make fairly accurate cuts simply by whacking with a brick hammer, but a do-it-yourselfer will have better results using a hammer and chisel.

Cutting Tips

Save time and hassle by designing paving or walls to minimize the number of cuts you need to make. If you need to trim only a few pieces, ask the store where you purchased materials to make the cuts for you. Whether you are using hand tools or power tools, practice on scrap pieces first until you get the knack. Some materials, such as hard stones and concrete pavers, are very difficult to cut by hand, so you should rent power equipment.

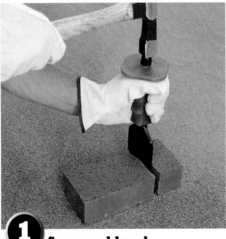

1 Score and break

- Place brick or block on a flat, resilient surface, such as a bed of sand.
- Hold a cold chisel firmly in place and tap it with a hammer to score a line.
- Score all four sides.
- Hold the chisel on the line with the bevel (the angled side of the tip) facing the waste side of the cut.
- Whack hard to break the brick.

2 Clean the cut edge

- Hit with a trowel or brick hammer to knock away any protrusions.
- Scrape away smaller protrusions, if needed.

Hand-Cutting Stone & Brick

For a casual surface where joints don't have to be precise, or if the stones are soft, you may cut with hand tools, perhaps with the assistance of modest carpentry power tools.

Crack apart

- To cut a large flagstone into smaller parts, draw lines roughly marking the sizes you want.
- Tap, then pound, along the lines using a hammer and chisel, or just a hammer.
- The resulting parts can be separated and will form neat-looking joint lines.

Using a Grinder

A handheld grinder can be used for a variety of masonry-cutting uses. However, it will create a good deal of dust and cannot be used for very precise cuts.

- Equip a grinder with a masonry blade or a diamond blade.
- Score lines so you can lop the waste material off with a hand sledge.
- You can also use a grinder to cut through rough tiles.

Score & break

- For somewhat more predictable results, first score a line using a chisel.
- Place a pipe under the score and then tap it with a hand sledge to break it.

Circular-Saw Cuts

If you have, say, 15 or fewer bricks or pavers that need precise cuts, perhaps use a circular saw equipped with a masonry blade. Be aware, however, that the dust may damage the saw if you cut too many bricks. Stop when you notice the saw heating up.

Cutting a concrete block

- Use a circular saw to cut about ½ inch deep on each side.
- Finish the cut with a cold chisel and a hand sledge.

Using a brick splitter

- A brick splitter makes fairly accurate cuts and can be rented for a modest price.
- Use it for natural brick only, as pavers are difficult to cut.

Clamp & score

- Attach a scrap board to the working surface to keep the bricks from sliding.
- It may work to clamp several bricks together and cut them at the same time.
- Cut bricks about ½ inch deep; cut pavers about ⅜ inch deep.
- Lower the blade and make another pass.
- Repeat until the cut is most of the way through, then break the brick with a chisel.

Curve-cutting Flagstones

To produce a flagstone patio that has consistent joints yet looks natural, you need to cut fairly precise lines, then chip the edges so they don't look man-made.

1 Cut wet

- Draw lines to accurately follow the contours you desire.
- Use a rented masonry saw to cut along the lines.
- Have a helper spray the blade with water as you work.

2 Break apart

- Cut with several passes so you cut through at most points.
- Tap with a hand sledge or hammer to break the pieces apart.
- Use the saw to cut away any unattractive protrusions.

Smoothing Surfaces

Always try to install masonry units so they form a level surface. Sometimes, though, you need to do a little smoothing after the installation is complete.

3 Roughen the edges

- Use a masonry hammer or a regular hammer to tap gently along the edges.
- Aim to achieve a natural-looking edge.
- Tap straight up and down and sideways.

Wet-cutting Tips

- Follow all instructions from the renter.
- Test to make sure the tray glides smoothly and is square to the blade.
- Check that you have all the guides you will need for making any angle cuts.
- Water must spray onto the blade constantly; otherwise the blade will dull.
- Replace the water every hour or so to keep the blade sharp.

Dry Cutting

If you don't mind the dust, you can use a rented masonry cutoff saw to make fairly straight cuts quickly.

- Make sure you are comfortable holding the saw.
- Step on the stone with one foot and position the other out of the blade's path.
- Don't push down; allow the saw's weight to supply the pressure as you cut.

Lipping

- If a stone is high at one or more points, hold a cold chisel nearly flat and resting on the adjacent stone.
- Tap it with a hammer to break off stone flakes as needed.

Scrape with a grinder

- To smooth out protrusions, hold a grinder nearly flat and scrape them away.
- Use a pulling motion, rather than a pushing motion, so you don't dig in.

Wet-cutting Masonry

You may buy an inexpensive wet saw, but it will cut only through thin tiles, not bricks and pavers. For serious cutting, rent a heavy-duty masonry saw, also called a tub saw.

Set up the saw

- A wet saw may be placed on a table or simply set on the ground.
- You might want to cover the saw with plastic to minimize spraying.

Straight cut

- Place a paver in the tray and hold it against the back guide so it is square to the blade.
- Turn the saw on and check that water flows to the blade.
- Slide the tray forward slowly to slice through the paver.

Angle cut

- Typical guides hold a paver at 45 degrees and other angles.
- Use an adjustable guide for off-angles.
- Hold the paver firmly against the attachment and slide it forward.

Cutout

- Make two cuts for a cutout or notch.
- Tilt the paver up so the bottom of the cut is slightly longer than the top.
- Hold the paver against the back guide to ensure a square cut.

Curve cut

- Hold the paver firmly with both hands and tilt it up so the bottom of the cut is slightly deeper than the top.
- Make a series of cuts up to the cut line.
- Press the paver gently against blade and move it from side to side.
- Remove only a small amount at a time until you have finished.

Cut a sliver

- This saw can make surprisingly precise and narrow cuts.
- For a very narrow cut, hold another paver against the side as you push forward.

Cutting Thick Stone on a Curve

Degree of Difficulty
● Moderate

Limestone, bluestone, sandstone, and other relatively soft stones are often cut into curved shapes to top off benches, walls, pools, and decorative features. Cutting calls for careful work but is not as difficult as you might imagine.

1 Mark the curve

- To determine the radius of the cut, have a helper hold a tape measure at one end while you follow along the desired arc at the other end.
- Have a helper hold one end while you mark one side of the slab.
- Poke a hole in the tape measure and insert the pencil into the hole, or just hold the pencil next to the tape measure.

2 Mark the sides

- To make two parallel lines, have the helper move his end the distance of the desired width, and mark again.
- Use the tape measure, stretched from the same location, to mark for cutting the sides.
- This will produce a cut line that is square to the curved lines.

3 Mark for a squared cut

- Use an angle square to mark the edge of the slab for a squared cut.

4 Use a masonry blade

- Equip a reciprocating saw with a masonry-cutting blade.
- Buy one or two extra blades, in case the first becomes dull.

5 Start the cut

- Holding the blade at an angle, cut upward from the bottom of the edge line.
- Take care to start out straight.

6 Finish the first cut

- Continue cutting; the work will go pretty slowly.
- If you go a bit off track, avoid making a turn that will bend the blade. You can fix mistakes with a grinder later.
- If the blade starts to heat up, take a break and allow it to cool.

 **Stuff to Buy**	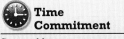 **Time Commitment**	 **Tools You'll Need**	**Related Topics**
Soft stone such as sandstone or limestone Masonry blade	Several hours	Framing square Grinder Reciprocating saw Tape measure	Cutting bricks, pavers, & stone, 48–49 Garden bench, 272–273 Natural stone, 14–15 Transporting heavy stones, 56–57

7 Cut the other side

- Cut the other curve in the same way.
- You may end up with excess at the center of the arc.
- Don't try to cut away the excess or you might wander inside the cut line.

8 Check for a squared edge

- Use a small square or a framing square to check the edge for square
- This will give you a general idea where to start grinding.

9 Grind the edge

- Equip a grinder with a rough grinding stone and work to remove excess stone.
- Work up to near the cut line.
- Periodically check with the square to make sure you are grinding in the right spots.

10 Fine-tune for square

- Slide the square along the cut edge, taking note of high spots.
- Continue grinding until the edge is nearly perfectly square and follows the cut line.

11 Belt sand

- Put a 60-grit belt onto a belt sander.
- Use only moderate pressure as you continue to smooth the edge.

12 Hand sand

- For the final touchups, use a piece of 80-grit sandpaper held in your hand.
- Sand the front edge, then also sand the top edge so it is not sharp.

Arranging Flagstones

A flagstone patio may look randomly arranged, but it actually takes a good deal of planning and noodling to get that pattern. Here we present some basic principles on how to cut and arrange flagstone.

The naturalist configuration of flagstones on this patio echoes the arrangement of stones around this backyard water feature.

Principles of Natural Design

When it comes to cutting and positioning flagstones, don't expect the natural look to come naturally. If you arrange the stones in any old order, you will likely end up with an unattractive layout. Here are some guidelines:

- Determine ahead of time the look you want and stick with it. For example, do you want joints that are consistent in width, or do you prefer a more casual look with joints that are often wider in some spots than in others?
- Sort the stones into piles of large, medium, and small pieces and create a layout that evenly disperses the various sizes. If you end up with three or four small stones next to each other, your work will look sloppy.
- Pay attention to color as well. Distribute stones of similar hue more or less evenly over the patio surface.
- Avoid using three-sided stones very often. In most cases, stones with four or more sides look better. If you have a large triangular stone, it is often best to lop off one corner.

- Unless you are going for a geometric look, avoid stones that appear square or rectangular. Again, you can cut off one of the edges to achieve a more natural look.
- If a joint line runs past two or more stones, it will draw too much attention to itself and result in a man-made look. Cut and replace stones as needed to avoid uninterrupted joints.
- Don't be in a hurry when sorting and laying out stones. Set them out in a dry run—without mortar, either on the ground or on a piece of plywood. Stand back from time to time, on a ladder if necessary, to examine your layout with a critical eye. Don't hesitate to make changes.

Split Flagstone

It is not unusual for a large piece of flagstone to arrive on a job site split in half horizontally. The resulting stones will be strong enough to use as long as they are at least 1½ inches thick.

Three Approaches

The photo on the opposite page shows a common type of flagstone patio. The photos below show three variants.

Formal
A formal patio has joints that are almost precisely consistent in width. This approach definitely takes more time, as it requires more cuts. Very few pieces will fit together without cutting.

Geometric
A geometric style violates some of the principles discussed on the facing page. Many of the stones are triangular or rectangular, and some lines extend along several stones. This can look great as long as it is maintained throughout the patio.

Room for Plants
If you plan to fill joints with lush crevice plants, then layout becomes simpler, as joints can be inconsistent in width.

Fixing a Layout Problem

Here is a typical layout problem and its solution. In the "before" photo, the stones are arranged in a trial pattern on a sheet of plywood. The layout is not too bad, but just above the middle two stones the upper horizontal line runs without a break past both stones, and the vertical line between them is unnaturally straight. The solution, as shown below, is to remove the left middle stone, cut two adjacent stones as indicated by the pencil lines in the "before" photo, and cut a new, larger stone to fit into the opening.

Before

After

Transporting Heavy Stones

While you'll want to minimize the need to move large stones and boulders, you may still have to pick up and set down very heavy objects. Here are some back-saving tips.

Using Small Tools

Arrange for delivery as near as possible to the final installation site, without damaging your yard or driveway. Some stones can be moved by hand or with the aid of simple tools.

Lift with your legs

- Joints and muscles in the lower back are susceptible to long-term damage, so lift and carry correctly.
- When lifting and carrying, keep your back straight and bend your knees. Do not bend your back.

Use a ramp

- To raise a large stone without actually picking it up, make a simple 2 × 12 ramp.
- Perhaps attach 2 × 2 crosspieces every 2 feet or so to keep the rock from sliding back.

Hand truck

- A hand truck with air-filled tires rolls more smoothly.
- Have a helper tilt the boulder back while you scoot the truck's base plate under it.
- Tilt the hand truck back until you feel no pressure, then roll forward or backward.

Motorized Wheelbarrow

Many tools are available to help homeowners move large, heavy objects. A motorized wheelbarrow like this can carry up to half a ton and fits through gates just 28 inches wide.

More elaborate ramp system

To move very large boulders, you can rent a ramp and cart designed to work together. Enlist helpers with the promise of a barbecue and a few cold ones after the job is done.

Working with a Skid Loader

A small earth-moving machine, variously called a skip loader or skid-steer loader, is the tool of choice when you need to move a number of boulders. A local rental store may have several to choose from. Tell the employees what you need to do, and they can rent you the machine best suited to your project. Some models have a bucket (see page 47) that can be removed and replaced with pallet forks, as shown in the photos below.

Adjust the forks

- If you need to, remove a bucket and replace it with pallet forks.
- Adjust the forks' positions to grab and hold the boulder.

Lift & carry

- Push the forks under the boulder and lift it.
- Tilt the forks back so the boulder will not roll off, then carry the rock.

Set it in place

- Tilt the forks down to allow the boulder to slide into position.
- With practice, you can position boulders accurately.

Push with forks

- To fine-tune the position, push the boulder with one of the forks.
- If you need to pull the boulder back, pick it up and start again.

Work with shovels

- Sometimes it helps to pry up one end with a shovel while the machine lifts or pushes.
- To help a boulder rest firmly, pull up with the machine and dig underneath with a shovel.

Use hand levers

- For final positioning, you may need to use hand tools.
- Use only fiberglass-handle shovels for this work, as wood handles may split.
- You may find that a digging bar works better in some situations.

Forming & Pouring a Footing

Any wall that is mortared, whether brick, block, or stone, must rest on a concrete footing that meets local code requirements. Otherwise, the mortared joints will almost certainly crack in a year or two.

About Footings

If you have freezing winters, you may be required to install a footing that extends below the frost line—the depth at which soil freezes in your area. In some locales, this may mean digging and pouring a footing that is 4 feet deep. However, if the footing will support only a modest garden wall, your inspector may allow a shallower footing that floats, meaning it will rise and fall slightly when the ground freezes and thaws.

At minimum, a footing should be 8 inches deep and twice as wide as the wall it will support. Unless you live in a dry climate, its top should be slightly above grade so rainwater cannot puddle. If the footing will abut an existing concrete structure, install an isolation joint to ensure the footing will not affect the structure.

If your soil and sod are firm, you can use the method shown in the illustrations on the opposite page. In this case, notches in the trench help hold the 2 x 4 forms in place. If your soil is loose, it may be better to set a firmly staked frame in place, then dig the trench inside it.

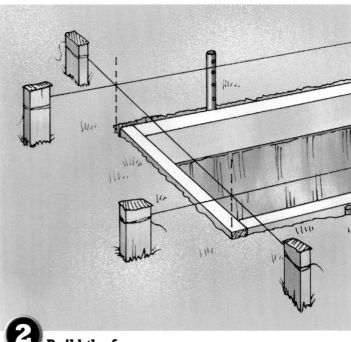

Even a low wall like this one needs a concrete footing if it will be mortared.

Building the Footing

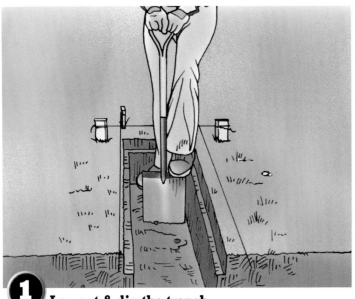

1 Lay out & dig the trench

- Use mason's line and wood stakes to lay out the outside perimeter of the 2 x 4 frame. This will be 3 inches wider than the formed concrete.
- Use sand or spray paint to mark for a curved footing.
- Dig the trench with a square shovel.
- Check with a carpenter's level to see that the sides of the hole are plumb.
- Scrape, rather than dig, the bottom of the excavation.

2 Build the frame

- Cut 2 x 4s for the frame and set them in place.
- Screw the boards together at the corners.
- Drive metal stakes or lengths of rebar to anchor the frame.

$ **Stuff to Buy**	🕐 **Time Commitment**	⚒ **Tools You'll Need**	◎ **Related Topics**
2 × 4s for forms and stakes Screws or duplex nails Concrete Reinforcement bar Wire rebar ties	A day to dig, form, and pour a footing 2 feet deep and 40 feet long	Hand sledge Lineman's pliers Saw for cutting rebar Shovel Swivel tool for twisting rebar ties	Calculating concrete needs, 170–171 Excavating, 46–47 Mixing & delivering, 172–173 Understanding concrete, 168–169 Working with rebar, 60–61

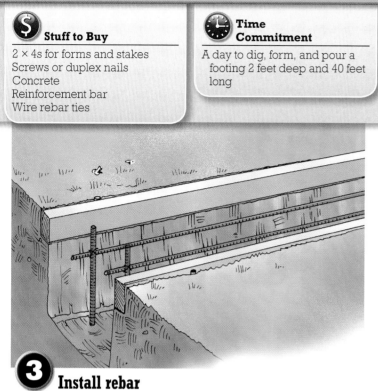

❸ Install rebar

- Reinforcement bar increases the concrete's strength and resistance to cracking.
- Typically, two horizontal pieces of ³⁄₈-inch rebar are sufficient, but check local codes.
- To suspend rebar in the center of the footing's depth, drive pieces of rebar into the ground and attach horizontals with wire or loop-end wire ties (see pages 60–61).

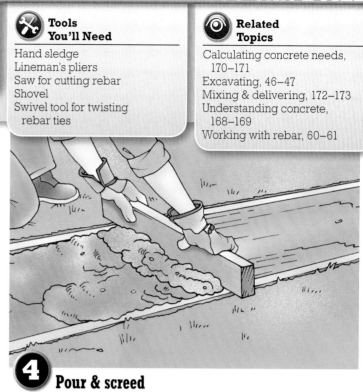

❹ Pour & screed

- Mix concrete and pour it into the trench.
- Poke a piece of rebar down into the concrete all along its length to reduce air bubbles.
- Use a length of 2 × 4 to screed the top.
- If part of the footing will be visible, smooth the concrete with a magnesium float.

Framing a Step-Down

If the site is sloped, you may need to step down the footing. (Don't try to slope the footing, as wet concrete is liquid.) Construct two frames, one for the upper level and one for the lower level, and fasten them together with pieces of plywood.

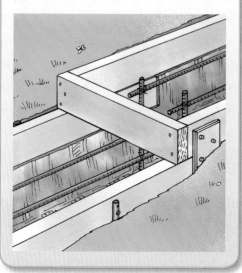

Staking for Strength

Stakes are typically made of 2 × 3s or 2 × 4s with 5-inch-long points at their ends. Vertically driven stakes often are not strong enough to hold the forms in place, so angled stakes are driven and attached for extra support. In the situation shown, where the ground is crumbly and difficult to cut accurately, 2 × 6s are used in some places for the form.

Get Help with Forms

Building a footing frame is often best done with two people. One person can check for the correct position of stakes and form boards while the other pounds the stakes. Be aware that stakes can angle as you pound them in, especially if the soil is rocky.

Working with Rebar

Consult your inspector or local builders to determine how much rebar to use and whether you should use ⅜-inch or ½-inch rebar. Most trenches are deep enough that you need to tie the pieces in place, as shown on these pages.

Cutting Rebar

Measure for horizontal rebar pieces that come to about 2 to 3 inches from footing ends. For the verticals, use 2- to 3-foot lengths, depending on the depth of the trench and the hardness of your soil. The pieces should be firm and secure when pounded a couple of inches below the top of the footing.

Tying Rebar

You can tie rebar together using lengths of wire, but pre-looped wire ties are easier. Buy a special swivel tool, which quickly twists looped ends together.

Cut using a reciprocating saw equipped with a metal-cutting blade. Firmly clamp the rebar to reduce sympathetic vibration, which is the bane of the reciprocating saw.

If you have a cutoff saw on site, cutting rebar is a snap, as well as a visual treat. Just hold the rebar in place with your foot.

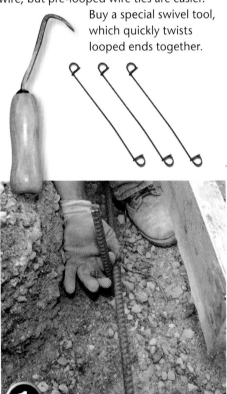

❶ Position & start to wrap

- Drive the vertical pieces of rebar every 4 feet or so.
- Position a horizontal piece at the correct height and with its end about an inch from the end of the footing.
- With your fingers, twist a loop-end wire around the two pieces of rebar.

❷ Tie with a swivel tool

- Insert the tip of a swivel tool through the two loops.
- While continuing to hold the rebar in position, move the tool in a circle to twist the loops together.
- Firm the attachment by grabbing the metal part of the tool and giving a final twist.

Well-tied rebar

Here's a good example of rebar that is securely fastened at the right positions. It will stay in place when the concrete is being poured. At a footing corner, horizontal pieces are stacked on top of each other.

Stuff to Buy

Reinforcement bar
Wire rebar ties

Time Commitment

A morning or afternoon

Tools You'll Need

Lineman's pliers
Saw for cutting rebar
Swivel tool for twisting
  rebar ties

Related Topics

Calculating concrete needs,
  170–171
Excavating, 46–47
Forming & pouring a footing,
  58–59
Mixing & delivering, 172–173
Understanding concrete,
  168–169

Rebar in a Footing

This footing is designed to support a low decorative retaining wall. It's built in a climate with mild winters and not much rain, so it does not have to be deep or raised above the ground.

Dig a trench at least 8 inches deep. Poke vertical pieces of rebar into the soil. Here, the rebar reaches up to support the block wall (see pages 224–225). Plan the positions of the vertical pieces so they will poke through open cells in the blocks. Bend horizontal pieces to follow the curve of the trench, and attach them to the verticals with wire ties. Mix and pour concrete. Use a scrap piece of lumber to generally smooth the concrete.

Tying to Existing Concrete

If the footing passes over an existing concrete footing, tie the two together. Use a drill with a 3/8-inch or 1/2-inch masonry bit to drill a hole down into the old concrete (top). Then drive a piece of rebar down into the hole (bottom).

Mixing Mortar

Whether you're installing stones, pavers, bricks, or tiles, it is important to use mortar that is just right—not too wet, not too dry, and with the right amount of portland cement. The next four pages show how to mix it right and how to apply it.

The Basics

For most projects, buy buckets of mortar mix, which is composed of portland cement mixed with sand and perhaps lime, if you live in a cold climate. For a very large job, you could buy the cement and sand separately and mix them yourself, but the money you'll save is usually not substantial.

Avoid working with mortar when the sun is shining directly on the site, as the mortar may dry quickly.

Mixing in a Bucket

A small amount of mortar can be mixed easily in a 5-gallon bucket. Stir it up with a heavy-duty ½-inch drill equipped with a mixing paddle.

Choosing mortar mix

- Type N mortar is strong enough for most projects.
- Buy Type S if pavers will stay wet for long periods or if you want extra strength.
- Another way to add strength is to buy a separate bag of portland cement and add a shovel or two to each bag of mortar mix.

Mix in a wheelbarrow

- Pour a gallon or so of clean water into the wheelbarrow.
- Add one or two bags of mortar mix.
- Use a pointed shovel to mix the mortar, scraping the bottom of the wheelbarrow as you work.
- Add water or dry mix as needed.

Mix

- Pour about 6 inches of water into the bucket.
- Add about half a bag of mortar mix.
- Poke the mixing paddle in and start mixing with short bursts.
- Finish by running the drill for 10 seconds or so, adding water as needed.

Pour

- Leave mortar in the bucket and scoop it out with a trowel, or dump mortar onto a board or hawk.
- The mortar should be just barely stiff enough to hold its shape.

Electric Mixers

With an electric mortar mixer, like this tub mixer, you just dump in the mortar mix, water, and colorant. The paddle stirs fairly slowly, so there is little spatter. Once you are done, you can simply tilt the mixer to dump the mortar out.

 **Time Commitment**
About 10 minutes to mix, per batch

 **Tools You'll Need**
Power mixer or drill with paddle
Shovel

 Related Topics

Mixing on Plywood

For a large amount of mortar, mix on a sheet of plywood. You can use bags of mortar mix, or mix portland cement and sand on the plywood.

Heating Cold Water

On cold days, pros sometimes heat the water with a torch. Very cold water will result in a mortar mix that takes a long time to set.

1 Pour and swirl
- Make a hole in the middle of the dry mixture and pour water into it.
- Using a shovel, start mixing with a swirling motion around the resulting pool.

2 Shovel dry mix
- Working all around the rim of the pool, scrape dry mix onto the pool.
- First scrape from the top of the pile, then poke deeper and scrape along the plywood.

3 Chop
- Use a chopping motion to work the dry mix into the water.
- Tap the plywood and scrape slightly as you chop.

4 Add water
- Keep chopping, then mix by scooping and turning the mortar over.
- If the mortar is too dry, splash water over its surface and chop again.

5 Finish mixing
- Scrape and turn the mixture over repeatedly until you achieve an even consistency.
- The mortar should be wet enough to stick for a second or so to a shovel turned upside down, but it should be dry enough to hold its shape.

Testing the Mix

For most purposes, mortar is the right thickness when you can cut ridges in it with a trowel and the ridges are just wet enough to hold their shape. The mortar is too dry if it appears crumbly.

Testing mortar thickness

- Another test is to scoop up some mortar with a trowel and hold it upside down at a 45-degree angle.
- The mortar should stick to the trowel for a second or two, then slowly slide off.
- If it is too wet, add dry mix.

Paving Techniques

Regular mason's mortar can be used to install flagstones, thick stone tiles, and bricks or pavers onto a concrete slab. To install thin tiles, use thinset mortar.

Ensuring a good bond

- To ensure that the mortar bonds with the concrete slab, spread liquid concrete bonding agent onto the slab and allow it to dry at least partially.
- Press stones firmly into the mortar.
- When you pull on the stone, it should feel secure.
- If it is not stuck, either butter the back of the stone with a thin coat of mortar or make the mortar wetter.

Spreading mortar for stones

- When setting large stones, first shovel mortar onto the slab.
- Spread the mortar with a trowel, estimating how high the mortar needs to be.
- Press the stone into place.
- You may need to remove the stone and add or subtract mortar to get the stone at the right height.

Using mortar at the edge

- On a sand-laid patio, it is often a good idea to set the perimeter pavers in mortar that has been laid on the sand.
- This will not be as strong as mortar on concrete, but it will definitely help keep things in place.

English-style paving

- Lay a bed of gravel and sand and tamp it firm.
- For each stone or tile, drop five dollops of mortar onto the sand.
- Press the stone into place and then step on it or tap it to achieve the correct height.

Embedding pebbles

- For a pebble mosaic, start with a concrete slab or a well-tamped surface of gravel and sand.
- Set the pebbles on a sheet of plywood first, in the desired pattern.
- Spread a small amount of fairly wet mortar.
- Press the pebbles into the mortar.
- As the mortar starts to dry, wipe the surface clean.

Tiles in thinset

- For a tile surface that is uniformly level, start with a concrete slab.
- Spread thinset mortar first with the flat side of a trowel, then with the notched side.
- Comb the surface smooth and then set the tiles.

Brick Walls

You might not be able to set bricks as quickly and as precisely as a pro, but with some practice, you can produce a modest brick garden wall that looks just fine and that will last a long time. Use mason's blocks and lines to maintain level courses.

Butter brick ends

- Most bricks need to be buttered on one end.
- Scoop mortar onto a brick trowel.
- Apply it with a scraping motion onto the brick end.

Strike the joints

- Choose the desired shape for the joints and use the appropriate striking tool.
- When you can leave a lasting impression by pressing with your thumb, the joint is ready to strike.
- Move the striking tool along the horizontal joints, then the verticals.
- Brush away any mortar crumbs.

Throw & furrow

- Scoop the mortar with a brick trowel and flick your wrist to make the mortar leave the trowel for a split second.
- Throw the mortar onto the footing or bricks with a sweeping motion.
- Make a furrow in the middle of the thrown mortar.

Block Walls

Standard or stackable concrete blocks can be stacked dry and then coated with surface bonding material to provide strength. Or the blocks can be set in mortar, as with a brick wall.

Filling cells

- Some of the holes in the blocks, or cells, can be filled with mortar and perhaps rebar to add strength.
- When you're joining two walls, cells are often filled, and bent rebar helps complete the connection.

Stone Walls

A mortared stone wall must rest on a solid concrete footing. Typically, the two faces of the wall are made of large stones, while the area between the faces is filled with smaller stones and mortar or concrete.

Placing stones

- Experiment to determine the layout for three or more stones before laying them.
- Spread thick mortar that is fairly stiff—just wet enough to stick to the stones.
- It may help to wet the stones to ensure stickability.
- Press the stones into place and wipe away the excess mortar.

Crevice Planting

The gaps between wall stones and the joints between flagstones and pavers can be filled with plants that make the scene softer and livelier. Choose plants that will thrive in your climate and survive your foot traffic.

Choosing Plants

Many nurseries have special sections for crevice plants that fill gaps, as well as "steppers," which can be walked on.

Desert plants like thyme and succulents need little moisture and can die if overwatered. For them, soil should be about half sand and should be well drained to a depth of at least 8 inches. If the patio is subject to puddling, the plants may not survive. Plants that require more moisture do best when planted in a rich potting soil.

Some crevice plants are hardier than others. In general, larger plants survive well only in low-traffic areas, while plants with small leaves are less crushable. Succulents look fragile, but some varieties are surprisingly hardy. Herbs like thyme and marjoram release a pleasant aroma when trod upon.

This patio is filled with geranium, blue sedge, heliotrope, and blue and white alyssum.

Moss pink, snow in summer, and silver lace do nicely on stairs.

Planting Tips

When you build a patio, keep the plants in mind as you prepare the substrate. Flagstones set directly in soil provide a natural growing medium. If you build a substrate of gravel and sand, choose desert plants or add some soil to the substrate. If the stones are 2 inches thick or thicker, filling the joints with soil may provide a deep enough medium for the plants.

For a neater appearance, limit plants within a pathway or on a wall to just one or two types. You may want to plant a greater variety initially and see what works best. Then thin out the slackers and transplant offsets of the plants that are doing well.

Remove all weeds completely before planting. Buy plants rather than seeds, as young shoots are very fragile. Break apart a plant into small portions, called plugs, and carefully dig deep enough so the roots don't have to be balled up.

If you don't mind spending the money and need instant gratification, fill patio joints completely with plants. If you space plants several inches apart, they should fill in within a year, given favorable conditions.

Planting on a Wall

When building a dry wall, add some soil between the stones where you will want plants. Break plants into roughly the shape of the gaps between stones, insert the plants, and gently tamp the soil around them.

Meadow foam softens this flagstone grid.

Propagating Moss

Moss usually works best in an area that is damp much of the time. You could cut up pieces of moss to fit and then set them on top of soil. Or you can make a moss slurry, in a blender or by hand, by mixing even amounts of moss with buttermilk or beer. Thicken it by adding clay or soil and perhaps also liquid fertilizer to encourage growth. Use a spoon to apply to crevices.

Do this . . .

. . . to get this.

The Elfin variety of Thymus serpyllum is perfectly suited for growing between pavers.

Blue star creeper blurs the line between a patio and the plantings that surround it.

How the Pros Do It

"If the soil under a patio has plenty of clay, we often dig it up with a pick, add coarse sand, then rototill to a depth of 4 to 6 inches. The resulting soil can be tamped firm to provide a good base for a patio or path, yet it is also a great medium for growing crevice plants."

Ken Coverdell, Blue Sky Designs

3

Quick & Easy Patios & Paths

In this chapter, you'll learn how to place flagstones and step-pingstones to create small patios and paths. We help you work with concrete, from existing slabs that can be recycled to new concrete that can be molded and colored. You'll also learn about boulders—where to purchase them, how to prepare for their delivery, how to safely move them about, and the ways to place them in a garden.

Chapter Contents

Casual Sitting Areas
page 70

Placing Flagstones
page 72

Steppingstones
page 74

Small Circular Patio
page 76

English-Style Paving
page 78

Paving with Recycled Concrete
page 80

Casual Sitting Areas

Flagstones and pavers can be set directly on soil, tamped gravel, or sand with no edging. As a result, paving materials are likely to sink, rise, or become uneven. If they shift, simply pick up the pavers, dig away or add soil or sand underneath, and reset them.

Stable Alternatives

Some patios look as if the flagstones were randomly dropped there, but in fact it takes a good deal of planning and work to achieve this effect. To stay in place, the stones may be mortared onto small concrete slabs or secured with invisible edging. If you want a patio that is relaxed in feel but more stable than the ones shown here, jump ahead to pages 92 and 144 for more techniques.

A short stone path surrounded by mulch leads to a quiet sitting area.

In this small space, irregular stones and recycled chunks of concrete have been set within a bed of plantless soil.

Scottish moss helps stabilize these flagstones, which were set on a bed of tamped soil.

The lack of edging alongside this path and patio softens the visual impact of so many hard stones amid the surrounding garden.

Gravel also makes a nice patio, such as in this reading spot in a small backyard.

Placing Flagstones

Flagstones can be set in a dry bed of sand and gravel or mortared onto a concrete slab. The easiest way, shown here, is to set the stones on soil.

Setting on Soil: Pros & Cons

If the future patio site is fairly level and has no nearby trees or roots that are near the surface, setting stones directly onto the soil is a good option for a number of reasons:

- Installation goes quickly. You don't have to lay a gravel and sand bed, and other than removing sod, you don't have to excavate.
- Since you won't be covering up the soil with gravel and sand, crevice plants can probably grow easily.
- A fair amount of water can drain through the patio, especially if the joints are fairly wide.

However, there are potential drawbacks:

- Over time, the soil will settle and some stones may become unstable or sink. When this happens, you will need to pick up a stone, remove or add soil, and reset the stone.
- If roots from a nearby tree are near the surface, the patio will develop humps and valleys.
- Weeds can grow up through the cracks, overpowering the crevice plants of your choosing. In that case, you will need to remove the weeds and replant.
- If the site does not slope consistently away from the house, you could end up with puddles after a heavy rain.

Buying Stones

Choose flagstones that are fairly consistent in thickness. Otherwise it will be difficult to achieve an even surface. Flagstones are sold by the ton, so you can save money by buying thin stones that are about 1¼ inches thick.

Flagstones in Sod

If the site is small and you want grass to grow in the crevices, consider setting stones individually in the sod.

1 Arrange stones & cut lawn

- Place the stones on the lawn, aiming for a pleasing arrangement.
- With a sharp spade or garden trowel, cut the outline of the stones into the sod.
- Remove each stone and dig away sod.

2 Set the stones

- Dig away soil to make a hole that roughly matches the bottom of the stone.
- Perhaps add a shovelful of sand to help level the stone.
- Replace the stones.
- Make sure they are low enough for lawn mowing.
- As needed, add or remove sand to help make the stones level and stable.

Stuff to Buy

Acrylic sealer
Crevice plants
Flagstones
Sand

 **Time Commitment**

A day for a 150-square-foot patio

 **Tools You'll Need**

Garden trowel
Grinder or masonry cutoff saw
Hammer and cold chisel
Hand tamper
Rake
Shovel

 Related Topics

1 Excavate & level

- Remove all sod and any roots or other organic matter.
- If needed, slope the site consistently away from the house.
- Scrape the bottom of the excavation to keep undisturbed soil intact.
- Tamp the area with a hand tamper or a 4 × 4 board.
- Gently rake to loosen the soil about 1/2 inch deep.

2 Sort & cut stones

- Set the stones on plywood or a driveway to protect the lawn.
- Sort the stones into three piles according to size.
- Some stones cut easily, while some are harder.
- If you have a very large stone, break it apart with a hammer and chisel and then space the pieces regularly on the patio.

3 Arrange stones

- Place stones in the excavated area and experiment with different arrangements.
- Aim to achieve joints that are fairly consistent in width.
- Cut stones as needed.
- If a stone protrudes beyond the excavated area, perhaps dig away the sod instead of cutting the stone.

4 Bed the stones

- Once you have arranged 10 square feet of stones, set them and then move on to the next section.
- To set a stone, stand on it or tap it with a rubber mallet to produce an impression in the soil.
- Tilt each stone and use a garden trowel to scrape away soil, or fill the area with soil or sand. Lay the stone back down and test it for stability.

5 Fill the joints

- Use a garden trowel or a pointed shovel to slip soil into the joints.
- Use soil that is slightly damp so it will stay in place but not smear.
- Add crevice plants if you want them.
- Add sand or potting mix depending on the crevice plants.

6 Spray, plant, seal

- Use a hose nozzle to mist the patio until the joints are soaked.
- Sprinkle seeds if you choose.
- Allow the soil to dry, then wet the seeds again.
- Coat the stones with acrylic sealer to prevent staining

Steppingstones

Here is a minimalist approach to paving that achieves a bucolic effect. Steppingstones are fairly inexpensive and can be installed quickly. The surface will not be smooth, but it will be just fine for a lightly traveled path.

Designing a Path

On a manicured lawn, steppingstones will be fully exposed. In other settings, nearby plants may partially cover the stones. If the stones are set on a lawn, you will most likely want them flush with the grass so you can run a lawn mower over them. If crevice plants will climb onto the stones, you may want to raise the stones a bit.

Steppingstones are not wedged together, so they need to be at least 2 inches thick to remain stable and not crack. Use stones that are at least 16 inches in diameter or width and not too bumpy. In addition to natural stones, you can buy precast concrete steppers in uniform square, octagonal, or round shapes. These may be formed and colored to look like natural stone, or they may have exposed-aggregate surfaces.

The Easiest Method

If the stones or pavers are heavy and the lawn is fairly smooth, you could simply set the stones directly on top of the lawn. In a few months the grass beneath will die and rot away, and the stone will settle. (Until then, use a weed whacker near the stones.) Depending on conditions, the stone may sink low enough to run a lawn mover over it, but you will likely need to add or subtract sand or soil to achieve stability.

Steppingstones can be orderly and uniform (top) or orderly and irregular (bottom). Either way, they create paths that are in harmony with the landscaping.

$ Stuff to Buy

Sand
Steppingstones

Time Commitment

Several hours for a 20-foot-long path

Tools You'll Need

Garden trowel
Pointed shovel
Rubber mallet
Square shovel

Related Topics

Natural stone, 14–15
Placing flagstones, 72–73

Arranging the Stones

There are two basic approaches to steppingstone arrangement. In the method shown here, stones are placed in a zigzag pattern that matches the natural gait of an adult. Another approach is to install closely spaced stones so you end up with a fairly solid-looking path.

1 Lay the stones

- A path should be 2 to 3 feet wide.
- Stretch string lines for a straight path, or use hoses for a curved path.
- Place stones within the lines or hoses, alternating left and right.
- Walk on them to determine a comfortable arrangement.

2 Slice the outline

- Set a stone in place and use a shovel to slice a line through the sod around it.
- Or leave all the stones on the lawn for a week and then pick up and slice away the yellowed areas.

3 Remove sod & dig

- Dig up and remove the sod.
- Also remove any roots or other organic material.
- Dig deep enough so the stone will be just below grade.
- Perhaps mix some sand with the soil to make it easier to work.

4 Bed the stone

- If a stone is uneven in thickness, roughly mirror the stone's contours in the hole.
- Set the stone in place and tap it with a rubber mallet or stand on it.

5 Fine-tune the bed

- Remove the stone and examine the bed as well as the bottom of the stone.
- Note where soil or sand needs to be removed or added.
- Scrape high spots and fill voids, then replace the stone.
- Walk on the stone and continue fine-tuning until it is stable.

Small Circular Patio

This small brick patio makes a big visual impact and can be built in as little as a day.
Tuck it into a corner of your yard to create a peaceful private retreat.

**A small detached circular patio like this could be built with a serious substrate and firm edgings, as described in chapters 4 and 5.
But if you don't mind a patio that might develop a few waves over time, you can opt for this decidedly simpler approach.**

Material Choices

To build this exact patio, which is 7 feet in diameter, you will need
134 standard-size bricks or concrete pavers, plus a round or octagonal center medallion. The medallion could be made of stone or a
cast-concrete paver. If you like, sprinkle the design with different
colored or decorative bricks.

Install bricks that are rated for use as pavers in your area. If you
live in a warm climate, you may choose to use wall bricks and perhaps protect them with a coat or two of masonry sealer.

$ Stuff to Buy

Bag of mortar mix
Bricks or pavers
Center stone or paver
Rough sand

Time Commitment

One or two days

Tools You'll Need

Hand tamper
Level and a straight board
Pointing trowel
Rubber mallet
Shovel

Related Topics

Applying mortar, 64–65
Brick, 16–17
English-style paving, 78–79
Excavating, 46–47
Invisible edgings, 100–101
Mixing mortar, 62–63

How to Do It

Here we show how to install a patio on bare soil. If you choose this option, finish by butting flexible invisible edging against the perimeter bricks and then planting sod up against the edging. If the area is grassy, mark and cut your sod in a fairly precise circle and butt the outside pavers against the grass.

Using a small amount of mortar will stabilize the patio but will not make it rock-solid. Filling more of the joints with mortar is not a good idea, as the mortar will likely crack. On a patio like this, you may occa-

Center Paver

Number of Bricks Per Row

28
44
19
16
13
14

Center Paver

1 Choose a pattern

- To determine the finished size of the patio, lay the bricks in a dry run on a level surface.
- You may want to add or subtract rows to change the patio's dimensions.

2 Mark & excavate

- Drive a stake in the middle of the patio area and make a simple compass out of a string and a smaller stake. Mark the perimeter with spray paint, lime, or flour.
- Dig away sod and roots, going deep enough for the base and bricks.
- Check for level.

3 Pour & tamp sand

- Add rough sand or paver base into the excavated area.
- Tamp it firm using a hand tamper or a 4 × 4.
- Recheck it for evenness and level.
- Spray it with a fine mist of water and tamp it again.

4 Set the pavers

- Set the medallion in the middle, then set the bricks in your desired pattern.
- Inspect and adjust the bricks as needed.
- Tap the bricks with a rubber mallet to bed them.
- Set a piece of plywood on top and walk on it to achieve an even surface.

5 Mortar the center & fill the joints

- Mix a small amount of mortar, pick up the center paver, apply dabs of mortar under it, and set the paver in mortar.
- Use a pointing trowel to slip mortar between bricks in the first row around the medallion.
- Pour sand onto the rest of the patio, then sweep until the joints are filled.
- Spray the joints with a fine mist, allow them to dry, and repeat.

English-style Paving

This method is used often by our friends across the pond, where winter temperatures can get down to freezing but are not severe. Stones are set in mortar atop a bed of tamped gravel, so a patio like this should stay stable and level enough for most situations.

The Logic of Five Dabs

In the United States, paving materials are usually installed in one of two ways. Either they are set in a dry bed of sand and gravel or they are mortared onto a solid concrete slab. The English method is a hybrid of the two, using mortar on top of a dry bed. It holds pavers more securely than sand or soil, so you do not need edging. The resulting patio is not quite as firm as one set on concrete, but installation is much easier if you do not already have a slab in place. This method also allows you to put plants in the joints.

Setting pavers in five dabs of mortar is a good technique when pavers are not uniform in thickness and the substrate is not completely even. The five dabs allow you to push down harder on one side or another to adjust for level.

Mortar or Plants?

Instead of filling the joints with soil and plants, you could fill them with mortar or coarse sand. Be aware, however, that the mortar may crack in areas of freezing winters.

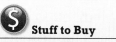 **Stuff to Buy**
Compactable gravel and sand for base
Crevice plants
Mortar mix
Paving stones or thick tiles

 **Time Commitment**
About a day for a 150-square-foot patio

 **Tools You'll Need**
Brick trowel
Carpenter's level
Hand tamper
Level
Rubber mallet
Shovel

 Related Topics
Applying mortar, 64–65
Crevice planting, 66–67
Cutting bricks, pavers, & stone, 48–51
Excavating, 46–47
Mixing mortar, 62–63

How to Do It

1 Arrange the stones

- Dig up sod and excavate 3 inches deeper than the lawn.
- Using scraps of 1-by lumber for spacers, set the pavers in a dry run.
- Use string lines to maintain straight joints.
- Experiment with arrangements to create attractively offset joints.
- You may choose to cut some pavers.
- For a ragged edge, allow some pavers to lap onto the lawn, then cut and excavate around them.
- Remove the pavers, numbering their backs to keep track of where they go.

2 Lay a base

- Tamp the soil with a hand tamper, a 4 × 4, or a vibrating tamper.
- Spread 2 inches of compactable gravel.
- Use a board to screed the surface even, then tamp it.
- Add 1 inch of sand and then screed again.

3 Five dabs

- Set some or all of the pavers in place with spacers.
- Mix a batch of mortar, barely dry enough to hold its shape.
- Pick up the paver that is highest and plop five dabs of mortar in the area below.
- If you are using large stones with more than four sides, you may use more dabs.

4 Bed the pavers

- Press several pavers in dabs of mortar.
- Tap with a mallet and a board to even the surface.
- If a paver is low, pick it up, add more mortar, and reset it.
- Scrape or wipe away any mortar that oozes into the joints.

5 Fill the joints

- Wait a day for the mortar to set.
- Apply a coat or two of acrylic sealer to make the pavers stain-resistant.
- Partially fill the joints with soil suited to your chosen plants.
- Insert crevice plants into the joints.

Paving with Recycled Concrete

One person's junk can become another's treasure. Here's a paving material you can likely get for free. Reusing old concrete is environmentally responsible, and the results can be surprisingly attractive.

Making Concrete Pavers

As long as it's not badly stained, old concrete has a pebbly charm. You can remove most stains by pressure washing the surface or scrubbing with a strong cleaner. Acid staining or sand blasting will expose the aggregate (pebbles), which may be the look you're after.

Concrete slabs, the raw material for your concrete pavers, generally range in thickness from 2 to 8 inches. If possible, dig to expose an edge of the old slab to get an idea of the thickness. Also, some slabs have metal reinforcement, which makes them more difficult to break apart.

Wear long clothing, gloves, and protective eyewear, as sharp chips can fly around. Heavy labor is involved, so start in an out-of-the way corner of the concrete to gauge the difficulty. Try whacking with a sledgehammer; the concrete may break apart with surprising ease. If not, insert a wrecking bar under the slab, use a stone or scrap board as a fulcrum, and pry up the concrete. Have a helper hold the concrete up while you beat it.

If the slab is reinforced with wire mesh, cut the wire with lineman's pliers or wire cutters. If you encounter 3/8- or 1/2-inch rebar, you'll need a pair of bolt cutters or a reciprocating saw with a metal-cutting blade.

For more precise shapes, cut first with a masonry cutting saw and then break the pieces apart. You may want to use a hammer to chip the edges for a more natural look.

When combined with crevice plants, pavers made of broken concrete can give a new patio or path a historical, time-tested appearance.

How to Do It

If the new patio will be in the same location as the current slab, break and then spread out the pieces to create fairly consistent joints. If the new patio will be in another spot, perhaps number the chunks so you can reassemble them in the same order.

Excavate the patio location to the depth of the concrete's thickness. If the chunks are nice and heavy, you can simply set them in soil, and no edging will be needed. If the chunks need to be held in place, use setting techniques shown in chapter 4.

To check the slab's thickness, dig away at its edge.

A wrecking bar and a sledge will handle most demolition projects.

Move chunks out of the way with a heavy-duty wheelbarrow.

Molded Concrete

Using sand-mix concrete and an inexpensive plastic mold, you can cast a stone path or small patio with neat-looking joints. Molds can also be used to create unique concrete steppingstones. When mixing concrete, add a tint to give your path or pavers color.

Molding Stones

At a home center you can find plastic molds for forming concrete into shapes that resemble bricks or flagstones. You'll find more options online if you search for "molded concrete pavers." These molds simplify the process, but they don't automatically make perfect stones. You will need to spend a fair amount of time smoothing the rough edges.

Shown below are some fairly straightforward molded faux stones. To achieve more artistic effects, see pages 260–263. To maintain your momentum and finish the project faster, purchase two or more molds.

These pavers can be set on well-tamped soil or on a gravel or sand bed. If you pour them in place, they will be stable. If you move them, you will need to adjust the substrate as you would for any flagstones or pavers.

How to Do It

1 Fill the mold

- Press the mold firmly into the soil or gravel so concrete can't seep out.
- Mix a batch of stiff sand-mix concrete. It should not be pourable.
- Perhaps add some fiber reinforcement to prevent cracks.
- Shovel concrete into the mold, then poke with a trowel to make sure all cavities are filled.

2 Trowel

- Use a brick trowel or margin trowel to smooth the surface.
- Scrape across the form in two or more directions.
- Remove any excess concrete.
- Wait at least 10 minutes before removing the mold.

3 Finish

- Once all surface water has disappeared, lift the mold straight up. You may need to shake as you lift.
- If a stone starts to crack as you lift, press the mold back down and wait 10 more minutes.
- Smooth the edges with a mason's brush or paint brush.
- Joints can be left as they are or filled with sand or fine gravel.

When choosing molds for pavers, think about colors and shapes that you will want to live with for a long time. For some people, a dozen pavers in the shape of green frogs might wear thin with time. For others, green frogs might give them something to smile about every day.

Rock Gardens & Boulders

You might think you can make a natural-looking rock garden by randomly strewing boulders here and there, but nature has an order to it that can be tricky to duplicate. When placing rocks in your landscape, try to take an architectural approach.

Stone Design Rules of Thumb

- In many natural settings, there is only one kind of stone. You may want to limit your design to one type as well.
- Boulders and large rocks usually look most natural if about one-third of each is buried. Alternatively, sink a rock into the ground to just beyond its widest point.
- Low, wide stones work as anchors or platforms, while wide, skinny ones stand as sentinels. Single boulders can be accents, while collections of stones suggest mountain outcroppings.
- When you are using large stones or boulders, odd-numbered groupings of up to nine stones look best. With more stones than that, a rock collection may seem too cluttered.
- Rocks may appear forlorn when you first lay them, but once crevice plants and larger plants have grown in, the rocks will look like they've been there all along. Coating rocks with moss adds to their patina.

Split-Boulder Effects

To simulate the ravages that time and weather work on stone, have a rock yard take a large boulder and split it lengthwise several times along its grain. Place the resulting slabs parallel and in order, but leave gaps of several inches between the slabs. Pack the gaps with soil mix and then plant miniature gardens in each joint, or leave enough room for a path.

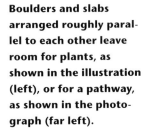

Boulders and slabs arranged roughly parallel to each other leave room for plants, as shown in the illustration (left), or for a pathway, as shown in the photograph (far left).

 **Stuff to Buy**
Stones and/or boulders

 **Time Commitment**
Varies by project

Tools You'll Need
Earth-moving machine
Shovel
Wrecking bar

 **Related Topics**
Crevice planting, 66–67
Transporting heavy stones, 56–57

Boulders in a Field

To capture the look of boulders in an open field, choose rocks and boulders that are somewhat chiseled in appearance rather than round. On a flat or gently sloped yard, lay stones in roughly parallel bands (see illustration, below left), or tilt the stones at the same angle (see illustration, below right). The more harmonious the composition, the more restful the landscape will feel.

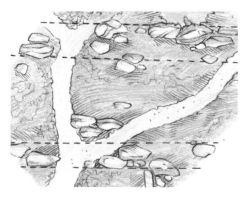

Outcroppings of rock in parallel bands

Top of each stone tilts at the same angle

Boulders with Scree

A typical natural scree is a pile of broken stone lying at the base of a cliff. To mimic the look, first establish boulders near the top of the rock garden. Plant shrubs and large perennials around the boulders. Cover the area around the plants with stones or gravel matching the color of the boulders.

Shopping for Boulders

Visit a number of stone yards with a camera and a tape measure. You may soon develop a love for stone and discover why people in the business often say they choose stones that "speak" to them.

Take snapshots and measurements of the stones you're considering. At home, stuff plastic garbage bags with newspapers to roughly create the same shapes and test the effects in your yard. Take into account the depth to which the boulders will be buried.

Large boulders are sold individually and may cost quite a bit. Some have regular horizontal lines that give a solid bedrock feeling, while others will look great pointing upward.

Arranging for Delivery

Stone yards typically offer a variety of delivery options. A person may go out to your house beforehand to verify that the moving equipment will work in your yard. You may need to remove part of a fence to allow room for a large truck. Make sure delivery will not damage overhead or underground power lines, overhanging trees, buried pipes, or a septic tank.

To set a large boulder precisely, a boom truck, with a crane arm that lifts individual rocks and sets them onto the ground, is often the best option. The weight of the stones is part of the calculation. For instance, a truck that reaches 40 feet with a 1-ton stone might be able to extend only 20 feet with a 2-ton stone. Delivery and placement will likely cost hundreds of dollars. A crane has a longer reach but is even more expensive.

A forklift or skid loader will fit through a 6-foot-wide gate. You can spend a few hours learning how to operate the machine yourself, or hire a skilled operator for a few hundred bucks to get the job done quickly and safely.

Safety Tip: Watch Your Back

You can make a small rock garden using hand tools. Be aware, however, that repeated lifting of medium-size objects can damage your lower back. This commonly happens to do-it-yourselfers who are not accustomed to physical labor. You may feel fine while doing the work, then wake up the next morning with lower-back pain that lingers for days or weeks. If you're not careful, you can do permanent damage to yourself.

To prevent a back injury, take plenty of breaks, keep your back straight, lift with your legs rather than your back, and consider hiring a couple of young, strong-backed helpers to do most of the lifting.

Planting Boulders

Boulders must be carefully planted into the ground so they look natural. Settle the stone so its widest circumference is even with the top of the surrounding soil. If one side of the boulder looks weathered or shows patches of moss or lichen, that side should face up. Otherwise, plant the stone with its smaller end down.

With a tall, columnar stone, carefully dig a hole that matches the circumference of the stone's base. About one-fourth of the column's height should be below ground.

Once a boulder is in the ground, it won't be easy to lift out. But you can pivot the stone or tip it slightly with a wrecking bar to change its appearance. Place a stone or a piece of wood underneath the bar to act as a fulcrum. Have a supply of rocks on hand so you can stuff them into the hole and wedge the boulder into position once you're satisfied with the placement.

Fieldstone Paths

A fieldstone is literally a stone found in a field, but the term can encompass almost any rock that wasn't recently blasted loose in a quarry or tumbled round on a beach.

Because it's been out in the weather for years, fieldstone is often flecked with patches of moss or lichen. These patches may wear away if stones are placed in a heavy-traffic area, but at least some greenery will likely remain.

A fieldstone path is not expected to be as smooth as a pavered area or even a flagstone patio. Still, set the stones as you would flagstones in soil, or provide a gravel-and-sand base below the stones and test each one for stability.

Loose Surfaces

Loose materials are the easiest type of paving to install, but you will probably want to enclose the patio or path with solid edging so the stones don't wander onto your yard. A gravel path can be surprisingly firm.

Where It Works

A loose-material surface is perfect in many situations. Because it allows rainwater to percolate into the soil, it is ideal next to an established tree. If growing roots cause waves, you can just rake the surface smooth.

A surface of rounded pebbles or large pieces of gravel is easily scattered and may make for loose footing. A surface of tiny irregular stones, such as crushed rock or decomposed granite, can become quite hard and stable once compacted.

This gravel dining and barbecue area is a casual, low-maintenance alternative to laid brick or mortared stones.

Steppingstones in Gravel

To make a gravel path easier to walk on, add flagstones or other pavers and space them to match your stride. They're best installed as part of the initial construction. Excavate, install edging, and lay a bed of well-tamped gravel that is a stone's thickness below the top of the edging. Set each stone so it is firm, perhaps adding sand for stability. You may want to set stones in mortar, English-style. Then install the finished gravel around the stones.

The scale of these steppingstones works well with larger pieces of gravel.

Sometimes bricks and stones can be combined to provide solid footing in gravel.

Smooth, square stone pavers create a stable pathway on round gravel.

Stuff to Buy	**Time Commitment**	**Tools You'll Need**	**Related Topics**

Compactable gravel
Edging material
Finish-material gravel
	A day for a 50-foot path	Compactor or drum roller
		Garden rake
		Shovels
		Tools for installing edging of
		   your choice
			English-style paving, 78–79
			Excavating, 46–47
			Lumber & timber edging,
			   102–103
			Other materials, 24–25

Building a Path or Patio

Excavate to a depth of 4 to 8 inches; the deeper you excavate, the better the drainage will be. If you get heavy rain or if your soil has enough clay that drainage is a problem, slope the excavation away from the house. Install the edging of your choice, then tamp the soil firm. If vegetation is lush in your locale, consider laying landscaping fabric at the bottom of the excavation, or between the two types of stone. Ask your supplier whether landscaping fabric is recommended.

① Lay a gravel base

- Shovel and rake a layer of compactable gravel, allowing 2 to 3 inches for the top layer.
- If drainage is a concern, use large non-compactable gravel instead.

② Compress the base

- Use a vibrating plate compactor to compress gravel 4 to 6 inches deep. You can use a hand tamper or a drum roller for gravel that is less than 4 inches deep.
- Thoroughly compress the gravel so less attractive stones will not work their way up to the surface.

③ Apply the top layer

- Use a rake to spread finish-material gravel.
- Take care not to disturb the base gravel.
- If gravel is small-grained, tamp it firm. Do not attempt to tamp rounded pebbles or large stones.

Stabilizing Gravel

To keep gravel from migrating onto your yard and to keep pets from digging in it, consider spraying it with an acrylic or vinyl acetate soil stabilizer. This binds the gravel and stiffens the surface. It won't work on rounded gravel, only on crushed or very small gravel that includes fine particles. Stabilized gravel sheds water, so slope the surface as if it were solid. Stabilizing products will leave your path looking like it's permanently wet, so test a small area first to make sure you like it.

Contain a gravel path with stones bordering bedding plant

Mixed Surfaces

Create a crazy-quilt pattern using just about any material that can survive in your climate. Take your time to develop a look that expresses your personality. Often, a few subtle rearrangements can transform a sloppy hodgepodge into an artistic design.

How to Do It

A mixed-material path or patio may be supported by a solid gravel-and-sand substrate, or it may be mortared onto a concrete slab. Here we show a casual surface, which has wood edging and a substrate of tamped compactable gravel. As a result, the lighter stones and gravel in the finished surface may need to be rearranged or replaced from time to time. The heavy stones and timbers will probably stay in place if subjected to no more than normal traffic.

Excavate the area. Some paths can be installed directly on tamped soil, but you may want to install a bed of tamped compactable gravel. You also may need to install an edging to keep paving materials in place. In the example shown here, 4 × 6 timbers are used to anchor the pattern and supply some stability. You may choose to use large flat stones instead.

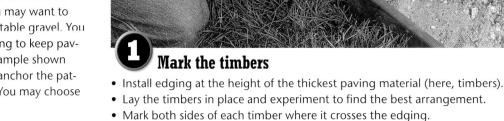

1 **Mark the timbers**

- Install edging at the height of the thickest paving material (here, timbers).
- Lay the timbers in place and experiment to find the best arrangement.
- Mark both sides of each timber where it crosses the edging.
- Use a square to extend lines upward, then mark the cutting angle across the top.

2 **Cut the timbers**

- If you have the skill, cut each timber with a chain saw.
- To cut with a circular saw, set the blade to its maximum depth and cut along a line on one side of a timber.
- Finish by turning the timber over, drawing another line, and cutting again.

3 **Add large stones**

- Between timbers, fill with compactable gravel, just high enough so large stones will be at the same height as the timbers.
- Push a large stone into the gravel, remove it, and spread a small bed of sand.
- Set the stone in the sand.
- If the stone wobbles, add or scrape away sand as needed.

4 **Fill with gravel & stones**

- Shovel decorative gravel around large stones and rake it smooth.
- Embed stones in the gravel.
- Tamp firm with a heavy board or a hand tamper.

Stuff to Buy
Gravel, stones, and anything else that suits you

Time Commitment
A weekend

Tools You'll Need
Basic carpentry tools
Rake
Tamper

Related Topics
Excavating, 46–47
Loose-material surfaces, 86–87
Lumber & timber edging, 102–103

Two Mixers for Gravel

Gravel is a generous host for materials of all sorts, as these two examples show.

Round wooden pavers resemble black polka dots in a pebble pathway. Remember to set the pebbles on a tamped surface (soil or gravel) before laying the pavers so they don't shift underfoot.

Here, brick is used to add graphic interest to gravel. In this case, only a few bricks are required to break up the path, making this an inexpensive option.

Paving Near a Tree

Keep solid paving at least 2 feet from tree trunks. The paving could cause the trees to die of thirst, and the tree's roots may cause the paving to heave. Before paving around a tree, consult a nursery to determine how fast the tree will grow, how much water it needs, and how close to the surface the roots will get. If you encounter large roots when excavating, be aware that cutting into them could cause part or all of the tree to die.

An even better paving solution near a tree is to use loose pavers, which are easier on roots than solid paving and allow water to get through.

How the Pros Do It

"People often injure roots because they can't see them. If you look straight up and see branches, you're probably standing above roots. To avoid damaging a tree, here's a very general rule of thumb: Measure a tree's circumference and keep a solid patio at least that far from the trunk. For more specific information, consult an arborist certified by the International Society of Arboriculture. A patio with gaps is preferable to one with tight joints, because some water can seep down. Finally, avoid paving with limestones or crushed limestone; it will raise the soil's alkaline level, which trees do not like."

Shawn Kingzette, The Care of Trees

Turf Blocks

Also called "drivable grass," turf blocks can be laid directly onto soil so that grass or other plantings can grow up through the gaps. The resulting surface will look like a lawn but remain strong enough support heavy vehicles.

Choosing Products

Turf block has wide gaps that allow water to get through, thereby solving most drainage problems. In fact, if you add sand to the underlying soil, you can make the area more permeable than it was before you installed the block. When excavating, you usually don't have to slope the area away from the house. Turf block is often used to cover small valleys that collect water.

A small amount of cast-concrete turf block has been around for decades, but now there is a wide variety of products to choose from. Most are made of cast concrete that is as strong as standard concrete pavers. Newer types come in mats, with individual pavers joined with fiberglass or other types of webbing. The overall surface is flexible, so the substrate does not have to be especially firm.

Installing Turf Blocks

The most popular use of turf blocks is in driveways. In this example, a homeowner's RV chewed up the lawn leading to a parking area on the side of the house. The solution was to excavate, lay the blocks, and then reseed (see instructions on opposite page).

To excavate, use string lines and stakes, a hose, or other methods to mark the area. (In this case, tire tracks in the lawn did a pretty good job of showing exactly where the turf blocks needed to go.) Then dig away sod and remove roots or other organic material to

ensure the block will be at grade. If you want to improve the permeability of the soil, add sand. At this point, you should also add fertilizer, mulch, and/or soil as needed, as well as an irrigation system, if desired. Screed the area to make it level and smooth.

Laying turf-block mats is not that difficult. Place all the full-size mats first. To cut a mat between individual blocks, use a hammer and chisel. To cut the blocks, use a masonry cutoff saw, grinder, or other power tool.

Before

During

After

 **Stuff to Buy**

Sand and soil as needed
Turf blocks

 **Time Commitment**

One day per driveway

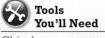 **Tools You'll Need**

Chisel
Garden rake
Hammer
Shovels
Sod cutter
Tamper (hand or power)

Related Topics

Planting Between Blocks

Fill gaps with a soil mixture to within ¼ inch of the top of the blocks. Broadcast grass seed over the area. Cover the seed with a light coat of organic material, filling to the tops of the blocks. Sweep the area smooth and water it regularly.

Other Uses

The driveway is probably not the only outdoor area around your house that gets a lot of traffic. Consider turf block for any problem area where a lawn has difficulty growing because of heavy use. In this case, a surface of turf blocks is probably better than this trash can deserves, but it could make the ritual of taking out the garbage a more pleasant experience.

Boat Ramp

Flexible turf blocks are an ideal material for a long and wide boat ramp. Prep is minimal, as long as the soil is already in good condition. The blocks install quickly and will support heavy trucks without cracking.

How the Pros Do It

"The finished surface will be only as good as the substrate it rests on. Most manufacturers provide detailed recommendations for tamping and the addition of sand or gravel, depending on your soil conditions and how heavy the vehicles will be."

Nick Jansson,
Soil Retention Products, Inc.

4

Dry-laid Patios & Paths

In this chapter, we show you how to install patios and paths without using mortar. You'll learn how to prepare a firm base so that pavers don't shift under your feet, as well as how to cut and set them. We give you lots of options for edging—from invisible edging to timbers and brick—and we show you how to build stairs so that your paths can handle slopes.

Chapter Contents

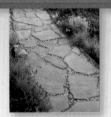

Stone & Brick Patio

page 122

Flagstones on a Tamped Bed

page 124

Pavers with Wide Joints

page 126

Permeable Paving

page 128

Paths

page 130

Designing Stairs

page 136

Steps

page 138

Dry Beauties

When a bed is solid and its edging is strong, a patio or path will last many years. We begin with patios, which are more challenging to build than those described in the previous chapter but are well within the reach of a motivated homeowner with a good set of tools. No special skills are required, but you will need to proceed systematically. Read on, and we'll show you how.

Rounding the curve of this running-bond patterned path, you can tiptoe past the tulips, then enjoy the garden from a strategically placed seat. Fairly wide joints between the pavers, as well as the occasional broken brick, lend a casual air. Rough boulders provide the edging.

A neat arrangement of bricks, also in a running-brick pattern, provides a level surface suitable for a dining area . The bluestone border brings out subtle blue-green hues in the brick.

Above: The traditional sidewalk leading up to the front door is replaced here by a charming pedestrian cul de sac that invites visitors to linger. A circular pattern like this uses pavers of several specific shapes and sizes, which are typically supplied in an ensemble.

Left: This brick patio is a seamless extension of its adjacent brick home. Despite the use of similar materials, the patio feels distinct from the walls that loom over it, thanks to the fact that the bricks are set at an angle to the house rather than parallel.

Laying Out & Planning

Depending on the edging you will install and the construction method you plan to employ, you may want to lay things out precisely, with perfectly square, exactly marked corners. In other cases, it's enough to generally indicate the contours of your patio.

If a patio abuts another patio, planters, raised beds, or other elements, run guidelines from those elements to help in excavating, as well as to develop a plan for laying gravel and sand to the correct height.

Order of Work

Building a dry-laid patio generally calls for five operations:
- Laying out and marking the contours of the patio.
- Excavating sod and digging down to a consistent depth.
- Pouring and tamping compactable gravel, then adding a top layer of sand.
- Installing edgings.
- Laying pavers.

These pages show some examples of patio-building methods to help you determine your order of work. The order in which you perform these tasks, as well as the methods you use, will depend on the type of edging and pavers, the shape of the patio, and other factors. For example, you may choose to set the pavers first, then add edging at the end. Or you may choose to install edgings first and set the pavers inside. Choose an approach that minimizes the need to cut pavers.

Leveling Tip

If your yard dips, use string lines when excavating and when laying the gravel and sand so you will not end up with puddles on the patio after a rain.

Using Batterboards

To precisely lay out for a rectangular patio with square corners, build a pair of batterboards for each corner. Position the batterboards 2 feet or so from the corner, stretch string lines, and check for square. Use a plumb bob or chalk line to reference down so you can mark accurately for the corner. If the corners do not need to be precise, you can simply use stakes and lines instead.

Free-form Installation

Here, the lawn has not been landscaped, and there is no sod. In this case, the initial layout does not have to be precise. Excavate any organic matter in the soil and make sure the site slopes regularly. Lay a base of compactable gravel, then a layer of sand. Install the pavers until you reach the end, then add the edging. In the example shown, the pavers were "run wild," slightly past the perimeter, and then a cutoff saw was used to cut a straight line. Invisible edging is being installed a half paver's length from the perimeter so that half pavers can fill in the gap. The surrounding yard will be landscaped to match the patio's height.

💲 **Stuff to Buy**
Edging boards, if required
Lumber for batterboards
Mason's line

🕐 **Time Commitment**
Two to three hours

🛠 **Tools You'll Need**
Shovel
Spray paint
Tape measure

◎ **Related Topics**
Measuring & laying out, 44–45

Pipe Screeding

In this example, two sides of the patio have been edged with bricks mortared onto a concrete footing. After compactable gravel has been laid and compacted, pipes used as screed guides are positioned so they are one brick's thickness below the edgings. A mason's line, stretched taut, indicates the height of the patio on the side where there is no edging. After the sand has been poured, a screed guide is run over the pipes to produce a smooth surface.

Screeding with Invisible Edging

If you are certain about the exact contours of your patio and want to use invisible edging, you can install the edging first, then pour and tamp the gravel base, then screed with pipe guides. The edging must rise above the pipes far enough to hold the pavers in place.

Excavating Inside the Edging

If the edging will be solid, you may choose to install it first, then roughly excavate the area inside. Run a grid of guidelines attached to the top of the edging to indicate the eventual height of the patio.

Adjusting the Edging

Often you can minimize the number of paver cuts by being a bit flexible with the edging. Here, the last piece of lumber edging is being moved over to meet the pavers. The other piece of edging will need to be cut, but that is much easier than making a stack of masonry cuts.

Complicated Areas

If the patio will have lots of curves and angles and abut an existing patio surface, layout methods meant for rectangular patios may not work so well. Stretch string guides from the existing surface whenever possible. In tight spots, you will first eyeball the excavation, then continually check with a level, which may be set atop a straight board.

Excavating

In most cases, you will begin building a dry-laid patio by removing sod and roots, then digging down to the correct depth so you can install successive layers of gravel and sand, followed by the pavers.

1 Remove sod

- For a small grassy area, use a square shovel to slice and roll up sod.
- For a larger area, use a sod cutter.
- Perhaps use the sod elsewhere on the lawn.

Removing concrete

- If a concrete slab needs to be removed, wear long clothing and protective eyewear.
- Smash the concrete with a large sledgehammer.
- If needed, use a wrecking bar to pry up the slab, then smash the concrete.
- If there is metal reinforcement, cut it with a reciprocating saw equipped with a metal-cutting blade.
- Cart the chunks away to an appropriate dump, or reuse them.

How to Do It

2 Dig

- Take care not to dig too deep, so soil will remain undisturbed.
- Start with a pointed shovel, then use a square shovel to scrape bottom of excavation.
- Use string lines or a level atop a straight board to check the depth.

3 Tamp

- Use a hand tamper or 4 × 4 to tamp a small area.
- Use a power tamper (vibrating plate compactor) for a larger area.
- If soil is composed of a lot of clay, little tamping is needed; if soil is loose, spend plenty of time tamping.

Using Landscaping Fabric

In some regions, it is common to lay landscaping fabric over a patio area to minimize weed growth. However, depending on soil conditions, climate, and the type of weeds, the fabric may or may not actually inhibit weed growth, so check with local builders. The fabric is often laid on top of the soil, under the gravel. Or it may be laid on top of the gravel and under the sand to keep the sand from filtering into the gravel.

 **Stuff to Buy**

Mason's line
Stakes

 **Time Commitment**

Varies depending on soil, size of patio, and depth of excavation

 **Tools You'll Need**

Earth-moving machine
Rake
Shovels
Sod cutter

Related Topics

Excavating, 46–47, 98–99
Paving with recycled concrete, 80
Planning drainage, 32–35

Excavating by Machine

A small rented earth-moving machine, sometimes called a scooper, cat, or front loader, can greatly speed up excavation. You may be able to hire an experienced operator to do the job, or have a rental company teach you how to operate a machine. Provide plywood paths to the area so you won't damage a yard or driveway.

1 Scoop

- Mark the area clearly. With practice, you can dig accurately.
- Have a helper watch and direct you.
- Scoop carefully, scraping rather than digging down, so you don't go too deep.

2 Off-load

- Prepare a place where you will put the excavated soil.
- Tilt the scooper up, back up, turn tightly, and proceed to the off-loading spot.
- Pile the soil carefully onto a spot in the yard, or deposit it into a refuse bin.

3 Scrape

- Once an area has been cleared, check for correct depth.
- Moving backward, use the bottom of the scooper to scrape the bottom of the excavation.
- With practice, you can scrape fairly precisely all the way up to the corners.

Radiant Heat

In cold regions, you can keep a patio ice-free by installing a radiant-heat system underneath. You may want to hire a company to install it. Once you have excavated the area and laid a bed of tamped gravel, the installers will lay the tubing and make the water connections. A system may use your existing water heater, or it may have its own heating unit.

1 Install tubes

- Lay protective fabric over the gravel.
- Run a grid of plastic tubing, anchoring it with special spikes.
- Make connections to the water supply and then test to make sure there are no leaks.

2 Cover with sand

- Make sure tubes are anchored tightly so they do not protrude above the sand layer.
- Pour sand over the area.

3 Screed

- Lay guide pipes or use screed guides that rest on solid edging.
- Check for protruding pipes as you screed the area.
- It's OK if a pipe is visible, as long as it does not rise above the sand surface.

Invisible Edgings

Once backfilled, this type of edging can often be completely covered with grass that surrounds the patio. It is often added after the pavers are laid, but it can be installed at the beginning of the building process.

When to Use Edging

If you're paving with flagstones or cut stone slabs, you don't need edging, as the pieces are heavy enough to stay put. You can also skip edging on concrete slabs or if you are setting pavers on a mortar bed atop a concrete slab. But for sand-set bricks, concrete pavers, or small stones, edging is essential if you want pieces to stay aligned.

This patio looks like it is being held in place by the lawn, but actually a hidden plastic edging strip keeps it firmly in place.

Firm but Hidden

Plastic or metal edging holds paving securely in place without drawing attention to itself. Some manufacturers specify that the compacted gravel base extend 6 to 8 inches beyond the pavers. In that case, hidden edgings must be installed on top of the gravel. In other cases, you can install the edgings first before adding the gravel. Either way, the edging must be in place before you go over the pavers with a vibrating plate compactor. Be sure to use edging designed to hold pavers. Landscaping edging is designed only to hold back mulch, and it is not generally strong enough for patios. Most edging can be installed in straight runs or bent to form curves.

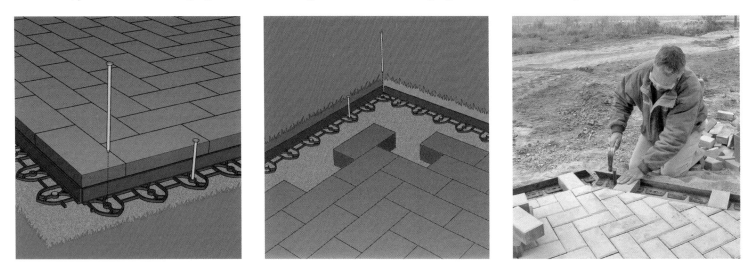

Installation Options

Often, invisible plastic edgings are installed with the flanges pointed out, away from the patio (above left). In this case, the area several inches beyond the patio must be cleared of sod to make room for the flanges. The area will need to be filled in with strips of sod after the pavers are set.

Another method is to point the flanges inward, toward the patio (above middle). This allows you to excavate right up to the sod so you do not need to replace a strip of sod after the patio is built.

Edging can be installed before the pavers, as shown on the next page, or it can be added when you install the last row of pavers (above right).

 **Stuff to Buy**

Plastic or metal edging
Stakes

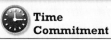 **Time Commitment**

An hour or so

 Tools You'll Need

Hammer or hand sledge
Shovel
Tin snips or hacksaw

Related Topics

Excavating, 98-99
Setting pavers, 116–119
Tamping gravel & screeding
  sand, 108–109

How to Do It

1 Check edging height

- Set the edging in place and check for square.
- The height does not have to be precise, but it should be enough to hold the pavers in place while not rising above them.

2 Drive spikes

- Along straight edges, drive spikes every foot or so.
- At a curve, drive spikes into every hole.
- If the soil is soft, drive extra spikes.

3 Adjust & backfill

- When you lay pavers, you may adjust the edging on one or two sides to minimize paver cuts.
- Once the patio is laid, fill in behind the edging with strips of sod.

Poundable Edging

Plastic edging that can be simply pounded into the ground is quick to install but is designed for landscaping purposes rather than patios. However, if your sod is firmly rooted and you do not have to excavate deeper than 5 inches or so, this edging will hold the pavers in place. The advantage is that you do not have to fill in the excavated space behind the edging with sod.

1 Drive the edging

- Lay 2 × 4s for guides on the lawn and hold them in place with stakes.
- Position the edging against the 2 × 4s and pound it into the ground.
- Join the pieces. Drive one partway, then start driving the next piece.

2 Check height

- Drive the edging level with the grass.
- Use a level to check that the edging is either level or correctly sloped.
- If a piece is too far down, pull it up with pliers.

3 Excavate & pave

- Excavate the interior, taking care not to dig so deep that the edging comes out.
- Add gravel and sand, then set the pavers.
- Remove the stakes and 2 × 4s.

Lumber & Timber Edging

Wood edging made of 2 × 4s or 2 × 6s gives a subtle homemade feel to a deck. Timber edging adds a more rustic touch. You can stain wood every year or so, or allow it to turn a silvery gray.

Two-by pressure-treated lumber creates an edging of modest width. The wood will weather to a discrete gray and will effectively resist rot.

Composition Decking as Edging

Instead of using natural wood, you could use composition decking material, available from many manufacturers. It won't rot, and high-quality products effectively resist fading and staining. It can also be bent to form wide curves. Because it is bendable, you will need to drive stakes every foot or so to keep it in place.

Lumber Edging

Wood edging is best made from 2 × 4 or 2 × 6 boards that are straight and free of large knots. Use pressure-treated wood rated for ground contact, or use the dark heartwood of redwood or cedar and apply two coats of sealer before installing it. If possible, buy boards long enough for each edge. If you must butt pieces, nail or screw a splice about 2 feet long to the outside edge of both boards. Support the edging with stakes every 2 feet or so.

Cut sod back 2 inches from the outside of the edging to make room for the stakes. Excavate deep enough to place at least 2 to 3 inches of gravel under the boards to help prevent rot.

1 Position boards

- Provide a gravel bed to minimize rotting.
- Cut the boards to length and set them in place.
- Align them with string guides, or use the boards themselves to check for square.
- Shift the gravel underneath or tap a board to achieve the correct height.

2 Drive stakes

- Cut stakes from pressure-treated 2 × 4s. The tips should be 4 inches long.
- The length of the stakes depends on soil conditions. It takes effort to drive them.
- Use a scrap board to prevent splitting as you drive stakes below the top of the edging.

3 Attach & backfill

- Recheck the alignment of the edging.
- Drive two 2½-inch deck screws through the edging and into each stake.
- Shovel gravel under the edging where needed.
- After the patio is installed, backfill with soil and sod.

 **Stuff to Buy**

Decking screws
2 × 4s, 2 × 6s, landscaping
   timbers
Rebar (½-inch)
Stakes

 **Time Commitment**

Three to four hours

 Tools You'll Need

Circular saw
Drill
Hand sledge

Related Topics

Excavating, 98–99
Laying out & planning, 96–97
Measuring & laying out, 44–45

Curved Wood Edging

For the sake of appearance, you may want curved edging to be the same thickness as any 2-by edging it abuts. For a gentle curve, you may be able to use two 1 × 4s, but for tighter curves you will need thinner material. A lumberyard can rip-cut benderboard pieces to ⅜ inch thick. Composite fascia board, typically ½ inch thick, is very flexible.

Because you cannot accurately measure the length of a curve, it is best to install pieces that are longer than you need and then cut them to length after they are fully installed.

1 Bend into position

- Drive stakes 1½ inches below the top of the edging, at the ends of curved runs, and on the outside of the benderboard.
- Bend the boards to the desired shapes.
- Drive temporary stakes on the inside to hold the edging in place.

2 Install permanent stakes

- Check that the edging is level or correctly sloped.
- Every 16 inches, drive a permanent stake on the outside, 1½ inches below the top of the edging.
- Drill pilot holes and drive deck screws to attach curved edging to permanent stakes.
- Remove the temporary stakes.

3 Cut the ends

- Where a curve ends and a straight line begins, use a square to draw a cutoff line.
- Cut with a handsaw or a reciprocating saw.

Timber Edging

You may be able to find railroad ties or other massive, weather-beaten boards to use as edging. They may not be straight, which is fine if you're after a rustic look. Or buy 4 × 4, 4 × 6, or 6 × 6 treated boards. Take care to select timbers that are straight, as there is no way to unbend them. Excavate a trench and pour several inches of gravel under the timbers.

1 Cut & position timbers

- To cut a timber, draw square lines all round it and cut along the lines with a circular saw. Cut the middle with a handsaw or a reciprocating saw or use a small chain saw.
- Set the timbers in a gravel bed.
- Check for correct height and alignment.
- Shift gravel as needed so the timbers are well supported.

2 Drill holes

- Equip a drill with an extra-long ½-inch bit.
- Drill holes in the center of each timber every 2 feet.
- If the drill gets hot or the bit smokes, stop and allow for cooling.

3 Drive anchors

- Buy pieces of ½-inch rebar, 3 feet long, or cut pieces using a reciprocating saw equipped with metal-cutting blade.
- Use a hand sledge to pound anchors down through the timbers and into the ground.
- If the rebar stops (you may hit a rock), cut the rebar flush with the top of the timber.

Brick or Paver Edging

Upright bricks, cobblestones, or concrete pavers make attractive edgings. They can match material used on the rest of a path or patio, or provide a pleasant contrast.

Installation Options

If your soil is firm and your grass is well established, paver edging can be held in place by the soil and sod; it helps to cut the lawn precisely. If the soil is sandy or soft, consider using invisible edging or lumber edging. Or set the edging in a bed of mortar, as shown on the opposite page. Install upright paver edging either before or after you put in the gravel base.

When bricks or other pieces stand upright with a thin edge facing the patio or path, they're called soldiers. Sailors face the other way, as if to catch the wind. Soldiers make stronger edging, but sailors require fewer pieces, so the installation is faster.

These concrete pavers come in an ensemble consisting of several sizes, making it easy to create a natural-looking, random pattern.

Masonry Edging for Gravel

If the path or patio will be made of gravel, the procedure is fairly simple. It helps to cut the sod and soil precisely so the bricks will have a firm surface to rest against.

① Excavate

- Dig just deep enough so the edging will be ¾ inch higher than the surrounding soil.
- Dig straight down along the edges so you won't disturb soil outside the path.

② Place edging

- Line the excavation with landscaping fabric, if you choose.
- Place the edging pavers in place.
- Tap the pavers with a board to create a smooth top surface and to slightly embed them.

③ Fill & tamp

- Fill half the excavation with gravel, then shovel and rake it level.
- Tamp with a hand tamper or vibrating plate compactor.
- Fill the rest of the excavation and tamp it.
- The gravel should be slightly lower than the edging.

 Stuff to Buy	**Time Commitment**	**Tools You'll Need**	**Related Topics**
Benderboard Gravel and sand Mortar Pavers or bricks	Half a day	Hand sledge Mason's line Screed guide Square shovel	Applying mortar, 64–65 Excavating, 98–99 Laying out & planning, 96–97 Lumber & timber edging, 102–103 Measuring & laying out, 44–45 Mixing mortar, 62–63

Upright Pavers

Depending on the depth of the excavation, the thickness of the gravel and sand base for the patio, and the height of the pavers, you may need to dig a perimeter trench for the edging pavers. Or you might need to add extra gravel at the edge to raise the edging up to the correct height.

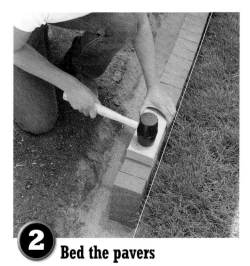

1 Trench & screed

- Stretch a guideline at the level of the patio surface.
- Dig a trench or add gravel. Pour and tamp the gravel so it is 1 inch more than a paver's length below the line.
- Make a screed guide out of a 2 × 4 and a 2 × 6 to mimic the length of the pavers.
- Pour sand and scrape it with a screed guide, slightly above the guideline, to form a smooth surface.

2 Bed the pavers

- Position each paver ⅛ inch from the guideline.
- Lay a straight board on top and tap to achieve a smooth, even surface.

3 Tamp

- Use a 2 × 4 to gently tamp the soil or gravel on the patio side.
- If you need to move pavers in toward the patio, use a 1 × 4 to tamp soil into the space between the pavers and the lawn.
- If the pavers won't stay put, temporarily stake a 2 × 4 to the outside edge.

Turning a Curve

To set edgings in a smooth curve, install benderboard edging supported with stakes. The joints between the pavers will be wider on the outside of the curve.

Sailors in Mortar

To add strength, which is often recommended if soil is loose or if you are installing sailors rather than soldiers, set the pavers in a bed of mortar. Stake a straight 2 × 4 along the outer edge, with its top at the correct edging height. Dig a 4-inch-deep trench, fill it with mortar, and set the edging pavers in the mortar.

In the example shown, the sailors are tilted for a decorative effect. Their uppermost corners should be at patio height. If they were higher, they would create a tripping hazard.

Concrete Edging

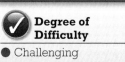

A poured concrete block makes very strong edging. Forming and pouring concrete edging is not as difficult as pouring a concrete slab and calls for no special skills. You can tint the concrete while it is wet, stain it later, or cover it with tiles.

Paver-on-Concrete Edging

Pavers, flagstones, or cobblestones can be set in or on concrete edging. You can allow the concrete to set, then set pavers in mortar. Or set pavers directly in wet concrete.

Mortaring onto cured concrete

- Pour concrete edging and allow it to cure.
- Set the pavers in a dry run on the concrete.
- Mix a batch of mortar and apply it with a trowel.
- Set the pavers in the mortar, checking for even height and straight lines as you go.

Setting in wet concrete

- Build concrete as shown above, but use 2 × 6s instead of 2 × 4s.
- Snap a chalk line one paver's thickness below the top of the form, minus ½ inch.
- Mix the concrete and pour it up to the chalk line.
- Set the pavers in the concrete, with ⅜-inch spacers for joints.
- Tap the pavers even with the top of the forms.

Forming & Pouring

The edging should be at least 6 inches wide and 4 inches deep. Anything less massive is likely to crack. If you plan to cover the edging with tile or pavers, make the edging an appropriate width.

1 Form & reinforce

- Dig a trench the width of the edging plus the thickness of the form boards.
- Shovel 3 inches of compactable gravel at the bottom and tamp with a 2 × 4 or 4 × 4.
- Build forms using 2 × 4s held in place with stakes.
- For a curved form, use composite decking or benderboard.
- Use fiberglass-reinforced concrete, or reinforce the edging with wire mesh or rebar (as shown).

2 Pour & screed

- Mix concrete in a wheelbarrow or trough.
- Shovel it into the forms.
- Poke with a piece of rebar along the forms to remove air bubbles.
- Screed the top by scraping and tapping with a scrap of lumber.

3 Trowel it smooth

- Finish by using a magnesium or wood float.
- Use a concrete edger (as shown) at the edges.
- When the concrete starts to harden, remove the forms.
- For a finished appearance, use a steel trowel or go over the edging with a broom or mason's brush.
- Cover it with plastic and/or spray it with a mist of water for a few days to slow curing and thus increase strength.

$ Stuff to Buy	Time Commitment	Tools You'll Need	Related Topics
Concrete mix Lumber Rebar	A morning	Concrete edger Hammer Magnesium or wood trowel Shovel	Calculating concrete needs, 170–171 Excavating, 98–99 Forming & pouring a footing, 58–59 Laying out & planning, 96–97 Measuring & laying out, 44–45

Tile Edging

Use floor tiles, not wall tiles, rated for outdoor use in your locale. For a slip-resistant surface, use unglazed tiles or small tiles. With small tiles, the grout lines will provide traction. Many tiles can be cut with a simple snap tile cutter, but some types require a wet saw or a grinder with a masonry blade.

Install concrete edging and allow it to cure. Mix and spread latex-reinforced thinset mortar using a square-notched trowel. Set the tiles in the mortar and use plastic spacers to maintain consistent grout joints. Wait overnight for the thinset to harden, then fill the joints with grout.

Short-Wall Edging

A short wall along the edge of a patio or on each side of a path clearly and attractively divides the masonry from the landscape. Plants can grow at will without encroaching on the patio or path.

If you leave a 1-inch space between the wall and the pavers, rainwater can run down through the joint. If the wall and patio are tightly abutted, be sure rainwater can easily run away from or alongside the wall.

Decorative Edgings

Almost any material that can be securely embedded can serve as edging. Edging that is uneven in shape is not a problem for a loose-material path or patio. You may choose to build the patio first, using invisible edging, then add the decorative edging. Many decorative edgings make it difficult to mow the lawn, so they work best next to flowers or shrubs.

Terra-cotta clay roofing tiles (below left) contrast handsomely with both plants and stone. The tiles are not strong and can crack during installation. However, they will form a durable edging if firmly embedded in well-packed soil. Carefully pack and tamp soil or sand on each side.

Boulders or cobblestones (below right) can be set in shallow holes. If you will install pavers, purchase semidressed stone with at least one flat side. You can achieve an inside edge that is fairly even, and you can adjust the positions of the stones when you lay the pavers.

Tamping Gravel & Screeding Sand

A solid dry-laid patio or path starts with a bed of solidly tamped soil, covered with a 3- to 4-inch-thick layer of tamped compactable gravel.

How to Do It

If possible, excavate down to soil that has not been previously excavated. If you cannot reach undisturbed soil—on some sites the ground was once excavated to a depth of more than 8 inches—be sure to use a vibrating plate compactor to tamp the soil.

Order compactable gravel—also known as aggregate base course, hardcore, and other terms—made to serve as a patio substrate. Your supplier will calculate how much you need based on the thickness of the gravel layer and the patio dimensions. If possible, have the gravel dumped directly into the excavated area. Otherwise, bring it in with wheelbarrows.

Remove any guidelines and spread the gravel to a uniform depth using rakes. Check for depth, then use a rented vibrating plate compactor to tamp the gravel down. Tamp systematically, as you would mow a lawn, to be sure everything is firm.

Strategic Renting

To save rental money, pick up a plate compactor an hour or so before the gravel is delivered. That way, you can tamp the soil, then the gravel, in a short time. If the patio is small, you may be able to install and tamp the pavers within the same 24-hour period.

Screeding with Pipe Guides

For adding the edging after the pavers are laid, it is common to use pipes as guides. For a 1-inch-thick sand layer, use ¾-inch plastic pipe, which has an outside diameter of 1 inch. For a 1½-inch-thick layer, use 1-inch plastic pipe. Cut the pipes to fit.

❶ Position pipes

- Space the pipes 4 to 6 feet apart.
- Check with a straight board to see that the pipes will follow an even surface that is sloped correctly.
- If needed, add or remove gravel under the pipes to adjust their heights.

❷ Spread sand

- Pour sand into the patio area and roughly smooth it with a garden rake.
- The sand should be slightly higher than the pipes at most points.

❸ Screed

- Lay a straight 2 × 4 across two or more pipes.
- Press the board onto the pipes and pull or push it across the patio to smooth the surface.
- Fill any low spots and repeat.

 **Stuff to Buy**

Long, straight board
PVC pipes

 **Time Commitment**

One to two hours

 **Tools You'll Need**

Rake
Shovel

 Related Topics

Excavating, 98–99
Laying out & planning, 96–97
Measuring & laying out, 44–45
Screeding with solid edging,
  110–111

More Techniques

Scrape with shovels

- For a big area, consider renting a long straightedge made for screeding.
- Have a helper or two use shovels to fill in low spots as you go.
- Your helpers can also scrape away excess sand ahead of the screed guide.

Fine-tuning

- You typically need to go over the surface several times to get it perfectly smooth.
- To fill in slight depressions, scatter sand with your hand, then screed again.

Removing pipes

- Lift and remove the pipes.
- Do this carefully so you don't disturb the sand.

Fill pipe trenches

- Fill the resulting trenches at least partially with sand.
- Take care not to raise the area.

Trowel edges

- Along an edge, level the surface.
- You may need to use a magnesium or wood trowel.

Scraping with a paver

- To make sure the edge is at the correct height, scrape with a paver, moving along the edging.
- Lightly scrape with a trowel to clean up the resulting ridge.

Screed with Solid Edging

Solid edgings—such as lumber, timber, concrete, or pavers on concrete—establish the height of the patio or path, so you can also use them as guides for excavating and screeding.

Preparing to Screed

Once the site has been excavated, the edging has been installed, and gravel has been spread and tamped (though not necessarily in that order), you can use the edging as a guide to spread and screed the sand that the pavers will rest on. If you plan to use invisible edging or install edging after you lay the pavers, follow the instructions for screeding with pipe guides (see page 109).

Local codes may specify using 1 or 2 inches of sand. If the gravel has settled, you may need to add more sand than originally planned. The pavers should end up about ¼ inch above the edging, making it easier to sweep the patio clean of debris.

1 **Tamp a gravel base**

- Measure and excavate the right depth for a gravel base, sand base, and pavers.
- You may use string lines stretched from the edging to help determine the correct depth.
- Pour and spread compactable gravel, then tamp it with a vibrating plate compactor.

Screeding Sand

Consult local builders for the right type of sand to use for screeding. It may be called torpedo sand, leveling sand, concrete sand, or screenings of a certain type of stone. Avoid limestone screenings. Limestone will leach alkaline into the soil, which can harm nearby grass and plants.

2 **Protect against weeds**

- Check with contractors or your building department to see whether landscaping fabric is needed.
- If so, roll heavy-duty fabric over the gravel base.
- Work carefully to minimize folds and bubbles.
- Cut pieces accurately and butt them tightly against the edging, where weeds may grow.
- Overlap pieces by at least 6 inches.

3 **Install a temporary guide**

- If the patio is less than 10 feet wide, skip this step.
- For a larger patio, cut a 2 × 4 to fit and anchor it 6 to 10 feet away from, and parallel to, the edging.
- Screw a temporary guide to the edging at each end.
- Anchor with 2 × 4 stakes driven every 4 feet.

4 **Make a screed**

- Cut a straight 2 × 4 or 2 × 6, 2 feet longer than the area to be screeded.
- Cut plywood to the thickness of the pavers, plus the width of the board, and 2 inches shorter than the area to be screeded.
- Attach the plywood so it extends below the board by the thickness of a paver minus ¼ inch.

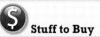 **Stuff to Buy**

Compactable gravel
Landscaping fabric
Lumber for screed guide
Rough sand for a paver base

 **Time Commitment**

About four hours

Tools You'll Need

Drill
Hand sledge
Mason's line

Related Topics

Edgings, 100–107
Excavating, 98–99
Laying out & planning, 96–97
Measuring & laying out, 44–45
Tamping gravel & screeding sand, 108–109

5 Spread sand

- Have course sand delivered to the site.
- Spread it with a square shovel.
- Rake it until it is slightly higher than the final level.
- The sand should be dry.

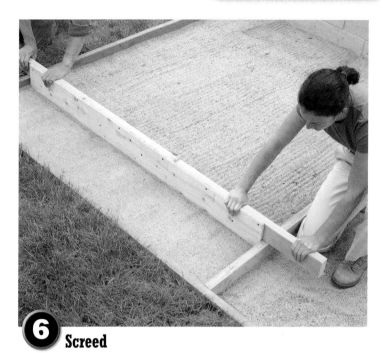

6 Screed

- Work with a helper if the screed is longer than 6 feet.
- Move the screed across the patio to smooth the sand.
- Test with a few pavers to be sure the height is correct.
- Fill in any low spots and screed again.

7 Attach guidelines

- To prepare for laying the pavers, stretch mason's line across the patio for a height guide.
- Pull the line taut so it does not sag.

8 Plan future screeding

- Once you have installed pavers for the first section, you will remove the temporary screed guide and screed the next section.
- You may need to change the length of the screed for this process.

Cutting Pavers

If you have 10 or fewer pavers to cut, you may choose to cut them with a chisel. To cut more pavers, rent a brick splitter or a masonry saw. If you have plenty of cutting to do, or if the cuts need to be very precise, rent a wet masonry saw.

Measuring & Marking

Even a few poorly cut pavers will give a patio a sloppy look, so take the time to measure and cut precisely. Whenever possible, install all the full-size pavers first, then hold pavers in place to measure for cuts. Where this is not possible, you may need to use a tape measure.

For an angle cut, hold the paver in place and mark both sides of the cut. Then draw a straight line between the marks.

Use a T bevel to capture the angle. Set it in place, then tighten the wing nut. Use this to check the angle for accuracy.

Hand Cutting

Some concrete pavers and some stones are so hard that you will have a very difficult time cutting them by hand. But with practice, you can make fairly accurate cuts in softer pavers.

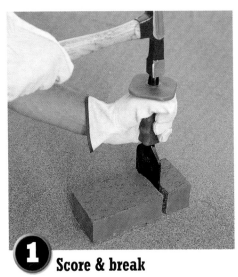  

❶ Score & break

- Place a paver on an even surface that has some give, such as a bed of sand or a board.
- Press a brickset chisel firmly onto the cut line and tap with a hammer to score a line on all four sides of the paver.
- Hold the brickset against a score line, with its bevel (the angled side of the tip) facing the waste side of the cut.
- Whack the brickset hard to break the paver.

❷ Clean the cut edge

- Cutting by hand is unpredictable. If the cut is inaccurate, throw the paver out and try again with another one.
- Chip or scrape away any protrusions along the cut edge, using a brick trowel, the chisel, or the sharp side of a brick hammer.

Cutting flagstone

- Some stones will split with just a tap or two, while others call for strenuous effort.
- Use a brickset to score a line on both sides of the stone.
- Position the stone with the scored line on top of a pipe or a scrap of wood.
- Hit the waste side with a hand sledge to break it off.

Related Topics

Flagstones on a tamped bed, 124–125
Other paver patterns, 120–121
Setting pavers, 116–119

Brick Splitter

A brick splitter makes fairly accurate cuts without generating dust or much noise, and you can rent one for a modest price. Mark the cut line and align it with the splitter's blade. Or use the splitter's ruler to measure for the cut. Press the brick snugly against the guide. Push down forcefully on the handle to break the brick.

Using a Circular Saw

If you have 15 or fewer pavers that need precise cuts, consider using a circular saw equipped with a masonry-cutting blade.

Cutting bricks or pavers

- Attach a scrap piece of wood to the working surface to keep bricks from sliding as you cut.
- Clamp several bricks together to cut them all to the same length.
- Set the saw blade to a depth of about ½ inch (deeper or shallower if the paver is soft or hard.)
- Press the saw down firmly on pavers as you cut.
- Lower the blade and make a second pass, repeating until you cut most of the way through.
- Break off the waste with a hammer and a chisel, or finish the cut from the other side for greater precision.

Carrying Pavers

Wear gloves when carrying a heavy stack of pavers. (But avoid wearing gloves when cutting with a power tool, because the gloves may catch on the saw blade.) A pair of brick tongs, also called a hod carrier, will make it easy to pick up and carry a stack.

Tool Tip

Be aware that the dust and strain you create by cutting masonry can eventually damage a circular saw, especially if the saw is an inexpensive model. If you notice the saw heating up, take a break to allow the motor to cool. If possible, work so that the wind blows dust away from the saw rather than into its housing. Perhaps use a shop vac to suck dust out of the saw's motor.

Scoring a concrete block

- Use the circular saw to score a line about ½ inch deep on each side.
- Finish the cut with a cold chisel and a hand sledge.
- For greater precision, lower the blade and make one or two more passes to cut all the way through.

Cutting with a Wet Masonry Saw

The quickest, easiest, and most precise way to cut pavers is with a wet-cutting masonry saw, also called a tub saw. You can rent one for a modest price.

Straight cut

- For a basic cut, place a paver in the tray and hold it against the back guide so it's square to the blade.
- Turn on the saw and check that water sprays onto the blade.
- Slide the tray forward slowly to slice through the paver.

Angle cut

- The saw will probably come with a guide to hold a paver at 45 degrees and other specified angles. Adjustable angle guides are also available.
- Hold the paver firmly against the attachment as you slide the tray forward to make the cut.

Cutout

- Make two cuts for a notch.
- Tilt the paver up to avoid overcutting the top.
- The bottom of the cut, which will not show, should be slightly longer than the top cut.
- Hold the paver against the back guide to ensure a square cut.

Curve cut

- Tilt the paver up so the bottom of the cut will be slightly longer than the top.
- Make a series of closely spaced parallel cuts up to the cut line.
- Break away the waste material with a hammer and a chisel.
- Clean up the cut by pressing the paver gently against the blade and moving it from side to side, removing only a small amount at a time.

Cutting a sliver

- When you are cutting only a small amount from a side, it can be difficult to keep the paver from moving as you cut.
- Press another paver against the paver being cut, as shown, for stability.

Cutting in Place

If you want to install a border along one edge or around the perimeter of the patio, it's usually best to install uncut pavers, snap a chalk line, and cut the pavers in place. A gas-powered masonry cutoff saw (above) will easily cut all the way through the pavers in one pass. Practice on scrap pieces until you are confident of your skill. Place a board on top of the pavers to avoid moving them as you cut. Get into a comfortable position, turn on the saw, and lower it onto the cut line. Let the saw's weight apply the pressure; don't press down.

You can also make an in-place cut using a grinder equipped with a masonry blade (above). It will take several passes to cut all the way through the pavers.

Cutting Flagstones

You can use a circular saw or a grinder to cut flagstones, but a masonry cutoff saw is easiest.

1 **Score the back**

- Mark the top of the stone, then transfer the cut line to the back.
- Score most of the way through the stone.

2 **Break off waste**

- Turn the stone over and position a pipe or a rod just to the good side of the cut line.
- Break off the waste with a hammer to produce a natural-looking, slightly chipped cut line.

Cut all the way through

- Keep the blade wet as you cut.
- Cut through the line.
- Chip the visible cut edge with a hammer to make it look more natural.

Setting Pavers

Once the area has been excavated and the layers of gravel and sand have been prepared, you are ready to install pavers. At this point you may have solid edging in place, or you may choose to install the pavers before the edging.

Bricks in basketweave

Choosing a Pattern

Rectangular bricks and pavers that are modular—exactly half as wide as they are long—can be arranged in any of the patterns shown on page 117. Some of these patterns will take extra time to install, but all can be accomplished by a do-it-yourselfer with patience and a wet masonry saw.

Jack-on-jack is the easiest to install, but only by a small margin. Half-basketweave and basketweave (with or without the 2 x 4 grid) are nearly as easy. None of these patterns require a lot of cutting. In fact, if you install the final two sides of edging after the pavers, you may get away without making any cuts at all.

For the pinwheel pattern, every fifth paver must be half-size. The running bond and 90-degree herringbone patterns also call for plenty of half-size pavers, which you can easily mass-produce using a wet saw.

The 45-degree herringbone pattern requires lots of 45-degree cuts of various sizes. However, if you love the look, don't let the extra work scare you. It's nearly insignificant compared with the other work you've done to get to this point.

Concrete pavers may have interlocking shapes, or they may be rectangular. In most cases, they come in a variety of colors that are mixed on the pallets so the colors are diffused more or less evenly.

Move Edging to Minimize Cutting

By adjusting the edging after laying pavers, you may be able to avoid cutting pavers along one or two edges of the patio. Install pavers until you're near the end of the patio, then move the edging to abut them. In the case shown here, 2-by edging is pushed up against the pavers, and stakes and screws are driven to secure it. Use a handsaw or reciprocating saw to cut the adjacent piece of edging flush.

$ Stuff to Buy

Edging materials
Pavers
Sand

Time Commitment

Half a day

Tools You'll Need

Broom
Level
Mason's line
Screed guide
Vibrating plate compactor

Related Topics

Cutting pavers, 112–115
Screed with solid edging, 110–111
Tamping gravel & screeding sand, 108–109

Paver Patterns

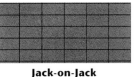

Jack-on-Jack

Running Bond

45-Degree Herringbone

90-Degree Herringbone

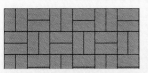

Pinwheel

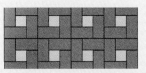

Basketweave

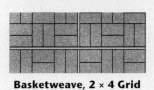

Half-Basketweave

Basketweave, 2 × 4 Grid

Laying Pavers

As long as the sand is screeded correctly, the pavers you set will be at the desired height. However, check with a mason's line to be sure. Take care not to walk on the sand or disturb it.

1 Lay the first pavers

- If you have solid edging, start in a corner. If the edging will be installed later, you may start in the middle.
- Use a level or a straightedge to see that the pavers are at the desired height.
- Set each paver straight down onto the bed, gently scraping the side of an abutting paver as you lower it. Avoid scraping the sand.

2 Bed the pavers

- After setting a section, place a 2 × 6 beater board on top and tap it with a mallet.
- If a paver is high, tap it directly with the mallet.

3 Continue laying

- Continue to lay and bed pavers, keeping them snug against each other.
- Avoid stepping or kneeling directly on the pavers near an edge. Kneel on a piece of plywood instead.
- Stretch a guideline every 4 feet or so to check the height and straightness of the pavers.

4 Screed the other side

- If you installed a temporary screed guide, work up to it, then remove it.
- Screed the other side, using the newly installed pavers as a height guide on one side.
- Work carefully so you do not push the pavers out of position.

Finishing the Job

1 Fill joints

- If the edging was not installed beforehand, install it now.
- Scatter fine sand or stone dust over the pavers.
- Use a soft-bristled broom to sweep sand into the joints.
- If the sand is damp, allow it to dry and then sweep again.

2 Power-tamp

- Run a vibrating plate compactor over the surface.
- Sweep more sand into the joints and repeat.

Troubleshooting

Here are some common issues you may encounter when installing a patio.

Right side up

- Some pavers are the same on each side, but some have only one face designed to show.
- On these bricks, the side with rounded edges is meant to show, even if it is rougher than the other side.

Spread to fit

- When border pavers are installed, they may not produce the correct length.
- In some cases, you can make up the difference by spreading them apart slightly.
- Use a margin trowel or a brick trowel to slightly increase the joint width.
- The resulting joints will be large but not noticeably so.

Mortaring edge bricks

- In some cases, you want a bit of extra strength to ensure perimeter pavers stay in place.
- Scrape away some sand and spread wet mortar to reach the desired height.
- Setting the pavers in the mortar will not make them strong enough to serve as edging, but it is a good idea in a situation like this, where they abut another paving surface.

Setting Pavers on a Large Surface

On a large patio, pavers can go noticeably out of alignment. Here are some common techniques used to keep things straight.

Level the sand

- On a large area, the sand may go out of level from time to time.
- Use a trowel, or a paver as shown here, to gently smooth the sand where needed.
- Take care not to produce new ridges or indentations.

Centerline

- Where there is a very long row of pavers, it's easy for them to wander out of alignment.
- Stretch a centerline at a point that is visually important.
- Install the pavers starting at the line rather than on one side.

Tap to a guideline

- Along a long line, stretch a guideline every 10 pavers or so.
- Tap with a rubber mallet as needed to keep the pavers straight.

When Pavers Won't Fit

If you need pavers to fill in a defined area, chances are they will not fit exactly. If they are slightly short of the distance, you can spread them apart slightly, as shown on the previous page.

In the example here, a measurement (above left) reveals that rows of full-width pavers would be too wide for the area to be filled. In this case, you could cut and install one row of pavers that is obviously narrower than the others, but many people would consider that unsightly. A more elegant solution, though more time-consuming, is to make four or five rows just slightly narrower. To cut the pavers, hold another paver against the one being cut, as shown above center.

The photo above right shows the result. You have to look closely to see that five rows in the center are made of pavers that have been slightly narrowed.

Other Paver Patterns

Don't compromise when it comes to the paver pattern. Laying a richly textured patio will probably take an hour or two more—small potatoes compared with all that work you put into excavating and preparing the site.

Pinwheel

The half pavers in the center of each pinwheel can be made from a different material, as long as they're the same thickness as the other pavers. It's all right if they are slightly smaller in width, as joints can be filled with extra sand.

Set one square—composed of four full pavers and one half paver—and then move on to the next square. Use a guideline every two or three squares to keep the pattern straight.

Angled Herringbone

If you install the edging and pavers very accurately, you will end up with a large number of cuts that are exactly 45 degrees. However, it is likely that things will go slightly out of alignment, so make sure your rented wet saw comes with an adjustable guide. This will enable you to tinker with the cutting angles. Or you can hold off on installing the edging. That way, you can use a cutoff saw to make a chalk line cut around the perimeter and then install the edging up against the pavers.

Framed Grid

Install a grid of 2 × 4s, then set pavers inside the grid's sections. Each section must be perfectly square (or rectangular) and just the right size to hold a certain number of full-size pavers. Use pressure-treated lumber, composite decking, or another very rot-resistant lumber.

❶ Build the grid

- Excavate and install a gravel bed.
- To measure for the grid, lay pavers in a dry run in both directions.
- Add a ¼-inch spacer for wiggle room in case future pavers are slightly larger.
- First install a series of 2 × 4s that run the entire length or width of the patio.
- Then install short boards between them.
- Fasten the boards with angle-driven 2½-inch deck screws.

❷ Screed & pave

- Cut a short screed that will fit into a grid section.
- Notch the screed so the sand will be ⅛ inch less than a paver's thickness below the top of the 2 × 4s.
- Pour sand and screed it in each section.
- You may need to use a trowel to finish screeding at the edges.
- Set the pavers, then fill the joints with fine sand and tamp it firm.

❶ Snap a layout line

- Install a tamped gravel base, then screed a layer of sand on top. Mark the center of the edging on parallel sides of the patio.
- If the edging is not yet installed, position temporary boards and mark them for center. Snap a chalk line between the two marks to indicate the centerline.

❷ Set the pattern

- With painstaking precision, install a V-shaped row of pavers along the line for about 5 feet.
- Paver corners should just touch the chalk line.
- Use an angle square to check the angle.
- Install abutting pavers.

 **Stuff to Buy**

Deck screws
Lumber
Pavers
Sand

 **Time Commitment**

An extra hour or two

 Tools You'll Need

Chalk line
Drill
Gas-powered cutoff saw
Mason's line
Wet masonry saw

Related Topics

Cutting pavers, 112–115
Setting pavers, 116–119

Filling a Small Area

In the example shown, the pavers are the same thickness as the level, so you can simply screed with the level. You will need to use a trowel to finish the screeding at the edges.

If you must fill a small area with a defined perimeter—so that you cannot move the edging—you will need to experiment with the paver placement. First try to center the pattern. But if you find that centering will lead to a number of very small pieces, you may need to move the pattern to one side, as shown below right.

Under an Obstruction

Where a patio meets an obstruction, such as a pillar, you could carefully cut pavers to fit around it. But a better solution is to remove trim or raise the obstruction. First install the pavers; you won't have to cut them precisely. Then install trim or lower the obstruction for a finished appearance.

Layout Tip

You can estimate the overall size of the layout, but chances are the exact dimensions will change once you install the boards and the pavers. Cut the outer edging boards or timbers larger than needed, then cut them precisely when you construct the grid. Or you may be able to wait until the sections are completed before installing the edging. One option is to build the sections, then install invisible edging up against the perimeter of the patio.

Stone & Brick Patio

A patio with two or more materials creates a rich appearance. In the example shown, a center section of large bluestones is surrounded by natural brick pavers.

Flagstones laid in a paisley curve make a bold statement in this brick patio. A lively design like this may require an extra day of work.

Mixed-material Options

Here, bluestones form a somewhat smoother and more formal surface than the bricks, which feature natural surface imperfections. This provides a pleasing contrast. Other material possibilities include rough-surfaced flagstones, adobe blocks, concrete pavers, and ceramic tiles.

Be aware of the challenges that you will encounter if the two materials have different thicknesses. In the example on these pages, the bluestones in the center are thinner than the bricks. This did not present serious difficulties. Once the bricks were installed, more sand was added to the bluestone area, and the brick surface was used as a guide for screeding. If the thinner material is on the perimeter rather than in the middle, screeding can be a bit more difficult.

1 Setting stones

- Screed the area to correct the height so the stones will be at the same level as the surrounding bricks.
- Determine the location of the stones.
- Working with a helper, set the stones straight down onto the sand.

2 Center the stones

- In this example, the bluestones are positioned at a 45-degree angle and centered in the patio.
- Stretch a string line over the first stones and check that it is perfectly centered and parallel with the paver lines.

3 Reposition stones

- To move a stone slightly, pry with a trowel.
- If you need to move it more than an inch, pick up the stone and set it back down to avoid disturbing the screeded sand.

Stuff to Buy

Gravel
Pavers
Sand
Stones

Time Commitment

Several days

Tools You'll Need

Chalk line
Cutoff saw
Mason's line
Rubber mallet
Screed
Wet masonry saw

Related Topics

4 Push stones together

- Once the first two stones are positioned correctly, set the others tightly against them.
- Set the stones down carefully so you won't have to move them more than ½ inch.

5 Straighten perimeter bricks

- When you reach the end of the stones, lay the bricks as needed to meet the stones.
- Use guidelines and a mallet to achieve straight lines of bricks around the stone area.

6 Cut triangles

- Measure for triangular cuts at the corners and sides.
- Cut triangles with a masonry cutoff saw.

7 Level the sand

- Because you must walk on the sand to install heavy stones, you will need to level the sand.
- Use a trowel to screed the sand for individual stones.

8 Level stones

- Getting the stones to form a level surface is a painstaking operation.
- To check for level, use a straight board stretched across the area, resting on pavers.
- As needed, pick up a stone, add or subtract sand, and lay the stone again.

9 Cut bricks as needed

- Chances are the stones will not fit precisely into the area.
- Where needed, snap a chalk line and cut pavers in a straight line to accommodate the stones.

Flagstones on a Tamped Bed

Flagstones can be set directly on soil, but laying them in a gravel bed will make for a more stable surface. Try to buy flagstones that are fairly uniform in thickness.

Because a tamped bed is a great surface for flagstones, it's also perfect for stone pavers, and even stone pavers combined with bricks, as shown here.

1 Install base & sort stones

- Excavate the area and install a gravel base.
- No sand is needed, but you should use fine gravel for the top inch or so of the bed.
- Move the flagstones near the work area.
- Separate out stones with a long, straight edge so you can use them along the perimeter.
- Sort stones according to size and color so they can be dispersed evenly on the patio.

2 Set first pieces

- If the paving starts at the house, choose large stones with a straight edge to go next to doors.
- Set the stones in position, but do not attempt to level them yet.
- Set some very large stones randomly across the paving.

3 Fill & cut

- Work in an area about 10 feet square.
- Find pieces that fit with little or no cutting, and assemble them like a jigsaw puzzle.
- Aim for joints that are fairly consistently about 1 inch wide.
- Cut stones as needed and chip the top edges for a natural look.
- Once the pattern is established, set the stones (see next step). Then move on to the next 10-foot-square area.

 **Stuff to Buy**

Fine gravel for top of base
Flagstones, at least 1½ inches
  thick
Rough gravel for base
Sand

 **Time
Commitment**

About a day

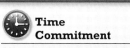 **Tools
You'll Need**

Broom
Level
Power saw
Pry bar
Rubber mallet
Vibrating plate compactor

**Related
Topics**

Cutting pavers, 112–115
Excavating, 98–99
Placing flagstones, 72–73
Tamping gravel & screeding
  sand, 108–109

4 Set stones

- Start with a stone next to a door to establish the patio's height.
- Pick up each stone and scrape away or add fine gravel as needed to achieve the correct height.
- It will likely take several attempts to set each stone.
- Step on the stones to make sure they do not wobble.
- If an edge needs a bit more support, lift stones with a pry bar and slip gravel underneath.

5 Check slope & bed

- For each stone, check with a straightedge to make sure it is fairly even with surrounding stones.
- Also check that the patio slopes gently away from the house. It should be level alongside the house.
- If a stone needs to be lowered slightly, try tapping it with a mallet, or pick it up and remove some gravel.

6 Fill joints

- Pour sand or fine gravel over the flagstones.
- Sweep with a wide push brush to work material into the joints.
- Sweep in several directions until all voids are filled.

7 Tamp

- Set plywood over a section of paving.
- Run a vibrating plate compactor over the plywood.
- Plant sod along the perimeter of the patio.

Pavers with Wide Joints

Large cut bluestones, adobe blocks, concrete steppingstones, square-cut flagstones, thick tiles, and even chunks of used concrete can be set with joints up to 2 inches wide, allowing ample room for crevice plants.

Moss-filled crevices echo greenery surrounding this patio, making the hardscape seem like an extension of its setting.

Where to Use Wide Joints

Use this method only if you are installing paving materials that are large and heavy—capable of staying put without edging. Large joints can be filled with fine gravel or rough sand, but you'll achieve a classic look by filling them with soil and adding crevice plants. The larger the pavers, the more lush the crevice plants can be.

For a stable surface, install a standard gravel-and-sand base. However, if the pavers are heavy enough, you can probably get away with tamping the soil firmly and adding a 1-inch-thick bed of sand or fine gravel. Keep in mind the soil needs of the crevice plants. If their roots go deep, they may not be able to penetrate a gravel base but will likely not find an inch of sand to be a problem.

The pavers may become wobbly over time, especially if the crevice plants have strong roots. However, you can easily lift and reset pavers.

Large slab-like concrete pavers, tinted a mellow pink, are separated by wide gravel-filled joints.

These capacious sandstone flagstones catch our eye because almost all of them are cut with curved edges.

 **Stuff to Buy**
Edging material
Gravel
Paving stones
Sand
Soil

 **Time Commitment**
About a day

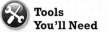 **Tools You'll Need**
Chalk line
Mason's line
Pry bar
Square shovel

 Related Topics
Crevice planting, 66–67
Excavating, 98–99
Tamping gravel & screeding sand, 108–109

1 Make a dry run

- Lay the pavers in a dry run with the desired joint widths.
- Check that the pavers will fit inside the edging, or plan to install edging later.
- If possible, adjust the joint widths instead of cutting the pavers.
- On the edging, mark the centers of every second or third joint.

2 Set pavers

- Using the marks made in step 1, tack small nails and stretch mason's line to form a grid of equally sized sections. Each section will hold about nine pavers.
- Place pavers in each section and adjust their placement to achieve fairly consistent joints.
- Use a straight board to check that the pavers form an even surface.
- Where needed, add or remove sand underneath the pavers.

3 Fill joints

- Check with a nursery to find the best type of soil for your crevice plants.
- Because the soil will get compacted and will receive more rain-water than a normal lawn, it's often best to add sand to improve drainage.
- Use a square shovel or a garden trowel to fill joints with soil.

4 Tamp & plant

- Sweep the surface using light strokes.
- Use a 1-by board to gently tamp the joints.
- Sow seeds or add plants to the joints.
- Add more soil as needed and sweep again.

Permeable Paving

Permeable paving allows rainwater to drain into a gravel bed beneath. It's an environmentally friendly option because the water percolates through the paving into the soil, reducing storm-water runoff that pollutes water supplies. It also prevents puddling on the patio.

Your Options

Installing permeable paving, also known as pervious or porous paving, is in many ways similar to standard paver installation. There are two basic differences: The pavers themselves have wide joints and voids—openings that allow water to flow through freely. And the bedding materials are crushed (or chipped) and washed stone chips, which allow water to flow through.

The illustration to the right shows a typical installation. However, you may not need to install all these components. If you have a modest patio and just want water to flow through it into the soil below, you will need to install only the bedding and base layers. For more serious drainage, or if you want to collect the rainwater for use in irrigation, you will need to install the subbase as well as drainage pipe.

The various sizes of chipped and washed gravel can be purchased at many stone yards or masonry supply sources. A subbase is 4 to 6 inches deep and made of stones 2½ to 4 inches in diameter. Sloped drainpipe is often embedded in this layer. The base layer has smaller stones, ½ to 1 inch in diameter. The bedding, which directly supports the pavers, is typically made of ⅜- to ⅛-inch stones. The bedding material is also used to fill in the joints and voids between pavers. No sand is used in a permeable installation.

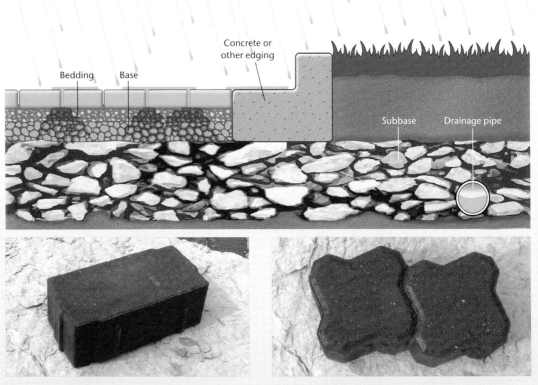

Permeable pavers come in many shapes and colors. All have slightly larger spacing lugs for wider joints.

Permeable pavers may be rectangular or interlocking. Both types feature gaps at the corners that allow for excellent drainage.

How to Do It

❶ Excavate & install subbase

- You may skip this step on a modest-size patio or where drainage is not a large problem.
- Excavate deeply to accommodate a subbase, base, bed, and pavers.
- Lay drainpipes, sloped to carry water as needed.
- Lay the 4- to 6-inch-thick layer of subbase rock, then screed and power tamp it.

❷ Lay the base & bedding

- Add a base layer of stones smaller than the subbase stones.
- Spread the gravel and power tamp it.
- Finish with a layer of fine bedding stones.

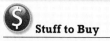 **Stuff to Buy**

Edging material
Gravel of various sizes
Permeable pavers

 **Time Commitment**

A weekend

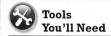 **Tools You'll Need**

Broom
Earth-moving machine
Masonry cutoff saw
Shovel
Vibrating plate compactor
Wet masonry saw

 Related Topics

3 Set pavers

- Here, the paving starts in the middle, but you may choose to install edging first and start in a corner.
- Chalk layout lines and/or use guidelines or a large square to determine the layout.
- Lay full-size pavers tightly together in the pattern of your choice.

4 Cut pavers

- Cut pavers with a wet masonry saw.
- Whether pavers are installed in rows or at angles to each other, there will be plenty of voids for drainage.

5 Keep it straight

- These pavers may go out of line after a few rows.
- Continue to use a large square and/or chalk lines to maintain straight lines.

6 Create patterns

- Where a pattern changes direction, you may need to improvise a bit.
- If cutting means that some of the joints do not have lugs to keep them wide, that's not a problem; a few tight joints will not matter.

7 Fill joints

- Sweep in the same gravel you used for the bedding.
- If you don't like the color of the bedding gravel, use crushed and washed stone of another color.
- For a large area, a power rotary sweeper makes the job go faster.

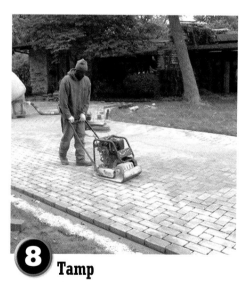

8 Tamp

- Run a vibrating plate compactor over the patio.
- If gravel sinks into voids, sweep in more gravel and compact again.
- If voids continue to sink and get clogged with dirt or leaves, clean them with a shop vac.

Curved Path

A curvaceous flagstone-and-gravel walkway edged with handsome redwood can be the perfect path to your front door. It is at once casual and elegant, and it adds richness to the landscape.

Material Options

Because flagstones are heavy and stable, they generally do not require a solid gravel-and-sand bed. A layer of sand atop tamped soil usually provides a stable enough substrate.

Shown here is redwood benderboard, which should be given several coats of sealer, plus plenty of stain, unless you want it to turn gray in a year or two. You also could use composite decking, which definitely will not rot. Invisible edgings are also a possibility.

A path with little foot traffic can be as narrow as 2 feet, but in order for two people to pass comfortably, a path should be at least 40 inches wide.

On this path, stones, edging, and gravel blend in a unified clay colored pattern. The plants along the edge seem to leap out in contrasting bursts of color.

Building with Plastic Edging

If you are using pavers, space the edging so you can use all full-size pieces. Set out a row of pavers, as shown, to the desired width. Cut a 2 × 4 spacer to ½ inch longer than the pavers run to accommodate minor discrepancies. Use the 2 × 4 as shown to check the spacing between the edgings. Every 3 feet or so, posi-tion the 2 × 4 between the edgings and drive stakes on each side.

A crowned walk sheds water quickly and ensures against pud-dles. To make a screed for a crowned walk, cut a curve along the working edge of the plywood strip. Screed the sand (below) and install the pavers as you would for a patio.

Casual Benderboard Path

Outline the path with a hose or spray paint. Excavate the soil 2 inches deeper than the average thickness of the stones and tamp the soil firm. To install benderboard edging, drive stakes the desired height of the edging at 3-foot intervals along the outline. Cut and screw the benderboard to the stakes.

❶ Landscaping fabric

- Consult local builders to determine whether landscaping fabric or plastic sheeting is recommended in your area.
- Cut fabric a few inches wider than the path. Roll the fabric onto the path and tuck it under or roll it up onto the edging.

❷ Spread sand

- Pour rough sand into the path.
- Spread it with a rake.

❸ Spray with a mist

- Use a hose nozzle set on mist to moisten the sand.
- Take care not to saturate the sand. Just moisten it.

❹ Tamp

- Use a hand tamper or drum roller to firm up the sand.
- Make several passes to pack it down.

❺ Cut & arrange stones

- Cut and arrange the stones, aiming for fairly consistent joints.
- Press each stone into the sand, then remove it to determine where you need to remove or add sand.
- Adjust the bedding until the stones are fairly even and stable when you step on them.

❻ Fill with gravel

- To create a stable surface, use crushed granite or another rough, small-diameter stone.
- Fill joints so the gravel is just below the level of the stones.

Brick Walkway

Bricks are individually light in weight, so they require a solid edging to keep them in place. Shown on the opposite page is a path with brick-on-concrete edging.

A rustic door is right at home with the timeless brick walkway leading to it.

The invisible edging holding this pathway in place is visible now but it will soon be covered with sod or mulch.

Setting Bricks in Mortar

As long as you are pouring concrete anyway, you may choose to pour a complete concrete sidewalk and then set the bricks in a mortar bed atop the cured concrete. See chapter 6 for instructions on mixing and pouring concrete. You don't have to make the surface very smooth. Simple screeding will do.

Experiment with a dry run and cut the bricks as needed to fit. Spread a 1/2-inch-thick bed of mortar onto the concrete. Use small pieces of 3/8-inch plywood for spacers, and set the bricks onto the mortar (below left).

The next day, use a mortar bag to fill the joints with stiff mortar. Then smooth the joints with a jointer (below center). Alternatively, mix a batch of wet, pourable mortar and spread it over the brick surface. Scrape away excess, then use a sponge to clean the bricks and fill the joints (below right).

Stuff to Buy

Boards
Brick pavers
Concrete dry mix
Gravel
Rebar
Sand (fine and rough)

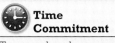

Time Commitment

Two weekends

Tools You'll Need

Mallet
Mason's line
Masonry trough
Shovel
Wheelbarrow

Related Topics

Applying mortar, 64–65
Concrete edging, 106–107
Cutting pavers, 112–115
Excavating, 98–99
Mixing mortar, 62–63

Path with Brick-on-concrete Edging

1 Build footings & pour

- Make forms from 2 × 4 lumber and put 1 × 2 stakes along the outside edges to hold the boards in place.
- Plan the edging so you can install all full-size pavers in the path.
- Run rebar down the middle, held up with stones or blocks.
- Mix concrete and shovel it into the forms.

2 Level concrete

- Use a piece of lumber as a screed to level the top of the concrete.
- Use a sawing motion as you move the screed along the form.
- When the concrete has hardened, remove the forms.
- Cover and wait for half a day or more.

3 Set the edging bricks

- Stretch a mason's line along the concrete. Position the edging bricks so you don't have to cut the inside bricks to fit.
- Spread a 1/2-inch-thick layer of mortar over the concrete.
- Set the edging bricks in the mortar. Butter each brick end to join it to the preceding brick.
- Smooth mortar joints on the edging bricks (see below).

4 Lay the bed

- Spread 2 inches of gravel over the path and tamp it firm.
- Add rough sand and screed it to one brick's thickness below the edging bricks.

5 Set bricks

- Set bricks in the sand, checking that they are at the same height as the edging and each other. Tap lightly with a rubber mallet to bed any bricks that are slightly high.
- Kneel on plywood as you work, to keep from disturbing the sand.

6 Fill joints

- Sweep fine sand into the joints between bricks.
- Tamp with a hand tamper or vibrating plate compactor.
- Fill in more sand as needed.

Gravel Path

Here's a relatively speedy way to build a gravel path. Metal edging naturally produces gentle curves and is unobtrusive in appearance. If you use the right stone, little if any tamping is required.

Path Options

Gravel that is made of small, sharp stones will provide a surprisingly stable walkway, especially if it is well tamped. Gravel referred to as "packing stone" will quickly compact when you walk over it.

If you expect not to use the path much, you may choose larger and rounder stones. They will escape more easily, but you may like the crunchy sound they make as you walk over them.

Shown here is metal ribbon edging, which can be attached snugly against cut-away sod. Some types of plastic edging can be installed this way as well.

How to Do It

1 Slice the outline

- Place a pair of hoses on the ground to indicate the contours of the path.
- If you want the path to be even in width, measure the distance between the hoses every 2 or 3 feet.
- Use a square shovel to slice through the sod along the perimeter.

2 Excavate

- A depth of 4 inches is sufficient for many types of packing stone, but you may want to dig deeper.
- Cut out any roots.
- Dig with a shovel and scrape the bottom of the excavation.

3 Stake edging on one side

- Metal ribbon edging is ideal for this application, as you don't have to remove sod outside the excavation in order to drive stakes.
- Position the edging against the excavation on one side and pound stakes to anchor the edging.
- The edging will form modest curves.

Related Topics

Excavating, 98–99
Loose-material surfaces, 86–87

Stuff to Buy

Metal edging
Landscaping fabric
Packing stone or crushed
  limestone

Time Commitment

Most of a day

Tools You'll Need

Hammer
Hand sledge
Hand tamper
Rake
Shovel
Vibrating plate compactor

4 Add other edging

- Skip this step if you don't need the edgings to be parallel.
- On a piece of 2 × 4, cut slices, just wide enough for the edging to slip into, spaced as far apart as the path will be wide.
- Slip the 2 × 4 over the two pieces of edging to keep them evenly spaced as you anchor them.

5 Check height & level

- The edging should be ½ inch or so above the future level of the gravel.
- Use a level to check that the edgings are even with each other.
- Where needed, pound down or pull up edgings.

6 Tamp ground & spread fabric

- Tamp the bottom of the excavation until firm using a hand tamper or a piece of 2 × 4 nailed to the bottom of a 4 × 4.
- Where appropriate, spread landscaping fabric or plastic to inhibit weed growth.

7 Pour gravel

- Purchase gravel in large bags. Have it delivered to the site or transport it in garbage bins.
- Pour the gravel into the excavation, taking care not to scatter stones on the lawn.
- Use a rake to spread the gravel.

8 Spread, tamp, backfill

- You can tamp many types of packing stone by simply walking on the surface. Other types you will need to press into place with a hand or power tamper.
- Backfill the trench outside the edging with soil and/or sod or plantings.

Fabric or Plastic?

In many regions, one or two thicknesses of landscaping fabric will keep weeds from growing. The fabric lets water seep through, though slowly. In areas with lush vegetation, the fabric may not be effective at preventing weeds.

You may consider using thick plastic instead. It will not allow water to drain, but that is usually not a problem on a narrow path. Water can simply seep to each side.

Keep in mind that neither fabric nor plastic will keep down large roots from nearby trees.

Designing Stairs

If a slope is gentle, stair construction can be casual, perhaps a few excavated level spots topped with stone slabs or pavers. However, a stairway of three or more steps should be planned carefully so all steps are consistent and at a comfortable height.

Calculating Step Dimensions

Steps should be at least 2 feet wide; make them 4 to 5 feet wide if you want two people to be able to pass each other or to have a comfortable place to sit and chat. Stair treads should be sloped at a rate of about ¼ inch per foot so rainwater can flow easily down the stairs or to the side.

A stair rise—the vertical distance from one tread to another—should be between 4 and 8 inches. For a step to be comfortable and safe, the horizontal run—the depth of the tread—should be at least 11 inches. A general rule is that the run plus twice the rise should equal 25 to 27 inches. See the simple line drawings below. If, for instance, the rise is 5½ inches (the thickness of a 6 × 6), the tread should be about 15 inches (5½ × 2 = 11, + 15 = 26). The higher the rise, the shorter the run should be. A step with a 7½-inch rise requires a run of about 11 inches.

Left: Stones of matched thicknesses form a natural-looking stairway. Above: These flagstones are set in a gravel bed that is held in place with lumber.

One common outdoor stairway configuration has rises of 6 inches and runs of 14 inches. The sum total of all the rises equals the stair's total height, and the sum total of all the runs equals its total length. As the illustration at far right shows, stair runs should be longer when the rises are shorter, and vice versa.

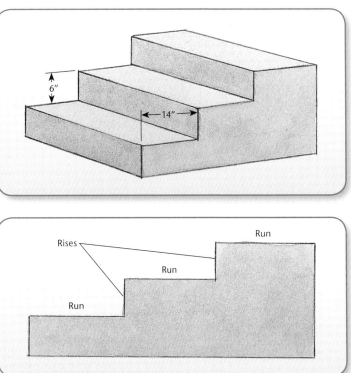

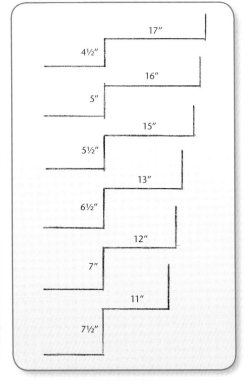

Measuring & Figuring

Time Commitment
Several hours

Tools You'll Need
Calculator
Level
Shovel
Tape measure

Related Topics
Faux railroad-tie steps, 142–143
Stone steps, 138–139
Timber-and-brick steps, 140–141

To lay out stairs, first determine the total rise and run. On short slopes, extend a level board across the slope and mark the beginning and end of the steps. The distance between these marks is the total run. Measure down from the end mark to determine the total rise. If the slope is long, divide the slope into shorter sections and add up individual measurements, or use a transit level, line level, or mason's line. Be sure to take into account the thickness of any landing pad at the bottom of the stairs.

Next, decide which riser height you'd like, keeping in mind the riser and run requirements shown on the previous page. Divide that into the total rise (in inches). Round off the fraction and you'll have the number of steps you need.

Divide the number of steps into the total rise. The answer is the exact riser height you need.

Divide the total run by the number of steps to get the run of each step.

If you can't get the calculations to result in steps with the proper dimensions, you might choose to excavate or add soil at the bottom of the stairs.

Slab Steps

Massive stones that are approximately equal in thickness make attractive steps. Where there is good access for heavy equipment, use flat pieces that are 4 to 7 inches thick, and deep enough so the back 3 inches of each step can support the front of the step above. Buy an extra piece for a foundation.

Because it's hard to predict precisely how high the top slab will be, it's best to build the stairs first, then build a patio at the top.

At the bottom of the slope, dig a foundation hole and set the bottom stone. You may choose to set stones in tamped soil or lay compactable gravel and/or sand as a base.

Excavate, add gravel or sand, and set each succeeding step in rising order. Rest the front of each stone on the back of the one below. If any stones wobble, add or remove sand or gravel.

Stone Steps

Building steps of variously sized stones is a slow, laborious process, but it creates a one-of-a-kind stairway that will be a pleasure to look at and walk on for many years.

Steppingstone Staircase

If you need just a few steps and can transport large stones to the site, build a simple staircase. Select flat stones at least 20 inches long and wide and 5 to 7 inches thick. Use another piece to serve as a foundation stone.

Starting at the bottom, dig a hole for the foundation stone. If your ground freezes, excavate 6 inches deeper and pack that space with compactable gravel. Add a 2-inch layer of compacted sand. Twist the first stone onto the sand, so it is slightly sloped and about 2 inches above grade.

Excavate for the second stone, and set it in a 1-inch-thick bed of sand. It should overlap the foundation stone by at least 1 inch. Twist and shim with small stones until it is slightly sloped for rain runoff.

Repeat for the other stones. When all the steps are in place dig back some of the band alongside the steps and embed large stones there to keep soil from washing down the steps.

Steps should tilt forward or to the side by ⅛ inch per foot.

Wide stones make for deep stairs, which are comfortable to walk on as long as they are not too thick.

A stairway that incorporates many small stones usually must be mortared onto a concrete base.

A stairway with few small stones can be set in a gravel base.

Stair Parts

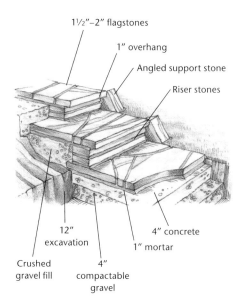

1½"–2" flagstones

1" overhang

Angled support stone

Riser stones

12" excavation

4" concrete

1" mortar

Crushed gravel fill

4" compactable gravel

Stuff to Buy

Concrete mix
Compactable gravel
Flagstones or cobblestones
Sand
Thick stones

Time Commitment

Several days

Tools You'll Need

Carpenter's square
Level
Masonry trough
Plumb bob
Shovel

Related Topics

Calculating concrete needs,
  170–171
Designing stairs, 136–137
Flagstones on concrete, 152–153
Mixing mortar, 62–63

How to Do It

Build these stair treads using flagstones, about 2 inches thick, mortared together, or use single, large slabs. For risers, use granite cobblestones or several layers of flagstones. This design calls for two rectangular stones to serve as support pieces on the sides of each step. You may choose instead to build up the sides with more roundish stones, as shown in the photo on page 138, lower left.

Though these steps are rustic in appearance, they should be a comfortable height and depth, and they should be consistent in size. Take the time to carefully plan the rises and runs.

Shown here is a stairway that is supported by compacted gravel, concrete, and mortar. Depending on the stability of your soil, you may need a base that is thicker or thinner. Consult local builders or your building department.

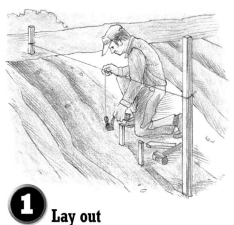

1 Lay out

- Use a board and level or a string and stakes to determine the locations and sizes of the steps.
- Mark off increments on the string or board to show the run of each step.
- Transfer the marks to the ground with a plumb bob or a chalk line and drive a stake into each spot.

2 Excavate

- Use a carpenter's square to lay out parallel lines and establish the other side of the steps. Drive stakes at these corners also.
- Using a shovel, remove enough soil to create the rough shape of the steps.

3 Lay the foundation

- Arrange flagstones for the bottom tread, which will be flush with the soil.
- Remove the stones and dig down 12 inches.
- Pack with 12 inches of compactable gravel.
- Mix concrete and pour a 4-inch layer over the gravel. Roughly smooth the surface and wait a day.

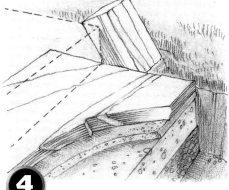

4 Add side stones & flagstones

- At each side, excavate and place rectangular cobblestones.
- Mix a stiff batch of mortar.
- Spread a 2-inch layer of mortar over the concrete and around the angled stone.
- Top with flagstones, tapping with a rubber mallet so they are even and sloped slightly forward.
- Fill the spaces between stones with mortar and clean it away when it starts to harden.

5 Add riser stones

- To build the next step, spread a 1-inch layer of mortar along the back of the finished tread.
- Place riser stones on top and fill between them with mortar.
- After the mortar sets, carefully dig a 6-inch-deep hole behind for the next step.

Timber-and-Brick Steps

This stairway is basically a series of small patios, each with timber edging and bricks or pavers set in a gravel-and-sand base. A 4 × 6 set on edge is 5½ inches tall—a good height for a step rise.

Thick and wide lumber, like these railroad ties, must be carefully chosen to make sure they are straight.

Here, the top "step" is actually an extension of the patio. You may choose to eliminate this portion of the patio and make it your first step down.

Timber-and-gravel Steps on a Slope

On a gently sloping site, you may choose to build several separate patios, perhaps with a step or two between some of them. The photo at left shows a more casual approach, using lumber and gravel. The steps vary in depth (the run), but in a predictable way: the lower steps all have runs of four feet, and the upper steps are consistently 18 inches deep. That way, a person only has to change gait once.

To build the stairway, firmly stake the timbers in place, using pressure-treated 2 × 4 stakes that are driven an inch below the tops of the timbers. Drive stakes as deep as possible, using a sledgehammer. Install a short masonry wall on each side, then fill the areas between with fine gravel.

 **Stuff to Buy**

4 × 6s
7" lag screws with washers
Compactable gravel
Pavers
Rebar in 2- to 3-foot-long pieces
Sand

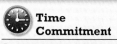 **Time Commitment**

A weekend or two

 **Tools You'll Need**

Circular saw
Drill with long bit
Hand sledge
Level
Shovel
Socket wrench

 Related Topics

Excavating, 98–99
Designing stairs, 136–137
Measuring & laying out, 44–45

How to Do It

❶ Build timber frames

- Purchase 4 × 6 pressure-treated lumber. Look for straight pieces that are not deeply cracked.
- On a flat surface, lay pavers in a dry run to determine the inside dimensions of the frame.
- Steps should be about 15 inches deep, including the front 4 × 6 but not the rear.
- Cut the timbers with a circular saw, and drill a pilot hole with a long bit at each joint.
- Tap the lag screws in, and tighten with a socket wrench.

❷ Lay the bottom step

- Place 2 to 3 inches of compactable gravel at the bottom of the stairway.
- Tamp, then check the height.
- Set the frame on gravel and see that it is sloped slightly toward the front.
- Remove or add gravel as needed so the frame is stable.

❸ Stack & anchor the frames

- Add succeeding frames one at a time, checking each for the correct slope.
- Excavate and add gravel as needed for each frame.
- In at least four places, drill pilot holes through both layers of timber.
- Drive rebar down through the timbers and into the soil until the rebar is flush with the top of the timber.

❹ Screed the base

- Check that all frames are stable, and pour compactable gravel to a depth of one paver's thickness plus 1½ inches below the top of each.
- Tamp with a 2 x 4. Shovel in sand and use a short piece of 2 x 4 to screed the sand.

❺ Set pavers

- Place pavers into the frames. Tap them with a board and a rubber mallet.
- Check with a board to see that the pavers are all at the same height as the framing.

❻ Fill joints

- Sweep fine sand to fill the joints.

Faux Railroad Tie Steps

Here's an inexpensive way to make nicely rustic steps: Construct rough forms and pour in tinted concrete. The resulting "loaves" can be wire-brushed or distressed in other ways to make them look like rough-hewn lumber.

How to Do It

❶ Build forms

- Construct crude forms to make faux ties about 8 inches wide and tall
- Here, scavenged pieces of structural metal are used, but you could use 2 × 10s as well
- Position two pieces of lumber between each of the future ties, and run a piece of rebar through them

Roughening Methods

There are various techniques to achieve a textured surface. You can scrape wet concrete with a scarifying tool, or a small board with nails poking out of it. If the form is made of rough-grained lumber, apply a concrete release agent or cooking oil to it before forming, and allow the concrete to set fully before disassembling the form.

❷ Mix & pour concrete

- Mix a batch of concrete; you may choose to color it
- Insert and work a square shovel along the edges, to remove any bubbles
- Scrape the top with a board to screed it

❸ Smooth the top

- Use a magnesium float or a steel trowel to smooth the top edge
- Wait a half hour or so before disassembling the form

❹ Disassemble & roughen

- Pull apart the form
- Use a reciprocating saw to cut through the rebar between the wood edge pieces
- Spray with a fine mist, then use a wire brush to roughen the surface

❺ Excavate & set ties

- Working with a helper, roughly excavate for each step
- Start from the bottom and work up

Stuff to Buy

Concrete
Concrete colorant
Crushed granite
Lumber for forms
Rebar

Time Commitment

A day

Tools You'll Need

Magnesium float
Pry bar
Reciprocating saw with metal-
  cutting blade
Rubber mallet
Shovel
Tools for mixing concrete
Wire brush

Related Topics

Calculating concrete needs,
  170–171
Designing stairs, 136–137
Mixing & delivering, 172–173

6 Keep things consistent

- Check that each step is at least close to level along its length; it should slope slightly along its width for rain runoff
- Maintain consistent rises and runs
- Here, the workers measure quickly for width using the length of a hammer

7 Pound ties in place

- To set ties firmly, pound with a rubber mallet, or set a scrap piece of lumber on top of the tie and use a hand sledge
- If a tie sinks on one end, lift it up, apply soil or sand, and reinstall

8 Pry & reposition

- If soil is soft, you may need to tamp it, then apply a layer of compactible gravel
- Use a large pry bar to keep the ties consistently aligned

9 Test for firmness

- Walk on the ties to make sure they do not wobble
- Adding gravel (next step) will firm things up somewhat, but it's best to get the ties firmly established now

10 Add crushed stone

- Excavate straight lines alongside the stairway
- Pour in crushed gravel or other decorative but compactible stone in the gaps between ties

11 Soak & tamp

- Spray the gravel with water to compact it
- Tamp with a 2 × 4, firmly but not so hard that you move the ties

5

Paving on Concrete Slabs

In this chapter, you'll learn how to freshen up existing concrete slabs, whether It's using decorative techniques such as acid staining and stenciling, or covering a worn-out-looking slab with flagstones or other pavers such as brick and tile. In our flagstone-entry project, we also show you how to work with stones of differing thicknesses to create a gentle step.

Chapter Contents

Resurfacing Concrete

Acid Staining

Stenciling

Flagstones on Concrete

Formal Flagstones with Tight Joints

Paving over Concrete
page 156

Mortared Bluestones
page 158

Outcropping & Flagstone Entry
page 160

Tiles on Concrete
page 162

Resurfacing Concrete

A growing number of products make it possible to cover drab or stained concrete with a fresh layer that can be left plain or textured and tinted. Some are available only to professionals, but many are sold to homeowners as well.

Application Methods

Buy a bag of resurfacing mix at a home center. Check the label to be sure you get the right product for the thickness of your application. Products made with white portland cement can be tinted to vibrant hues, while less expensive products made with gray cement can be tinted to more muted colors.

Clean the old concrete and patch any cracks. Pour when the sun is not shining directly on the surface. In a bucket, mix with a drill and a paddle mixer, or mix small batches by hand with a margin trowel. Achieve a mixture that is just thin enough to pour easily.

Pour it out, then apply it with a magnesium float or a large squeegee. Or use a special gauge roller (right), which automatically spreads the mixture to a specified thickness. If the slab is wide and you cannot reach across, use kneeling boards like the ones shown below right, which leave only pinhole marks in the topping.

Gauge Roller

Mixture Options

Some micro toppings are only $1/16$ to $1/8$ inch thick. Stamp overlays tend to be $1/4$ to $1/2$ inch thick, depending on the stamp. Self-leveling overlays can be $1/4$ to 2 inches thick, enough to level and smooth out a moderately damaged surface. The formulas all consist of cement, sand, and any of a number of adhesives that often go by the broad designation of polymer. Consult the dealer to find the product that works best in your climate.

Kneeling Boards

Application with Forms

If you need to apply a thick coat to even out a damaged slab, forming the edges can be difficult. Install simple forms made with 2 × 4s butted against the existing slab, at a height to produce the desired overlay thickness. Mix and spread the resurfacing product with a large squeegee, as shown, or use a bull float or magnesium float. Most materials are self-leveling, meaning they will smooth themselves out to a certain extent.

Coloring & Patterning

You can tint the product before applying it, or allow it to dry and then apply an acid stain. Similarly, you can use stamps or stencils during application, or wait for the product to dry and then score lines using an angle grinder, with a straight board as a guide.

Stuff to Buy

2 × 4s
Colorants or stamps
Resurfacing mix

 **Time Commitment**

Less than a day

 **Tools You'll Need**

Kneeling boards
Squeegee, trowel, or gauge roller

 **Related Topics**

Acid staining, 148–149
Repairing concrete, 286–289

Epoxy Garage Floor Finish

At a home center or hardware store, you can buy do-it-yourself supplies, often in a kit, to apply a durable and decorative garage floor finish. You will need acid to wash the floor, two-part epoxy base coat, a small bag of color chips, and topcoating material. Instructions vary by manufacturer, but the steps shown here apply generally. Start by ensuring that the floor is sound. Fill and smooth any cracks with repair concrete and allow it to cure fully before you proceed.

1 Clean & etch

- Thoroughly clean away any oils and dirt.
- Use a recommended acid wash to etch the concrete, opening its pores to ensure a secure bond with the epoxy.

Floor grinder option

- If the floor is heavily stained or has been coated with a sealer, rent a floor grinder.
- Turn on the machine and slowly move it around the entire floor.
- When you are done, the floor should look like rough sandpaper.

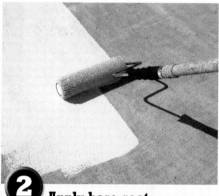

2 Apply base coat

- Thoroughly mix the two components of the base coat epoxy.
- Starting at the farthest corner of the room, apply the base coat to the perimeter with a brush, then use a roller to apply it to an area about 6 feet square.

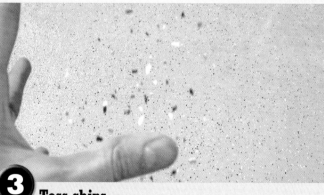

3 Toss chips

- Grab a pinch of color chips between your thumb and index finger.
- Throw the chips upward, as if tossing a basketball, and allow them to fall gently onto the base coat.
- Aim for an even dispersal of color chips, with no clumps or bare spots.

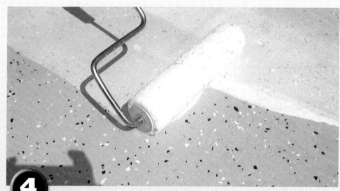

4 Top coat

- Wait overnight for the base coat to cure.
- Mix the two components of the topcoat and apply it with a brush and roller.
- The topcoat will appear milky white at first, then dry clear.

Acid Staining

Acid-stained concrete can be attractive enough for interior floors and countertops. While interior applications are usually best left to the pros, with the right materials and careful preparation you can successfully stain an outdoor surface.

Working the Stain

- After you have applied acid stain once, wipe some water over it to see how it will look with sealer. For a darker color, apply a 3–1 stain-water solution.
- Acid stain is nasty stuff, so take care not to get it on your skin. Place a towel over the top of the pump sprayer before unscrewing it, so it does not spatter.

Beneath the Surface

By penetrating beneath the surface, acid stain creates a durable finish. A local paint store or home center may carry acid stain, but you will find a wider range of colors online.

Acid stain produces fairly consistent color as long as the concrete is smooth and clean. On a rougher surface, the color will be more variegated. Small cracks will appear as marble-like veins. The final color depends on how light or dark the concrete is, as well as its alkali content. If the concrete has been patched, the patched areas will almost certainly end up a different color. To get an idea of the finished appearance, apply both stain and sealer to a small spot.

If the concrete is very rough, with exposed pebbles, acid stain will not produce vivid color. In this case, you may want to first apply an overlay, which is basically a resurfacing material.

Professionals can produce artistic creations by overlaying several colors, by using acid for certain areas, and with elaborate masking. Shown here is a basic application with a modest pattern.

How to Do It

1 Prep the floor

- Use a heavy-duty cleaner—but not acid—to clean away all oily residue.
- To remove paint, scrub it with paint remover, then with a mild detergent.
- Rinse with a pressure washer, using a fan tip.
- Where there is built-up residue, use a power sander.

2 Mask a pattern

- Allow the floor to dry completely.
- Use a tape measure and a pencil to map out a pattern for the floor.
- Working with a helper, stretch masking tape in straight lines to produce the pattern.
- Press the tape down firmly at all points.

3 Apply acid gel

- Use hydrochloric acid gel rather than liquid acid, which will seep behind the tape.
- Paint the lines inside the tape.
- Wait an hour or so and then gently rinse the surface with a damp sponge.

 **Stuff to Buy**

Acid stain
Ammonia
Concrete sealer
Hydrochloric acid gel
Overlay material

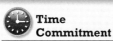 **Time Commitment**

Most of a day

 **Tools You'll Need**

Bristle broom
Flat trowel
Masonry brush
Pump sprayer

 Related Topics

Repairing concrete, 286–289
Resurfacing concrete, 146–147

4 Remove tape

- Once the etched area is dry, pull the masking tape straight up.

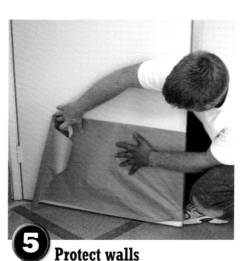

5 Protect walls

- Sprayed acid stain will spatter, so clear the area completely.
- Unless you plan to paint the wall, cover it with wide masking paper.

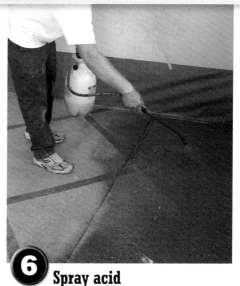

6 Spray acid

- Start with an 8–1 stain-water solution. You may use a heavier solution for a second application.
- Using a figure-eight motion, keep the spray head moving at all times to avoid puddles.
- Saturate the entire surface evenly.

7 Clean

- To neutralize the acid, mix a 1–10 ammonia-water solution.
- Pour the solution onto the floor and scrub with a soft bristle brush.

8 Vacuum & dry

- Use a wet-dry shop vac to suck up as much liquid as possible.
- Wipe with dry towels to dry the surface evenly.

9 Seal

- Allow the acid stain to dry completely.
- Apply a solvent-based concrete sealer, or two coats of water-based sealer.
- You may choose to top the surface with a sacrificial barrier, such as paste wax or acrylic floor sealer.

Stenciling

With materials purchased online or at a specialty supply store, you can create fanciful or geometric designs on a concrete floor.

Materials & Methods

Stencils ranging from simple to elaborate enable you to stain, etch, or paint patterns on a concrete floor. Buy all the materials together, and choose the colorant that works best with each particular type of stencil.

Vinyl stencils, which are self-sticking and can be used only once, are generally 4 mils thick. Stenciling works best on a concrete surface that is smooth, with little or no visible aggregate. If the surface is rough, use a heavier stencil, 10 or 25 mils thick. The stencil must be burnished—rubbed firmly at all points onto the concrete—to ensure that the color will not seep under it. Often, a special gelling (or thickening) agent should be applied to the stain to keep it from wicking under the stencil.

There are many application methods:

- Acid-stain the entire floor, then apply a stenciled pattern and use gelled acid to remove (or lighten) color from the stencil's exposed areas.
- Apply positive color by applying gelled stain to the exposed areas with a brush, squeegee, or sprayer.
- Apply very light coats of thin (ungelled) stain using a Preval sprayer, which is powered by CO_2 cartridges and is available at a paint store.
- Create an embossed (raised) pattern by applying a colored cement over the stencil.

About Large Installations

On a large job with colored cement rather than paint, most of the steps are the same as for a basic installation, but the size of the sheet calls for somewhat different techniques. When applying the stencil, you may need to burnish half the sheet, then peel back and cut the backing paper (right), then position and burnish the remaining half. The photo at far right shows the application of colored cement rather than paint. Apply the cement with a putty knife or squeegee, pressing downward, rather than scraping across, as much as possible. Allow the cement to harden but not fully cure. Then carefully peel back the transfer paper (right).

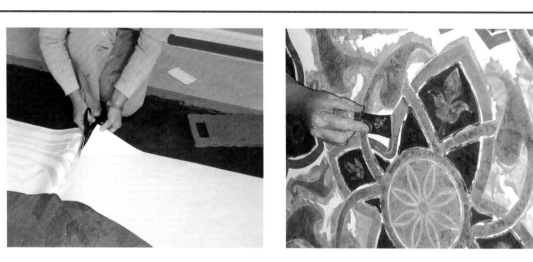

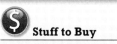 **Stuff to Buy**

Acid stain, colorized cement, or another coloring agent
Adhesive stencils
Gelling or thickening agent

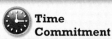 **Time Commitment**

A full day

 **Tools You'll Need**

Sprayer
Squeegee
Trowel

 Related Topics

Decorative effects for concrete, 180–187
Repairing concrete, 286–289

How to Do It

1 Position & burnish

- Tape the stencil to the floor.
- Check for correct position.
- Burnish (rub firmly) with the burnishing tool supplied by the manufacturer, to firmly affix the stencil.

2 Remove paper covering

- Peel off the backing paper.
- Watch the pattern as you peel, to be sure it is adhered firmly at all points. If it's not, lay the backing paper down and burnish again.

3 Burnish again

- Use the burnishing tool again to make sure the pattern is stuck firmly.
- Hold the tool nearly flat so you don't peel the pattern up.

4 Apply color

- Using a daubing stenciling brush—not a regular paintbrush—spread the paint or colored cement over the stencil.
- Daub the paint, rather than brushing or smearing it, to keep it from seeping behind the stencil.

5 Peel transfer paper

- Follow the manufacturer's instructions to wait until the color is dry or mostly dry.
- Gently peel back the transfer paper.

6 Pry out small bits

- Some patterns have narrow or small pieces.
- Use an awl, a small screwdriver, or a tool supplied by the manufacturer to carefully pry these pieces up.

Flagstones on Concrete

Flagstones can be set on soil or on a bed of gravel and sand, but for the sturdiest installation, mortar them onto a solid concrete slab. If you work patiently and carefully, the patio will be as elegant as it is natural feeling.

Contrasting colors of flagstone create a patchwork-quilt approach to a stone-surrounded front door.

Mortaring onto Gravel

Where the climate is mild, mortaring onto a bed of tamped gravel will produce a patio that is strong enough for foot traffic. Consult local builders to make sure this method will work in your area.

Excavate and tamp the gravel firm using a vibrating plate compactor. Spread mortar (or sand-mix concrete) as you work, checking for an even height. Allow the mortar to harden, then fill the joints with more mortar.

Planning & Preparing

You can lay a new slab for mortaring the flagstone, or use an existing one. Inspect any existing slab to make sure it is sound. Mortaring stones on top will give the entire structure additional strength.

If you want to install edging, you will need to cut most of the perimeter stones. This is best done with a masonry cutoff saw after the stones have been installed. However, you may allow the stones to overhang the slab by as much as 2 inches for a naturally uneven look with no edging.

Choose stones that are similar in thickness. It's best to have a variety of sizes. Consult a stone dealer to choose the best mortar for your type of stone. You may use a combination of thinset and brick mortar, or simply mix portland cement and sand.

These two pages show an informal-looking surface, with joints that vary a bit in width. For a more formal and precise arrangement, see the next two pages.

How to Do It

1 Apply bonding agent

- Clean the concrete by scrubbing it with TSP or a mild muriatic acid solution and then rinsing it thoroughly.
- To ensure adhesion, brush liquid latex concrete bonding agent over the slab.
- Wait for the agent to dry at least partially before applying mortar.

Mixing with a Machine

A small rented mixing machine like this can make it easy to mix mortar. If you add liquid colorant, be sure to use exactly equal amounts of colorant and mortar with each batch so the color will be consistent.

2 Mix mortar

- Avoid working in bright sunshine, which can dry mortar too quickly.
- Mix a batch of mortar, using dry mortar mix or 6 shovelfuls of sand combined with two shovelfuls of portland cement.
- The mortar should be fairly stiff, just wet enough to stick to the stones and the slab.

$ Stuff to Buy

Flagstones
Gravel to fill joints
Latex concrete bonding agent
Mortar

⏰ Time Commitment

A weekend

🛠 Tools You'll Need

Broom
Chisel
Power masonry saw
Rake
Shovel
Trowel
Wheelbarrow

◎ Related Topics

Applying mortar, 64–65
Arranging flagstones, 54–55
Cutting bricks, pavers, & stone, 48–51
Mixing mortar, 62–63
Pouring a concrete patio, 174–179

3 Set a large stone

- To provide a reference point for height and to help ensure an even distribution of large stones, shovel out mortar and set a large, thick stone near the middle of an area about 8 feet square.
- Check that the stone is level, or sloped in the direction that the slab is sloped.
- Press the stone into the mortar, taking care not to push it down too far.

4 Make a dry run

- You will spend most of your time shuffling, rearranging, and cutting stones to achieve a pleasing pattern.
- Aim for joints that are fairly consistent in width.
- Allow stones to overhang the slab by as much as 2 inches.
- To mark a stone for cutting, hold it in place and draw a cut line.

5 Cut stones

- If you choose to cut by hand, expect stones to break the way you want them to about 70 percent of the time.
- Move the stones to an area where you can easily sweep away chips.
- Using a cold chisel and a hand sledge, tap along the cut line to score each stone.
- With the chisel tip on one of the score lines, deliver a sharp blow to break the stone.

6 Spread mortar

- Every 15 minutes or so, remix the mortar with a shovel. If it starts to stiffen, throw the batch out and mix a new one.
- Pick up one dry-laid stone and set it to the side, oriented so you can replace it.
- Shovel mortar onto the concrete.
- Estimate the needed thickness of the mortar and spread it with a trowel.

7 Bed stones

- As you set stones, check that each is close to level and at the same height as its neighbor.
- Every few stones, use a straight board to check stone heights.
- If a stone is low, pick it up, add mortar, and reset it.
- If a stone is too high, tap it down and scrape away any excess mortar that oozes.

8 Fill joints

- Wait a day or so for the mortar to set.
- To fill joints with finely crushed stone, sweep the gravel into the joints.
- Wet the surface by spraying it with a mist. Allow the gravel to settle, then sweep in more gravel as needed.

Formal Flagstones with Tight Joints

If you want a flagstone surface that is nearly smooth, with pieces that fit together like those of a jigsaw puzzle, you will need to cut most of the stones. Very rarely do two edges fit together all along their edges.

1 Mark stones

- Position one stone near or on top of another in order to mark for an accurately parallel line.
- Either directly trace a line along the side of one stone or use a tape measure to draw a line 2 or 3 inches away, as shown here.

2 Cut stones

- If you have only a few stones to cut, a circular saw with a masonry blade might work. Otherwise, rent a masonry cutoff saw.
- Keep the blade wet as you cut.
- After cutting, tap with a hammer to chip the upper edge to make the cut look natural.

3 Assemble a dry run

- Piece together either all of the stones, or all of the large stones in an area of about 10 square feet.
- Tap with a mallet to align the stones precisely.
- You will often need to modify cut lines in order to achieve the correct fit.

4 Shovel mortar

- With practice, you will learn how to estimate the amount of mortar needed for each stone.
- Mix a batch of stiff mortar, just wet enough so it sticks to the stones.
- Use a shovel to drop mortar onto the area.

5 Spread mortar

- Take note of the shape of the stone, as well as how thick it is at various points.
- Spread plenty of mortar onto the site, using a mason's trowel.

6 Test the bedding

- Set the stone down and press it into place.
- If you can tap it to the desired height, you can move on to the next stone.
- Remove mortar that oozes out into the joints, especially if it threatens to smear on the top of a stone or if it is a different color than the joint mortar will be.

7 Adjust the bed

- Chances are good that the bed will be too thick or too thin.
- Tilt the stone up and remove or add mortar.
- Use the indentations left by the stone as a guide for where to add or remove mortar.

8 Bed the stone

- Tap with a rubber mallet to adhere the stone firmly to the mortar.
- Use a level or a straight board to check that the stone is at the same height as its neighbors.

Mortaring Flagstone Joints

Wait a day for the mortar under the stones to harden, then fill the joints with mortar. Some masons use a mortar bag, but most simply work with a trowel, jointer, and brush.

1 Slip mortar into joints

- Mix a batch of stiff mortar, adding colorant if desired.
- Use a margin trowel (as shown) or a pointing trowel to slip mortar into the joints.
- With practice, you can shoe-horn mortar down into the joints without smearing the tops of the stones.

2 Tool joints

- Use a jointer to press the mortar down and create even joints.
- Aim to press the mortar just slightly below the surface of the stones.

3 Scrape excess

- After a few minutes, the mortar will start to harden and become crumbly, so it is less likely to smear.
- At this point, and before the mortar starts to harden, use a trowel to scrape off excess mortar.
- Where voids appear, add a bit of mortar and go over the area again with a jointer.

4 Brush joints

- Use a small brush to achieve even joints.
- Brush gently so you remove dry crumbs but don't spread wet stuff.

Wet-mortar Method

1 Spread mortar

- Mix a batch of fairly wet mortar so it can seep down into the joints.
- Use a trowel to lather the joints with mortar.

2 Wipe

- As soon as some of the mortar starts to dry, wipe it with a wet sponge.
- Avoid the joints themselves and concentrate on the tops of the stones.
- Continually rinse the sponge with clean water.

3 Joint with sponge

- Use a damp (not wet) sponge for this step.
- Ball the sponge up tightly.
- Use the sponge to create mortar joints that are just slightly below the stone surface.
- Repeat the processes. Once the mortar dries, you may need to clean the stones with a mild muriatic acid solution.

Lipping

Once the mortar has dried, you can remove some surface imperfections and make the total surface smoother by lipping. Hold a cold chisel nearly flat, with the beveled edge up, and tap it with a hammer to remove flakes of stone.

Paving over Concrete

Bricks or pavers make a handsome covering for a concrete slab. You can install edging along the perimeter for the sake of appearance, but the bricks will stay firmly in place without it.

How to Do It

Inspect the slab to be sure it is in solid condition. You will spread a thick layer of mortar over it, so it does not need to be very even. Mortaring pavers on top will increase the strength of the slab.

Once you are finished, the patio will be 4 inches or so higher than the concrete. As a result, you may need to raise the level of the surrounding lawn, or you may choose to add a flower bed.

Set the pavers in any pattern you choose. At the edges, you can let the pavers overhang, then snap a chalk line and cut them with a power saw.

Lay pavers in a dry run on the concrete. You may choose to adjust the thickness of the joint lines or allow the pavers to overhang the slab by an inch or so if that will reduce the number of cuts you need to make. If you install edging, the pavers should end up ¼ inch above it to make sweeping easy. Clean the slab and apply latex concrete bonding agent.

1 Spread mortar

- To make a guide for a 1½-inch-thick mortar bed, stake temporary boards on each side of the slab and use a straight board as the screed.
- If you have permanent edging, construct a screed using a straight board and a piece of plywood that extends below the edging by a paver's thickness minus ½ inch (the pavers will settle down into the mortar by about ¼ inch).
- Mix mortar and shovel it onto the slab.

2 Set bricks

- Using scraps of plywood as spacers, set pavers in the mortar.
- The bricks should feel stuck when you lay them. If they do not, perhaps spray the bricks or dip them in water before setting them.
- Lay a flat board on top of the pavers and tap it with a hammer to bed the pavers and produce a flat surface.
- The mortar should ooze up a bit but should not rise to the surface.

3 Grout

- Wait a day or two for the mortar to set.
- Mix a batch of wet mortar, stirring in colorant if you choose.
- Pour the mortar over the surface.

4 Push into joints

- Use a grout float to push mortar down into the joints.
- Work the float in at least two directions for each joint.

5 Spread

- Using long, sweeping strokes, spread mortar across the surface.
- Tilt the float up and scrape away most of the excess.

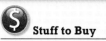 **Stuff to Buy**
Colorant for joint mortar
Edging
Latex concrete bonding agent
Mortar mix
Pavers or bricks

 **Time Commitment**
Several days

 Tools You'll Need
Grout float
Jointer
Lumber screed guide
Sponge and bucket
Trowel
Wheelbarrow

Related Topics
Applying mortar, 64–65
Cutting bricks, pavers, & stone, 48–51
Mixing mortar, 62–63
Repairing concrete, 286–289
Setting pavers, 116–119

Outside edges
- If you have an outside edge, as you would with a stairway, wait for the mortar to become a bit stiffer.
- Use the short side of the float to press mortar into joints.

6 Scrape
- Use a trowel to scrape up excess mortar.
- Try to expose each paver. The more mortar you remove now, the easier the next steps will be.

7 Wipe
- With a damp sponge, gently wipe the surface.
- Aim to mostly clean off the pavers without indenting the joints.

8 Rinse sponge
- Continually rinse the sponge in a bucket of water. Replace the water when it gets very murky.
- Repeat this gentle wiping, taking care not to drag joint mortar onto the paver surfaces.

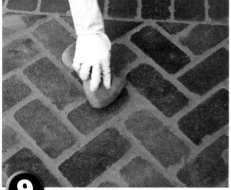

9 Joint with sponge
- Use a balled-up sponge to gently scrape joints, creating even lines.
- If a void appears, press in some mortar with your thumb and tool again.

Jointing an edge
- The thin mortar you applied to the edges earlier will probably not fill the joints.
- Mix a small batch of stiff mortar.
- Press the mortar in with your thumb, then use the jointer.

10 Acid-clean
- The next day, mix a solution of 1 part muriatic acid to 3 parts water.
- Scrub the bricks with the solution to clean off the haze of mortar.
- Rinse with water.

Using a Mortar Bag
Instead of the grouting method shown at the left, you may choose to use a mortar bag. Mix fairly stiff mortar and shovel it into the bag. Carefully squeeze the mortar into joints, making sure it sinks down to fill them. Once the mortar is dry enough that you can press it with your thumb and leave a permanent impression, tool the joints with a jointer. When the mortar becomes crumbly, brush the crumbs away.

Mortared Bluestones

Large, thick bluestones that are cut to fit precisely produce a formal yet natural surface. The gray and blue tones of the stones make for a subtle patchwork effect. This work calls for very accurate cutting and setting.

The Challenges of Cut Stone

Bluestone, limestone, and other large cut stones are usually installed by pros rather than do-it-yourselfers, as they must fit together tightly and form a very even surface. If you have gained some basic cutting and setting skills, you may want to tackle a small area with this material.

Start with a sound concrete slab. Because the mortar bed is thick—from 1 to 2 inches—the slab does not have to be even.

The project shown on these pages has perimeter pieces of bluestone already installed. Any edging must be precisely level or consistently sloped so you'll have reliable reference points for installing an even surface. The first pieces must be level, as any unevenness will be amplified as you continue laying stones.

Mortar should be just the right consistency—wet enough to stick but stiff enough to support heavy stones. Cuts must be accurate, so you might want to cut cardboard or plywood templates for the more difficult angles and shapes.

The precise lines of cut bluestones add natural beauty and a sense of order to this rambling patio.

How to Do It

1 Cutting stones

- Stones will probably be too large to cut with a wet saw.
- Mark cut lines carefully, then use a masonry cutoff saw or a circular saw equipped with a masonry blade (shown).
- If you are using a circular saw, vacuum dust as you cut to prevent damaging the saw's motor.

2 Plan & sort cuts

- Usually, it's best to cut a few stones at once.
- Number the backs to keep track of which stones go where.
- Don't cut the smallest stones yet. Cut them after the others are installed.

3 Bevel edges

- Because the stones will fit together tightly, check that the cuts are square, or slightly beveled for easy fitting.
- Sand corners so you can shoehorn them in more easily.
- Use a grinder to slightly bevel the cut edges so each stone is slightly smaller at the bottom than at the top.

4 Make a dry run

- Set a number of stones in place to make sure they will fit.
- Recut stones that are a bit too long. If one is too small, use it elsewhere and cut another one.
- Set stones off to the side so you can easily reassemble them.

 **Stuff to Buy**	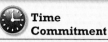 **Time Commitment**	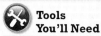 **Tools You'll Need**	**Related Topics**
Bluestone slabs Latex concrete bonding agent Mortar mix or portland cement and sand	Several days	Grinder with masonry wheel Level Masonry cutting saw Trowel	Applying mortar, 64–65 Cutting bricks, pavers, and stone, 48–51 Mixing mortar, 62–63 Repairing concrete, 286–289

5 Mix mortar

- Apply latex concrete bonding agent to the slab and allow it to dry at least partially.
- Mix a stiff batch of mortar.
- Keep the mortar in a shaded spot so it won't dry out.

6 Dampen stones

- To ensure that a stone will stick to the mortar, wipe the back with a fairly wet sponge.
- If the stone soaks up moisture immediately, moisten it again.
- The stone should be damp, not dripping wet.

7 Spread mortar

- Scoop mortar onto the area where the stone will go. Estimate how thick it should be.
- Use a trowel to scrape away an angled portion around the perimeter so the stone can settle without forcing mortar up through the joints.

8 Set stones

- Carefully lower each stone into place.
- Lower it straight down so you don't move adjacent stones.
- Use a straightedge, mason's line, or level to check each stone for correct height.

9 Bed stones

- Tap with a mallet to make stones level and perfectly flush with adjacent stones.
- If a stone is too low or too high, remove it and add or remove mortar.
- Do not allow mortar to ooze up to the surface.

10 Adjust positions

- Joints generally should be tight, but if you need to move a stone over by 1/8 inch or so, it will not be noticeable.
- Constantly check for an even surface as you work, making adjustments right away, before the mortar starts to harden.
- Fill the joints with very fine sand.

Outcropping & Flagstone Entry

Degree of Difficulty

● Challenging

Thick outcropping stones at the front edge of the porch create the illusion that the entire porch is made of thick stones. They also subtly make the entire assemblage, including the pathway flagstones, feel more substantial.

How to Do It

This project has three elements, each with its own installation method, shown in several places in this book: thick outcropping stones at the face of the porch, flagstones mortared onto a concrete slab, and dry-laid flagstones for the path.

The massive outcropping boulders, which look like stones you often see sticking out of a hillside or overhanging a river, must be chosen carefully so they fit the opening and are similar in shape and color. They may need to be cut to fit at a stone yard.

On a mixed-process job like this, some people can work on the dry-laid stone path while others cut and mortar the porch stones.

1 Set outcropping boulders

- Excavate and lay a tamped gravel bed in preparation for a concrete slab behind the boulders.
- To position the boulders, use a skid loader or other earth-moving machine.
- Install concrete reinforcement bar. Here, it's anchored to an existing concrete footing.
- Attach isolation joint material against the house to separate the new concrete from the house.

2 Pour concrete

- Cover the stones with plastic to protect them from wet concrete.
- Transport the concrete by aiming the truck's arm at the site, by using wheelbarrows, or (as shown) by pouring with a scooper.
- Shovel the concrete to roughly level it.

3 Float concrete

- Use a wood or magnesium float to smooth and level the area.
- The slab does not have to be very smooth, because thick mortar will be applied over it.

 Stuff to Buy

Compactable gravel
Flagstones
Isolation joint material
Mortar
Outcropping stones
Rebar
Sand

Time Commitment

Four or five days

Tools You'll Need

Level and mason's line
Magnesium float
Mallet and hand sledge
Masonry cutoff saw
Trowels

Related Topics

Applying mortar, 64–65
Arranging flagstones, 54–55
Pouring a concrete patio, 174–179
Cutting brick, pavers, & stone, 48–51
Mixing mortar, 62–63
Transporting heavy stones, 56–57

④ Prepare dry bed

- When using large flagstones of varying thicknesses, you need only generally mark the outlines and roughly smooth the surface.
- Tamp a bed of compactable gravel.
- Spread a layer of rough sand.

⑤ Cut next to outcropping

- To give the illusion that the boulders rest on the flag-stones, cut the stones next to the boulders precisely.
- Place a flagstone near the outcropping and scribe a cut line.
- Cut flagstone with a masonry cutoff saw.

⑥ Cut apart a large stone

- If a stone is very large, you may want to cut it apart into two or more stones.
- Mark a random-looking cut line, which can be slightly curved at points.
- Cut with a cutoff saw.

⑦ Chip top edge

- For a natural look, tap with a hammer along the cut lines.
- Aim to create chip marks and indentations at irregular intervals.
- Stand back to examine your handiwork, then chip more if needed.

⑧ Use level guides

- Here, the path will follow the contours of the yard rather than being level or following a consistent slope.
- Stretch mason's lines between stakes to serve as guides for maintaining an even surface.

⑨ Assemble porch stones

- For the porch stones, make a dry run on a level surface.
- Aim for a natural-looking arrangement, with few lines that carry through from one joint to the next.
- Recut and/or reassemble until you are satisfied with the arrangement.

⑩ Set porch stones

- Set several stones in place in a dry run.
- Pick up one stone, shovel and roughly smooth mortar, and set the stone.
- Take care to maintain an even surface and consistent joints.
- Wait a day or two for the mortar to set, then fill the joints with mortar.

⑪ Finish flagstone path

- Continue assembling flag-stones, supporting them with sand and gravel and working to maintain an even surface.
- Fill the joints by sweeping in gravel.

Tiles on Concrete

A tiled outdoor surface lends an air of grace and order. For most tile installations, the underlying concrete slab must be at least fairly flat and even.

Cutting Tile

Consult the dealer on the best way to cut your tiles. Some can be cut straight with a snap cutter, but you will need a power saw to make notches or cutouts. Others require a masonry saw.

Snap cutter

- Position a tile in the cutter and lower the cutting wheel onto the cut line.
- Press down on the wheel as you push or pull the handle along the cut line.
- Allow the cutter's wings to rest on each side of the line, then push down to break the tile.

Wet saw

- A rented wet-cutting tile saw works much like a wet masonry saw.
- Make sure water is spraying onto the blade at all times.
- Position the tile firmly against the guide.
- Turn on the saw and slide it forward slowly to cut the tile.

Bold black tiles break up the uniformity of this expansive patio.

Cutting notches & cutouts

- Use a snap cutter to score the front cut line.
- Hold each tile at a steep angle so the blade will cut deeper on the back side.
- Make a series of closely spaced cuts.
- Finish by breaking out the waste with a tile-nibbling tool.

Stuff to Buy

Latex concrete bonding agent
Plastic tile spacers
Sanded grout
Thinset mortar
Tiles

Time Commitment

Several days

Tools You'll Need

Chalk line
Drill with mixing paddle
Laminated grout float
Sponge
Square-notched trowel
Tape measure
Tile cutter
Wheelbarrow

Related Topics

Repairing concrete, 286–289
Tile, 22–23

Mixing Mortar

Ask your dealer for the best type of mortar to use. In most cases, tiles are set in thinset mortar. Polymer-modified thinset is mixed with water, but standard thinset should be mixed with latex additive to prevent cracking.

Setting Small Tiles

Be sure to use floor tiles (not soft wall tiles) proven to survive winters in your area. Tiles with a glazed surface are slick when wet, while quarry tiles and other types have a slip-resistant surface. If the tiles are small enough, the many grout lines will provide traction. Below is an installation of tiles on a stairway, which involves setting vertical and horizontal tiles.

1 Mix thinset

- Pour a few inches of liquid into a 5-gallon bucket.
- Pour dry thinset mortar mix into the bucket.
- Mix with a heavy-duty drill equipped with a mixing paddle.
- Use short bursts at first and add water or thinset mix as needed.

2 Test mix

- The thickness of the mix is critical.
- It should be wet enough to pour and just thick enough to stick to a trowel for a second or two when held upside down.
- Wait 10 minutes, then briefly mix the mortar again.

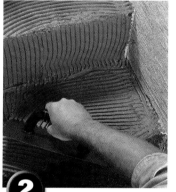

1 Lay a dry run

- Place tiles in a pleasing arrangement.
- For some types, use plastic spacers to maintain consistent joints.
- See that all joints, both vertical and horizontal, are the same thickness.
- Cut tiles as needed.

2 Trowel thinset

- Mix thinset mortar just stiff enough to hold the ridge shapes created by the trowel.
- If the mortar starts to harden, throw it out and mix a new batch.
- Using a square-notched trowel of the size recommended for your tile, push as you spread the mortar.
- Pass over the surface with less pressure, to create an even surface.

3 Set tiles

- If you are installing vertical tiles, support them with plastic spacers or pieces of cardboard to keep them from slipping downward.
- Press tiles into the mortar, then pull back gently to make sure they stick.
- Tap with a straight 2 × 6 to achieve an even surface.

4 Grout

- Allow the tiles to set overnight, then mix a batch of sanded, latex-reinforced grout.
- Holding a grout float nearly flat, push grout into the joints, using diagonal strokes in at least two directions.
- Tilt the float up and scrape away most of the excess grout.
- Use a large sponge to wipe the surface gently. Rinse and repeat several times.

Determining the Grid Size

These tiles are laid in 3-foot-square sections, each of which holds nine tiles. Whichever grid size you use, test to make sure it will lead to grout lines of the width that you want. (On an exterior installation, wide grout lines, up to ¾ inch, are the norm.) Lay three tiles next to each other, spaced as you like. Measure the width of the three tiles and then add the width of one more grout line. This will give you the length of the sides of each square in your grid.

Setting Irregular Tiles

Handmade Saltillo tiles are popular in the West and Southwest, where winters are generally warm. Because the tiles are soft, they cannot survive frigid winters. In a colder climate, you may opt for quarry tiles, porcelain tiles, or ceramic tiles made for outdoor use.

If the tiles are manufactured precisely, you could install them using plastic spacers. These Saltillos, like other handmade tiles, vary slightly in size and shape and are not perfectly flat. For tiles like that, the grid method shown on these pages works best, as it allows you to adjust tile positions to suit the eye.

Inspect the slab to be sure it is sound, and repair any large cracks or indentations. Wash the slab clean of oils and debris using a strong cleaner or a weak muriatic acid solution.

How to Do It

1 Mark for grid lines

- If the slab is not square, draw square lines and make all your measurements from the lines, not from the edges of the slab.
- Measure the length and width of the installation and then plan your tile locations.
- Avoid narrow slivers of cut tiles along any edge.
- Mark for the locations of grid lines.

2 Snap grid lines

- Measure for and mark line locations at both ends of the lines.
- Snap chalk lines between the marks.
- Check that the squares are all the same size and have square corners.

❸ Spread mortar

- Use a trowel with large notches, at least ³⁄₈ × ¹⁄₂ inch.
- Using the flat side of the trowel, spread a 1-inch-thick coat of mortar inside a grid square.
- Use long, sweeping strokes to produce a surface that is fairly level.

❹ Trowel mortar

- Turn the trowel over and use the notched side.
- Comb the surface of the mortar.
- The notches should not scrape the concrete.
- Work to achieve an even surface with no globs or gaps.

❺ Position tiles

- Position tiles inside the grid.
- Tiles on the edges should sit half a joint's width from the grid lines.
- Stand back, eyeball the layout, and adjust the tiles as needed so they look evenly spaced.

❻ Bed tiles & check adhesion

- Gently tap the tiles with a hammer over a block of wood or with a rubber mallet to embed them in mortar.
- Every once in a while, pick up one tile and check its back.
- Mortar should stick to at least three-quarters of the back surface.
- If it doesn't, spread a bit more mortar on the back of the tiles.

❼ Cut tiles

- You can cut a limited number of tiles with a grinder or a circular saw equipped with a masonry blade.
- Clamp a scrap of wood to the tile along the cut line.
- Run the grinder's blade along the wood.
- Make several passes, then break the tile.

❽ Grout

- Wait for the mortar to harden.
- Mix a batch of sanded, latex-reinforced grout.
- First hold the grout float nearly flat and press grout into the joints, pushing in at least two directions.
- Tilt the float up and scrape away any excess grout.
- Use a damp sponge to wipe away excess mortar and produce even grout lines. Go over the surface several times.

6 Pouring Concrete Slabs

I n this chapter, we show you how to pour a new concrete slab.

To help you plan for, or execute, this challenging task, we give

you the formulas to calculate the amount of concrete you will

actually need, so that you don't mix or order too much or too

little. You'll also learn how to frame before you pour and how

to create smooth surfaces and edges.

Chapter Contents

Understanding Concrete
page 168

Pier
4" radius

Footing
8" radius

Calculating Concrete Needs
page 170

Mixing & Delivering
page 172

Pouring a Concrete Patio
page 174

Decorating Effects for Concrete
page 180

Understanding Concrete

Pouring and smoothing concrete is challenging. The work is physically demanding, and all the operations must be well planned and performed on time, before the surface is, well, set in concrete. Start by gaining a basic understanding of concrete.

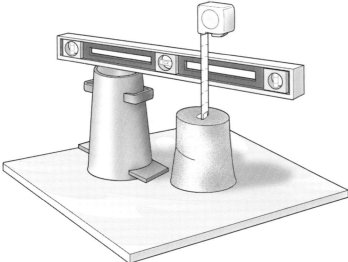

An inspector may test concrete for "slump" by using a testing cone. A sag of 4 inches indicates the right consistency for most jobs. You can do this yourself with a plastic cup. First cut the bottom off. Fill the resulting cylinder with wet concrete, turn it upside down, and pull it away. If the concrete slumps to about three-fourths of its former height, the mix is right for pouring into a form.

Basic Mix

Many people use the terms "cement" and "concrete" interchangeably, but actually cement is an element of concrete, which is a mix of portland cement, aggregate (gravel and sand), and water.

CEMENT

Portland cement is the glue that holds it all together. The more cement, the stronger the concrete. To strengthen a small batch of concrete, add more cement. When ordering ready-mix concrete

from a company, specify how much cement you want. A "six-bag mix," for example, contains six bags of cement per yard of concrete, strong enough for most projects, but local codes may require more cement.

AGGREGATE

Gravel and sand take up most of the space in concrete and also provide strength. A range of particle sizes works best because small pieces fit between big ones. The largest gravel stones should be no larger than one-fifth the thickness of the slab; avoid the temptation to throw in large rocks to fill space. If you are mixing for a surface that will be 3½ inches thick, stones should be no larger than ¾ inch in diameter. For surfaces less than an inch thick, use sand mix, which has no gravel, only sand.

It you mix your own concrete, use sharp stones and gravel rather than round pebbles or play sand. If dirt gets into a concrete mix, the concrete will be weakened.

WATER

Wet concrete is easy to pour and shape, but extra water weakens the mixture. Excess water also increases the risk of tiny cracks appearing on the surface. So in general, aim for a mix that is pretty stiff but still pourable. To be sure you have it right, use a slump test, as shown at the left, or a squeeze test, below.

Once concrete stiffens, giving it several days of abundant moisture is good. Water allows hydration, the chemical reaction that cures concrete, to continue. So keep the slab moist for at least three days. Once the concrete dries, however, hydration ceases, and adding more water will not restart the reaction.

Properly mixed concrete is completely wet but not soupy. Wearing gloves, pick some up and squeeze. It should roughly hold its shape, and liquid should not drip from your fingers.

Bagged Mixes

Labels on bagged concrete mixes help point you to the right product for a specific job. The strength (shown as psi, or pounds per square inch) refers to crush resistance but is also an overall indicator of durability and abrasion resistance. The higher the psi number, the better.

A high-early-strength concrete mix contains a higher percentage of cement, plus sand, gravel, and additives. Use it for added strength and ease of finishing.

Concrete resurfacing mix contains portland cement, fine sand, polymers, and other ingredients. Use it up to ½ inch thick as a layer over old concrete. The material is quite fluid, so you can spread it with a trowel, brush, or squeegee.

Sand mix contains no gravel, just one part portland cement and three parts sand. Use it for steppingstones or pavers that will be 1½ to 2 inches thick, or for topping old concrete. Toppings can be as thin as ½ inch if you replace half the water with acrylic or latex fortifier.

Basic dry concrete mix combines portland cement, sand, and gravel and is suitable for slabs at least 2 inches thick. It is a standard strength. To increase its strength and make it easier to trowel, add a shovel or so of portland cement.

Additives

A number of extra ingredients are available to help you solve specific problems.

- If you live in an area with freezing winters, water that seeps into concrete and then freezes can cause cracking. To minimize this problem, consider ordering air-entrained concrete. The mixture forms tiny bubbles that act as safety valves, giving winter ice crystals room to expand without damaging the concrete. If you are mixing your own, replace some of the mix water with acrylic or latex fortifier and make a stiff mix.
- If it's hot and sunny, or if you have a large slab to pour, the concrete may set sooner than you want. Ask the ready-mix company to add a polymer retarder to shorten the setting time.
- If you order concrete with a water-reducing additive, the concrete will be stronger because it has less water. It will also be easy to pour and finish.
- Don't neglect reinforcement, which may include metal rebar or mesh, or polypropylene fibers, as discussed on page 171.

Safety Tip

Dry concrete mix is dusty and can damage your lungs, and set cement is about as caustic as lye. Wear a dust mask when working with dry cement. When working with either dry or wet concrete ingredients, wear gloves. Wear tall boots if you are pouring into an area wider than you can reach across. Rinse any spilled concrete from your skin immediately.

Calculating Concrete Needs

Whether you are ordering concrete from a ready-mix company or mixing it yourself, you will need to figure out how many cubic yards you will need and also determine which types of base material, reinforcement, joint materials, and additives the job calls for.

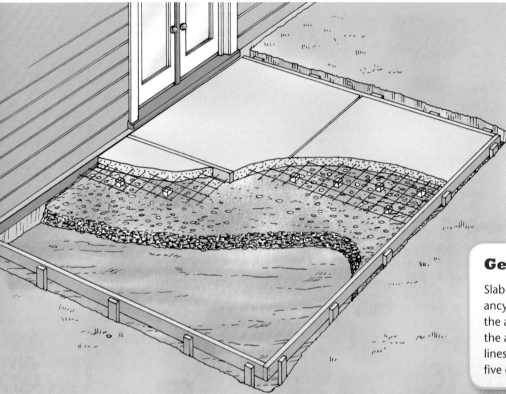

Anatomy of a Slab

To be free of cracks, a concrete slab should rest on a stable subsurface, typically a 4- to 6-inch-thick layer of compactable gravel. Firmly staked 2 × 4 forms hold the concrete in place while it is being poured.

You may need an isolation joint at the house to keep the slab separated from the house, and perhaps also some material for control joints in the middle of the slab to minimize cracking. An isolation joint may be made of a heavy fibrous material, or it may be polyethylene foam.

Getting the Thickness Right

Slab thickness is a critical measurement; a discrepancy of even 1/2 inch can make a big difference in the amount of concrete you'll need. To determine the average thickness your slab will be, stretch taut lines across the area and measure the thickness in five or six places.

Calculating Concrete by the Yard

Concrete is usually sold by the cubic yard, also called just a yard. A yard fills an area 3 × 3 × 3 feet. For small projects, you may choose to measure cubic feet instead. A 60-pound bag of concrete mix produces 1/2 cubic foot; a 90-pound bag yields 2/3 cubic foot. (There are 27 cubic feet in a yard.)

For a rectangular shape, calculate the area by multiplying width in feet times length in feet. To figure the area for a circular slab, multiply the radius in feet squared times pi (3.14). If the patio will be an irregular shape, divide the area into rectangles and portions of circles, as shown at right. Measure the thickness in inches.

With these two figures—area plus thickness—a supplier can quickly calculate your concrete needs. To figure it yourself, grab a calculator. Multiply area in feet times thickness in inches. Divide that number by 12 to get the number of cubic feet. Divide the number of cubic feet by 27 to get the number of cubic yards. For example, if a slab measures 12 × 14 feet, it covers 168 square feet. If the slab is 3 1/2 inches thick:

- 168 × 3.5 = 588
- 588 ÷ 12 = 49 cubic feet
- 49 ÷ 27 = 1.8 cubic yards
- Add about 10 percent for waste and order 2 yards.

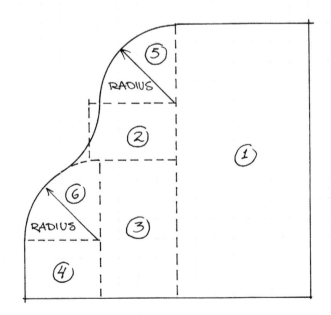

Calculating for Cylinders

Determine the amount of concrete in a cylinder with this formula: radius squared × inches of depth × 3.14 = cubic inches. Divide cubic inches by 1,728 to obtain the number of cubic feet. In the example below, the pier contains 1,809 cubic inches and the base footing 1,608 cubic inches, for a total of 3,417. Divide this by 1,728 to reach the total of 1.97 cubic feet, calling for roughly four 60-pound bags of dry concrete mix.

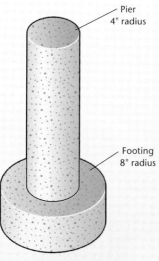

Pier
4" radius

Footing
8" radius

Pier volume: 4" squared × 36" × 3.14 = 1,809 cubic inches

Footing volume: 8" squared × 8" × 3.14 = 1,608 cubic inches

Small cracks like these can result from lack of reinforcement or from too much water in the mix.

Reinforcement Materials

The concrete should meet local codes for strength and should be at least 3 inches thick for a patio or walkway. For reinforcement, you may use wire mesh, which comes in very large rolls. Or, if local codes allow, you may simply order the concrete with polypropylene (or fiberglass) reinforcement added. The delivery driver should add at least one 1-pound bag of fibers for each yard of concrete.

If a slab will be used to support a structure, the inspector will probably require a perimeter footing that is thicker than the rest of the slab. The footing should be reinforced with concrete reinforcement bar, as shown below.

Fiberglass reinforcement

Rebar

Mixing & Delivering

Depending on the size of the patio, you may choose to mix the concrete yourself by hand, mix it yourself using a small machine, or have it delivered by truck.

Mixing Options

For a slab that needs less than half a yard (or 13½ cubic feet), you may choose to mix bags of concrete in a wheelbarrow. However, be sure to work in small sections or have plenty of help on hand so you can finish the concrete before it hardens. For

moderate amounts of concrete, you can rent a power mixer to speed things up.

You may find, however, that truck delivery does not cost much more than mixing yourself. Truck delivery can save a great deal of work, especially if the chute (typically 18 feet long) can reach the site and so save you the trouble of wheeling concrete. Some concrete companies will not deliver for less than the cost of a full yard. Others have special trucks designed to mix smaller amounts at the job site. Call around to find a company that meets your needs.

Money-saving Tip

Most hand mixing is done with bags of dry concrete mix. If you have a lot of mixing to do or live in a remote area, you can save a bit of money by mixing your own dry ingredients. Haul in a pile of cement, a pile of gravel, and a pile of sand and measure the mix by the shovelful.

Hand Mixing

You can mix in a wheelbarrow (left) or in a trough (below). Because a wheelbarrow is elevated and a trough rests on the ground, each offers a different working angle. Pour the dry ingredients into the container, add water, and mix with a hoe, a mason's hoe, or a shovel.

Paddle Mixer

Mix small amounts of concrete for a craft or decorative project using a half-inch drill and a paddle mixer. Use a large measuring cup to make sure you add the same amounts of water, colorant, and other ingredients from batch to batch.

Small Mixing Machine

A rented electric or gasoline-powered mixer saves labor and works quickly. Spray several inches of water into the hopper, cleaning the sides as you do so. Add two bags of dry mix, turn on the machine, and gradually add water until the mix is just pourable. Pour it directly into the form or into a wheelbarrow.

Truck Delivery

Consult the sales staff at a ready-mix company for tips on making delivery go smoothly. Typically, you will have to pay extra if the driver has to wait around for more than half an hour, so study pages 174–179 carefully to make sure you'll have everything ready.

Also ask the company about the best additives. You may want to add polypropylene fiber reinforcement for strength, air entrainment to minimize cracking in a freezing climate, or retarder if you will pour on a hot, sunny day.

Plan the path for the truck carefully. Ideally, you will be able to pour directly into the formed area using the truck's chute, but often you will need to pour into wheelbarrows. Low-hanging wires, a narrow street, or other obstructions may make it difficult if not impossible for the truck to go where you need it.

Wheelbarrowing

Use only professional-quality wheelbarrows with air-filled tires, as lesser barrows may break. For a medium-size patio, have two wheelbarrows with two strong-backed helpers on hand. For a large patio, you may want three of each. Be sure to plan and lay wood wheelbarrow paths so you do not damage your lawn.

A Beginner's Strategy

If you are a beginner, or if you cannot line up enough help to pour and finish an entire patio at once, make the job easier by dividing the project into smaller sections. This will also allow you to mix the concrete yourself in small batches.

Build a grid of permanent wood dividers from pressure-treated 2 × 4s rated for ground contact (not rated "above ground"), or use composite decking boards. If sections are larger than 3 feet square, install stakes, as shown. Drive 3-inch deck screws partway to firmly anchor the concrete to the boards. Masking tape protects the wood from smears.

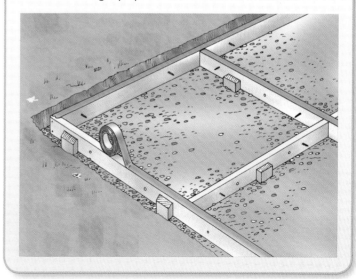

Pouring a Concrete Patio

Building a patio large enough to warrant ordering ready-mix concrete from a truck is an ambitious undertaking that involves hard physical work and intricate orchestration. The reward, though, is an amazing transformation of your yard in short order.

Before You Begin

Read through the instructions on the next six pages and make sure you have everything planned and in order before the truck comes.

- Get a permit from your local building department and schedule inspections.
- Line up helpers and make sure they have the right work clothes and safety gear.
- Decide who will do what. You may need two people for wheelbarrow duty and two more in the formed area to spread and screed the concrete. Ideally, hire someone with concrete-finishing experience to smooth the surface. If you want a smooth finish, hire a professional finisher.
- There may well be extra concrete, so decide where it will go.
- Have all needed tools on hand, including any rented gear. You'll probably need two wheelbarrows, several shovels, a bull float, one or two magnesium or wood floats, a screed board, a jointer, an edger, a broom, one or two kneeling boards, plastic sheeting, and perhaps a steel trowel.
- Check the forms for level or proper slope, and make sure you have all the metal reinforcement and isolation joints in position.
- If you will need to move the concrete in wheelbarrows, test the paths to make sure they are stable.

This concrete slab patio has been subtly tinted so it nicely complements the stone counter.

❶ Excavation & form

- Lay out the site, remove sod, and excavate to the correct depth.
- Build the form out of 2 × 4s. Use pressure-treated lumber if the form will be permanent.
- Anchor form boards with stakes every few feet.
- Drive stakes slightly below the top of the form boards.
- Check that the form is level or correctly sloped.

❷ Framing curves

- If the form will be permanent, use benderboard for a tight curve.
- If it is temporary, use two layers of fibrous isolation membrane (shown) or two or three strips of ¼-inch plywood.
- You can easily smooth the edges later, when you remove the membrane or plywood.

❸ Middle screed guide

- If the form is wider than 8 feet, it will be difficult to screed across.
- Install a temporary screed guide in the middle.
- Anchor the guide with a stake near the house and drive screws through the form at the other end so you can easily remove the guide later (step 11).

❹ Spread gravel

- Pour compactable gravel into the site, to a depth of about 4 inches.
- Use a garden rake or a gravel spreader (shown) to spread the gravel to a consistent depth below the top of the form.
- Tamp the gravel firm.

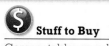

Stuff to Buy

Compactable gravel
Concrete
Isolation-joint material
Lumber
Rebar

Time Commitment

A weekend

Tools You'll Need

Bull float
Circular saw
Concrete edger and jointer
Hand sledge
High rubber boots
Lineman's pliers
Magnesium float
Shovel and rake

Related Topics

Calculating concrete needs, 170–171
Measuring & laying out, 44–45
Mixing & delivering, 172–173
Understanding concrete, 168–169

Forming a Long Curve

For a long, sweeping curve, use ¾-inch plywood or composite decking. At one corner of the form, drive stakes on both sides of the form material. Work your way along the edging, driving more stakes as you gradually push or pull the form into the shape you want.

Where a curve ends and a straight side begins, screw the curved edging to the side of a stake, as shown above. Then screw through the face of the stake into the end of the straight 2 × 4 form. Drive another stake behind the first. Trim the stakes level with the edging.

Reinforcing Concrete

Local codes may allow you to simply add fiber reinforcement to the concrete mix, or they may require some sort of metal reinforcement. One approach is to install a grid of ½-inch reinforcement bar (rebar). Tie the pieces together by twisting wire with a pair of lineman's pliers or a swivel tool. To position the rebar in the middle of the slab's thickness, you will pull it up when you pour the concrete (see page 177). Another approach is to use wire reinforcement mesh. Unroll the mesh, then roll it backward to straighten it out. Cut with lineman's pliers to fit it within 1 inch of the forms. Use a metal bolster or a chunk of stone to raise the mesh to the middle of the slab's thickness.

Attach or Isolate?

If the slab will abut an existing concrete foundation or slab, ask your inspector whether you should attach the new concrete to it, or isolate the new concrete from it.

To tie a new slab to a foundation, use a hammer drill with a masonry bit to bore ⅝-inch holes into the foundation every 2 feet or so. Slip rebar into the holes.

To isolate a slab from a foundation, snap a chalk line to indicate the height of the slab. Use construction adhesive to attach a strip of isolation membrane to the house. Glue it firmly so it stays put when you screed and finish the concrete.

"It's not unusual for a beginner to tip a wheelbarrow over. Ask the truck driver to fill the first wheelbarrow only halfway. Once you get used to wheeling concrete, you can ask for heavier loads. While wheeling, if you start to lose control, don't try to right the wheelbarrow; you will almost certainly lose control. Instead, push down hard with both hands to set the wheelbarrow firmly on the ground. Then pick up the handles and start again."

Ralph Bus, Benson Concrete Construction

5 Make wheelbarrow paths

- Determine where the concrete truck will go and where its chute will be positioned to fill wheelbarrows.
- If possible, arrange to pour directly into the formed area.
- Otherwise, provide a smooth running surface for wheelbarrows using 2 × 10s or 2 × 12s.
- Use scrap pieces to make a stable bridge over the form so the form will not get bumped.

6 Load wheelbarrow

- Set a wheelbarrow on a stable surface under the truck's chute.
- Firmly step on the wheelbarrow's rear frame to keep it from tipping.
- Have the driver pour, then use a scrap of lumber to scrape the chute so it doesn't drip.

7 Pour into forms

- Have shovelers ready in the formed area, wearing tall rubber boots.
- Wheel the concrete into a far corner of the area and pour it out.
- Scrape the wheelbarrow, then go back for more.

8 Fill the form

- Use a shovel to spread the concrete until it is even with, or slightly above, the form boards
- Fill the form up against the far end, then work forward toward the wheelbarrow path.

9 Screed

- After you have filled part of an area, start to screed. You will alternate between filling and screeding.
- To screed, set a straight 2 × 4 on the form boards and/or the temporary screed guide.
- It's usually easier to screed with a helper.
- Drag the 2 × 4 across the surface with a sawing motion.

10 Fill voids

- Also pull and push the screed board up and down to create a somewhat level surface.
- Where the concrete is low, sprinkle on small amounts using a shovel or your fingers.
- Screed again.

11 Remove temporary guide

- If you installed a temporary screed guide, fill and screed one section.
- Remove any screws, then use a shovel to pry out the temporary guide.

12 Finish screeding

- When screeding the other side of the slab, let one end of the 2 × 4 rest on the screeded concrete while the other rests on top of the form.
- Fill in any low spots and screed again.

Quick Concrete Tips

- Be sure the form is completely full before you say goodbye to the driver. If he's friendly, he may help you spray-clean your wheelbarrows.
- Pour some leftover concrete into a 5-gallon bucket. You may find that you need a little more when you finish the surface.

Centering Metal Reinforcement

If you are using metal reinforcement and it is not held up with bolsters or chunks of stone, use a rake or shovel to pull it up as you pour, positioning it in the center of the concrete's thickness.

13 Bull float

- Screw on as many handle extensions as needed to reach across the slab.
- Gently set the float on concrete near you and push forward, with the front edge slightly raised.
- Pull back over the same area with a series of tugs that produce slight ripples. This pushes the stones down and fills small holes.
- Move to the next section, overlapping your strokes slightly.

14 Magnesium float

- Wait for the surface water (called bleed water or cream) to mostly disappear.
- Where you must kneel on the surface, use one or two pieces of plywood to support your knees and toes.
- Hold the magnesium float so its leading edge is slightly raised, and press down gently as you smooth the surface.
- Use long, sweeping strokes. You will need to go over the surface several times.
- Float when the surface is slightly wet. Don't float if there are puddles or if the surface is so dry that you start to roughen it.

15 Cut edges

- Slip a mason's trowel or margin trowel between the inside of the form and the concrete.
- Using a sawing motion, slice all along the perimeter.
- This helps eliminate pockets of air that can weaken the concrete.

16 Tap form

- Tap the form boards with a hammer all along their length.
- This further eliminates air pockets and separates the form boards from the concrete.

17 Round edges

- Run an edging tool along the outside edges and both sides of any permanent wood dividers.
- Use a back-and-forth motion at first.
- Then switch to long strokes to achieve neatly rounded edges.

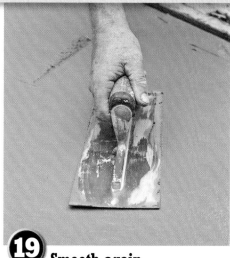

18 Cut control joint

- Make a control joint in the middle of any section of patio wider than 10 feet.
- Set a straight board on top of the concrete as a guide.
- Run the jointer back and forth several times until the concrete is smooth on both sides of the joint.
- Smooth down ridges using a magnesium float.

19 Smooth again

- If you opt for a broom finish, use a magnesium float again.
- For a smoother "hard" finish, have an experienced finisher use a steel trowel.
- Use wide, sweeping strokes with moderate pressure, barely bringing moisture to the surface.

Control Joints

A large concrete slab is likely to develop cracks. Cutting a control joint makes it likely that the crack will occur below, where it will not be visible.

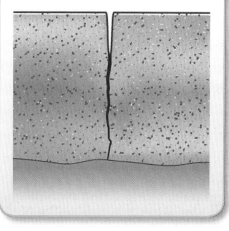

20 Broom finish

- Using a soft-bristled push broom, pull it toward you—never push—to produce a lightly textured surface.
- If the bristles don't dig in, try wetting the broom.
- Avoid overlapping strokes.

21 Cure slowly

- The slower concrete cures, the stronger it will be.
- Keep finished concrete moist for a week or so.
- Cover the slab with plastic, or spray it with a fine mist several times a day.
- After a day, pry away temporary forms.

Decorative Effects for Concrete

Degree of Difficulty
● Moderate

Concrete need not be plain and industrial in appearance. You can add color, create a stone-like texture, tool a design, expose pebbles on the surface, or imprint a pattern with stamps or stencils.

Before You Begin

If you are confident in your ability to pour a basic concrete slab, you can add a decorative finish as you pour, without a lot of extra work. The projects shown on the next six pages are all fairly do-it-yourself-friendly. Other methods may call for professional experience.

Try these techniques on a small area first, then move on to larger sections as your comfort level permits. You can also decorate concrete by pouring a plain slab, waiting for it to cure, then acid-staining it.

Travertine Finish

This technique produces a nice stone look. Be sure to work while the concrete is good and wet. That way, the added texture material will settle down into the concrete. There will also be few, if any, voids where water can seep in and cause problems in areas with freezing weather.

Pour, screed, and float the surface with a bull float and a magnesium float. Use an edging tool to round off the perimeter.

Mixing Colors

If you color the finish mixture so that it contrasts with the underlying concrete, the effect will be heightened.

1 **Apply texture**

- In a bucket, dry-mix 1 part portland cement with 2 parts sand.
- Add enough water to make a fairly stiff mix.
- Once most of the surface water has disappeared, dip a mason's brush into the texture and dash it all over the surface.
- Aim for an even mix of large and small blotches throughout the slab.

2 **Knock down**

- Once the mix starts to stiffen, gently scrape the surface with a steel trowel.
- Hold the trowel nearly flat and use long, sweeping strokes.
- Aim for a texture that is fairly smooth on the high spots and rougher in the low areas.

Stuff to Buy
Concrete pigment
Decorative aggregate

Time Commitment
Two to three hours

Tools You'll Need
Brush
Magnesium float
Pressure washer
Pump sprayer
Stamps or stencils
Texture roller

Related Topics
Acid staining, 148–149
Pouring a concrete patio, 174–179
Stenciling, 150–151

Seeded Aggregate

Have bags of decorative aggregate on hand. Ready-mix companies sell some types, but you may find a wider selection of colors at a stone yard. Colors usually run from brown to tan. For more interest, add pebbles of another color, such as black or red. Buy more aggregate than you expect to use, as you'll really be stuck if you run short.

Give Yourself Time to Work

This process takes longer than a standard broom finish, so unless you are working in a very small area, arrange for a retarder to be added to the concrete so you'll have extra time to work.

1 Scatter aggregate

- Pour and screed the concrete, making sure all voids are filled.
- Once bleed water disappears, use a shovel or your hands to scatter damp aggregate over the surface.
- Aim for a single layer of aggregate stones.
- Perhaps add accent stones as well.

2 Embed

- Use a flat board to press the stones gently into the concrete.
- Rest both ends of the board on the edging to ensure it does not create a dent.
- If pressing down with your hand does not work, try walking on the board.

3 Float

- If the slab is large, cover part of it with plastic to keep it wet.
- Work the surface with a magnesium float so a thin layer of cement without any gravel works its way up and barely covers the aggregate.
- Avoid overworking the surface. Produce as little bleed water as possible.
- Use an edger to round off the perimeter.

4 Brush & clean

- When concrete starts to stiffen, spray it with a fine mist over a small area and brush away the top layer.
- Stop as soon as the aggregate is exposed.
- If stones start coming loose, wait for the concrete to harden further, then try again.
- When the concrete is hard, spray it with a mist of water.
- Allow the concrete to cure slowly, then wash it with a mild acid solution, if needed, to remove any haze.

The red areas of this driveway and basketball court were colored and poured first, followed by the tan areas. Because the pigment is in the concrete, the court lines will never wear off.

Preparing for a Design

For the most part, concrete that will be tooled, stamped, or stenciled is installed with standard methods. However, there are some differences.

Order a pea gravel mix, one that does not contain large stones. A mix with large stones needs to be floated and troweled more than you want. A small-stone mix can be floated quickly and then tooled or stamped. The machine shown above is a pump with a grate that filters out the larger stones. You don't need a machine like this, as long as the stones are small to begin with.

If one part of the patio is wet while you are working it and another part is dry, then the pattern will not be even. So aim to keep the concrete at the same consistency throughout (above). Work on a small area, or have a retarder added to the mix, and avoid working in the sun on a hot day.

To test that the concrete is the correct consistency for working, press and remove a finger (above). The concrete should be soft but not overly sticky. Little of the concrete should adhere to the finger. The concrete should feel about as firm as the palm of your hand.

Coloring Concrete

Tinting concrete while mixing it is the most reliable way to achieve consistent, integral color. A ready-mix company may do this for you, or you can do it yourself if you are mixing your own concrete. Tinting the surface after the concrete has been poured produces a mottled or streaked effect. For either technique, the color will be more vibrant if you use white portland cement rather than the standard gray.

Unless you have a reliable recipe, experiment with sample batches and give them time to cure to reveal the final color. Mix a small amount of liquid or powdered colorant with a gallon of water (below left). Add the mixture to bags of concrete mix.

To tint after pouring, first bull-float the surface. Strew the powder over the surface using your hands (below center), letting the color sift through your fingers as you scatter it. Or dip a mason's brush (below right) into a bucket of colorant and flick it over the surface. Work the surface with a magnesium float.

Tooled Flagstone Design

This decorative touch is easiest to create on a path that you can reach across. A flagstone design looks best if the concrete is tinted or if it is stained after it has cured. Begin this technique after you have floated the surface with a bull float, edged the perimeter, and floated with a magnesium float.

❶ Tool surface

- Using a convex jointer made for striking joints on a brick wall, press a design into the surface.
- Pull the tool toward you instead of pushing it.
- For a flagstone look, distribute small and large sizes throughout the surface.

❷ Even surface

- Gently run a magnesium float over the surface to knock down most of the crumbs and any exposed gravel.
- To correct small raised pieces or voids, press in with the tip of the float or with your finger.

❸ Brush joints

- Use a paintbrush to gently clear away any remaining crumbs and to produce a finely textured broom finish.
- You may choose to go over the entire surface very gently with a mason's brush or a fine-bristled broom.

Stamping

Stamping a design is simple in concept: Set down textured mats, press on the back, and peel them off to reveal the design. But complications can arise, such as spaces where mats don't fit, and imperfections caused by concrete sticking to the mat. The concrete's texture should be just right when you stamp—soft enough to form but not wet enough to stick. If you have a large job, you may want to hire a professional finisher with experience in stamping.

You can buy stamps and powdered release agent at a concrete-supply company. Show a drawing of your job to a salesperson to make sure you get all the tools and materials you need. Most mats butt against each other to create a continuous pattern, so you should have at least two, and preferably three, mats, which you may be able to rent. Seamless mats can overlap, so they can be used in no particular order. You may need a flexible mat for hard-to-reach places and edges, and perhaps an old chisel or margin trowel to create lines where even those mats cannot reach. There are also edging stamps to create the look of brick or stone edging. Be sure to get a hand tamper as well.

Arrange for the concrete to be integrally colored. Also buy a bucket of powdered release agent, which keeps the mats from sticking. Release agent also adds or affects color, so it imparts a two-toned mottled or streaked look. Ask the supplier for a picture of the final appearance.

Before you pour the concrete, measure and mark the forms so you know the best place to begin stamping. After pouring, screed the concrete, go over it with a bull float, edge the corners, and smooth the surface with a magnesium float. Test that the surface is ready (see page 182). Then it's time to stamp.

If the area is large, a crew is needed to keep the job going. One person applies release agent to the concrete and to the back of the stamps, while two others position the stamps and press them in.

Concrete stamps come in a variety of shapes and textures.

❶ Apply release agent

- Once bleed water evaporates, broadcast release agent over the surface at the recommended rate.
- Broadcast enough release agent to stay 10 or 15 minutes ahead of the stamping. Otherwise, it can soak in and lose effectiveness.
- Also apply release agent to the bottom of the mats.

❷ Position & stamp

- Align the first two mats carefully. A slight error will be multiplied as you set future mats.
- Walk on the mats and use a hand tamper to make an impression in the surface.
- If the concrete sticks, you need to wait for it to dry a bit, or add more release agent.

③ Continue stamping

- Work quickly so the concrete does not harden.
- As soon as a mat has been stamped, pick it up, apply release agent to the back, and leapfrog to the next stamping position.
- If the concrete starts to harden, you may need to pound the mats with a rubber mallet.
- Touch up the joints using the techniques shown below.

④ Wash & seal

- Cover the concrete with plastic for a week or so.
- After a day, pull back the plastic and spray the surface with a pressure washer.
- Use a fan nozzle held about 2 feet above the surface, and move it slowly.
- This will remove excess release agent and reveal a two-tone color pattern.
- After the concrete has cured for a week or so, apply acrylic sealer.

How the Pros Do It

"The real art of concrete stamping lies in fixing mistakes and filling in details that stamps can't reach. Some installers pound with a special chisel after the concrete is pretty hard, but I don't recommend that for a homeowner—it's too easy to screw up. Instead, be sure to fix the little things as they happen rather than waiting until the concrete starts to harden."

Steve Williamson,
SoCal Custom Concrete

Fixing & Filling

You'll encounter many places where standard mats just don't reach all the corners. Or your stamping technique may not be perfect every time. So continually examine the surface and attend to the small voids and imperfections that need touching up. Avoid the temptation to wet an area. This may make it easier to work, but it could also cause the concrete to flake or bubble when it cures.

For many patterns, you can rent a seamless touch-up mat (right) to continue a pattern in a small area. Use a roller tool (far right) to quickly make a new line or to sharpen an imperfect line. Tilt it to make the line a bit wider. A pointing trowel or brick trowel (below right) has a sharp point that can reach into small places. You can drag it, or simply press it into the concrete. A pool trowel also comes in handy. Sometimes it works to use even the palm of your hand.

If the concrete hardens so that the stamp cannot make an impression, you may need to tap with a hammer and chisel. Work carefully, so as to make impressions rather than digging up, which will produce a ragged edge.

Seamless Touch-up Mat

Roller Tool

Pointing Trowel

Stenciling

With paper stencils you can create a surface that looks like flagstone, cut stone, or brick. You'll also need a texture roller and a mixture of cement, fine sand, and pigment to trowel onto the surface. Stenciling is in some ways easier than stamping. It is easy to modify patterns to fit the area—simply snip a stencil with scissors. From a concrete supplier, purchase the stencils, color hardener, stain (if using), and release agent. Also buy or rent a texture roller. All the things you need may be available in a kit.

Pour the concrete and go over it with a bull float. Round over the edges. Now you're ready for the stencils.

Choosing Colors

The poured concrete's color will appear under the stencils, meaning it will be the color of the faux joints. So you may want to pour untinted concrete, or you may prefer concrete that is tinted tan or dark gray. Consult your dealer to choose color hardeners, stain, and release agent. You may choose two or more colors, perhaps one for edging "bricks" and one for the "field stones." The final appearance will change after the surface has been cleaned and sealed.

This patio features concrete that was treated with a buff pigment. A paper stencil was used to create the look of grout lines, and a textured roller provided the rippled-surface effect.

1 Place border stencils

- While the concrete is still fairly wet, work with helpers to position the stencils.
- Here, a ribbon of small rectangles goes around the edge. Cut with scissors to accommodate a curved edge.
- These border stencils are also placed across the middle of the slab, where control joints will be cut later.
- As you place stencils, gently smooth them down with a finger so all edges adhere.

2 Apply field stencils

- These come in long rolls about 3 feet wide and have ragged edges that interlock.
- To keep a long roll airborne until it is in the right position, have a helper in the center lift the stencil with a pole.
- Pull fairly taut, then set the stencil down into the concrete.
- Use a trowel or a stencil roller to smooth stencils and adhere them to the concrete.

3 Broadcast color hardener

- With all the stencils in place, broadcast color hardener over the surface.
- Apply different colors to different sections using a piece of cardboard or plywood as a shield to prevent a color from drifting to the wrong area.
- Apply a generous amount, as recommended. It acts as a topping.

4 Work in hardener

- With a magnesium float, press down and smooth the hardener to incorporate it into the slab.
- Use short strokes and be careful not to lift any stencils.
- Work in sections, making sure the topping becomes moist before you move on to the next section.

5 Stretching across

- If you cannot reach to the middle of the slab, perhaps use a pole with a pool float attached to the end.
- Or work on a board or scaffolding plank positioned above the surface.
- You can also use a kneeling board. Just be careful not to lift any stencils when you move the board.

6 Hardener & release agent

- Broadcast a second coat of color hardener over the surface and work it in as you did the first coat.
- Toss handfuls of release agent over the surface until it's completely covered.
- Release agent is very fine, so work upwind or wear a dust mask.

7 Texture surface

- Go over the surface in several directions with a textured roller.
- You may also want to use a small edging roller for curves.
- If you need to walk on the surface to reach the middle, wear textured pads over your boots.
- If your boots or the roller starts to stick and pull up the material, apply more release agent.

8 Remove stencils

- After the surface has hardened, pull up the stencils.
- Cover the slab with plastic for several days.
- Pull up the plastic and rinse the surface with a pressure washer.
- Cut control joints using a circular saw with a masonry blade.
- Re-cover the concrete and keep it moist for a few more days.

9 Clean & seal

- Following the manufacturer's directions, clean away any haze using a mild muriatic acid solution.
- Rinse thoroughly.
- Apply two coats of acrylic concrete sealer.

7

Stone & Paver Walls

In this chapter, you'll learn how to go vertical with garden and retaining walls made out of everything from stacked pavers to mortared boulders. We show you how to provide for drainage, so the soil behind a retaining wall can drain, and since solid-stone walls can get quite costly, we also show you how to achieve expensive looks with stone veneers.

Chapter Contents

Boulder Retaining Wall
page 202

Stone Veneer
page 204

page 196

Beautiful Masonry Walls

This chapter shows you how to build modest walls made of natural stone and wall-paver units. Building with natural stone allows you to get creative, but it can also be a lot of physical work. Paver blocks are easier to work with, and some achieve the look of stone.

A low stone wall is the perfect choice for a raised bed. The roundish rubble stones in the wall above have been mortared for strength, while the flat flagstones in the wall at the right were easy to dry set.

Above: Thin sandstone veneer, in various hues of brown and taupe, are cut to fit neatly and then mortared onto a concrete block wall. Left: Large stones with angular sides are carefully stacked without mortar.

Stackable Paver Retaining Wall

Degree of Difficulty
● Moderate

Once the trench is dug, these retaining blocks stack quickly. They can be used to build a serious retaining wall or to create a flower bed.

Interlocking blocks fit together neatly to form a sturdy and attractive wall.

Choosing Retaining Blocks

Home centers and brickyards carry several styles of concrete block that interlock when stacked to form a solid retaining wall. The wall will batter (lean back) toward the soil that it retains. Most stackable blocks have a lip at the bottom rear, which slips over the top back edge of the block below it. Some types anchor via grooves or even fiberglass pins.

Drainpipe

This drainpipe empties onto the side of a hill. Because it is exposed, a hinged grate is installed to keep critters out.

If your region has normal precipitation, you can simply backfill with soil, and rainwater will seep through the face of the block wall. If your area tends to get very wet, you may want to backfill with gravel and cover the gravel with landscaping fabric. A perforated drainpipe can carry water away to a dry well or another location.

Flagstone Retaining Wall

You can make a simple garden bed or modest retaining wall by stacking flagstones. Batter the stones by an inch or so per course, until you reach the top. You may choose to adhere the top course with construction adhesive.

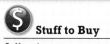

Stuff to Buy	**Time Commitment**	**Tools You'll Need**	**Related Topics**
Adhesive Compactable gravel Landscaping fabric Perforated drainage pipe Stackable blocks	A weekend	Hammer Level Rake Shovel	Cutting bricks, pavers, & stone, 48–51 Excavating, 46–47 Planning drainage, 32–35

How to Do It

1 Dig & fill trench

- Dig a trench about 4 inches deep and twice as wide as the blocks.
- Fill it with compactable gravel, then an inch or so of coarse sand.
- The sand does not have to be level, but it should be evenly sloped so it forms a smooth surface.

2 Set bottom course

- Place the bottom course of blocks with their lips facing down.
- Press the blocks tightly against each other.
- Check that they form a flat surface with no waves.

3 Add courses

- Place the blocks of the next course centered over the seams of the course below.
- Backfill with soil or gravel as you stack.

4 Trim blocks

- If the wall curves, you may need to trim the retaining lips for a tight fit.
- Wearing safety glasses, hold a block at an angle on the ground and strike the lip with a hammer.
- Aim to build a wall with all full-size blocks, but cut them with a power saw when needed.

Adhere Top Blocks

For a more secure installation, apply squiggles of construction adhesive before setting the top blocks.

Dry-stacked Retaining Wall

✔ **Degree of Difficulty**
● Challenging

The basic strategy for a dry-stacked wall is simple. Always put two stones over one, and one over two. In practice, however, you will need to spend plenty of time arranging stones in order to achieve a wall that is strong and artful.

How to Do It

Here we show how to build a dry-stacked retaining wall with rounded stones, often referred to as rubble. This appealing wall stacks quickly because the stones are large. The challenge is getting them to nest securely on top of each other. You may choose instead to stack flagstones, partially cut stones, or split boulders.

You will need to pick up, place, remove, and retry placing these heavy stones quite a few times. So enlist some strong-backed help, and plan to take plenty of rest breaks.

Using a Batter Gauge

A dry-stacked stone retaining wall must slope back, or batter, toward the soil it retains, usually about ½ to 1 inch per vertical foot. A simple gauge made of a level, 2 x 2s or 2 x 4s, and duct tape allows you to check the batter as you build.

Using Landscaping Fabric

If your soil is clay-heavy, drape landscaping cloth over the gravel so the soil doesn't work its way into the gravel and clog your drainage pipe.

1 **Excavate & lay out**

- Excavate to a depth of several inches along the base of the wall.
- Nearby, set out large stones for the first course.
- Install drainage pipe if needed.
- Drive stakes every few feet to mark the wall's front face.

Stuff to Buy

Drainage pipe
Gravel
Mortar
Stones

Time Commitment

Several days

Tools You'll Need

Mason's line
Rake
Shovel
Skip loader

Related Topics

Dry-stone garden wall, 196–197
Excavating, 46–47
Planning drainage, 32–35

2 Set base course

- Place the first course of stones inside the excavation, aligned with the stakes.
- Nest pieces snugly together.
- To raise a stone, add gravel, not soil, underneath.
- It will take several attempts to get all the stones stable and firmly supported.

3 Check alignment & backfill

- Stand back and check that the front faces create a straight or smoothly curved line.
- Make adjustments as needed.
- Fill behind the stones with gravel and perhaps add drainage pipe.
- Pack gravel into crevices between stones.

4 Add more stones

- Continue adding gravel until it's level with the tops of the base stones.
- Starting at the ends and working toward the middle, add a second course, then a third.
- If you place several small stones on one layer, bridge them with a large stone on the next course.
- To make the stones stable, tap chinking stones (small stones used as wedges) into crevices from the front or back.

5 Top with soil

- Backfill with gravel as you add more courses.
- When you near the top of the wall, tuck landscaping fabric, if you are using it, over the top of the gravel.
- Fill the top 4 inches with soil and pack it firm.

6 Top layer

- Stretch a mason's line at the final desired height.
- Use fairly flat stones for the top course.
- Fit the stones to achieve a fairly straight or artfully curved top line.

7 Finishing touches

- Backfill with more soil and perhaps add sod or plantings.
- Test the stones for stability and add chinking stones as needed.

Dry-stone Garden Wall

A dry wall, composed of carefully stacked stones with little or no mortar, can be surprisingly durable. Throughout the world, many have lasted centuries. The key is in the stacking. Allow plenty of time to experiment so each stone rests solidly.

Even today, the ancient art of stacking stones can inspire one-of-a-kind creations. Maybe that's because the techniques have changed little over time.

A freestanding stone wall batters inward on both sides. Large stones tie everything together, and small stones and rubble fill in the gaps.

Interconnect the front and back of the wall with tie pieces at both ends and every 4 to 6 feet along the wall's length. If possible, use tie stones that span the wall's thickness. Otherwise, select pairs of stones that each reach three-fourths of the way through. Set them so they project inward from opposite sides and butt tightly.

Planning & Preparing

A stone wall calls for plenty of heavy lifting, so work carefully. Avoid stones that weigh more than 50 pounds. Have the stones delivered as close to the site as possible, and enlist some strong-backed assistance.

It is possible to build a freestanding dry wall with roundish rubble stones, but it is very difficult. Choose stones that are at least partially squared off. You will need a large number of tie stones (also called bond stones) long enough to span the thickness of the wall. Sort the stones into three or four piles according to size. This will make it easier to find the stones you need. Reserve plenty of large stones to use in the wall's cap.

Make a simple batter gauge out of 2 × 2s or 2 × 4s and a level so you can quickly check that the sides lean inward. Based on the amount of batter and the height of the wall, calculate how wide the bottom and top of the wall will be and make sure you have stones of the right sizes.

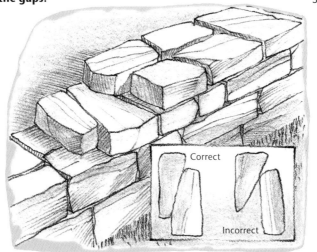

Correct

Incorrect

 **Stuff to Buy**

Gravel
Mortar mix
Stones

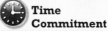 **Time Commitment**

Several days

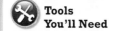 **Tools You'll Need**

Chisel
Level
Hammer
Power saw
Rake
Shovel

 Related Topics

Applying mortar, 64–65
Cutting bricks, pavers, & stone, 48–51
Excavating, 46–47
Mixing mortar, 62–63

How to Do It

① Lay base stones

- Remove sod and any roots from an area about 3 inches wider than the bottom width of the wall.
- Dig a trench several inches deep, either level or evenly sloped.
- Tamp the soil firm.
- Lay a tie stone at each end of the wall.
- Fill in with stones laid in two wythes (horizontal rows).
- Fill the space between wythes with tightly packed stones.

② Lay additional courses

- Continue to lay stones, keeping the courses level.
- Set large stones on each side and fill the middle with small stones.
- Always lay one on top of two. Avoid having a joint directly above another joint.
- Use a batter gauge to check that the wall leans inward on both sides.
- Every third or fourth course, install tie stones every 4 to 6 feet.

③ Mortar the cap

- Fill gaps in the side of the wall by gently tapping in small chinking stones.
- On the top, dry-fit large, flat cap stones that overhang the sides of the wall.
- Mix a batch of stiff mortar and lay a 1- to 2-inch-thick bed.
- Press stones into the mortar and level them.
- Fill joints with mortar.

Strap-and-pin gate hinges

- Install the hinge pins first, then build the gate and attach strap portions to fit.
- At the height of the lower hinge, leave a space.
- Mix mortar, fill the space, and set the pin in mortar.
- Check that the mortar is plumb, and allow it to set.
- Build the wall end plumb, then install the upper hinge in the same way.

Split-boulder Raised Bed

Split boulders are flat on one side, so they are easier to stack than round rubble stones. For a raised bed, dig a trench about 4 inches deep and wide enough for the bottom stones. Set the bottom course flat side up, then lay other courses in whatever configuration is most stable. As you build, fill joints with soil and perhaps crevice plants as well. Backfill with garden soil as you stack. The top stones should be flat side down.

Mortared Stone Wall

Unless you possess unusual stacking skills, a garden wall made with rounded stones should be mortared. A wall built this way can be freestanding or used as a retaining wall.

Building with mortar allows you to use roundish rubble stones that would be difficult to stack. Aim for mortar joints that are consistent in width.

Though mortar will hold the stones together, you should still stack the stones for stability, placing one on top of two and avoiding joints that stack on top of each other. Lay tie stones, which span the thickness of the wall, every 4 to 6 feet on every third course, and more often at the ends. Where a stone needs to be held up temporarily until the mortar sets, use wood wedges.

How to Do It

① Prep for foundation

- Excavate a trench about 4 inches wider than the wall's base at least 6 inches deep (deeper if you need to go below the frost line).
- Spread compactable gravel and tamp it firm with a vibrating plate compactor or a hand tamper.
- Position several lengths of ⅜-inch rebar in the trench, bending it into curves where needed.

② Pour foundation

- If needed, build forms to hold in the concrete. Otherwise, just pour concrete into the trench.
- Mix concrete so it is barely pourable, then pour it into the trench.

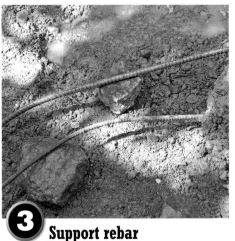

③ Support rebar

- As you pour, pull the rebar up to the middle of the footing's thickness.
- Or place stones under the rebar to hold it up.

Stuff to Buy	Time Commitment	Tools You'll Need	Related Topics
Concrete Mortar mix Rebar Stones	Several days	Mason's line Rake Shovel Trowel Wheelbarrow Wood shims	Applying mortar, 64–65 Excavating, 46–47 Forming & pouring a footing, 58–59 Mixing mortar, 62–63

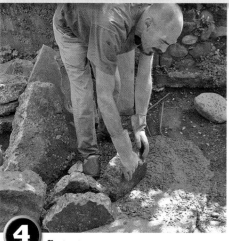

4 Set stones

- As you form the foundation, position damp stones along the less visible side of the wall.
- You can use used chunks of concrete for this, if they won't be seen.
- Mix a batch of mortar.

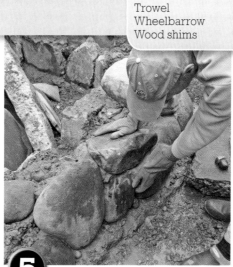

5 Place face stones

- Place stones along the most visible face of the wall.
- Position the stones so they would be stable even without mortar.
- Set small stones and chunks of concrete in the interior and pack mortar into gaps.

6 Add courses

- Dry-fit several stones for an upper course, then set them aside in order.
- Spread mortar, dampen the stones, and set the stones in mortar.
- Every 6 feet or so, install a large tie stone that spans the thickness of the wall.
- Where needed, use chunks of stone or wood wedges to hold a stone in place temporarily.

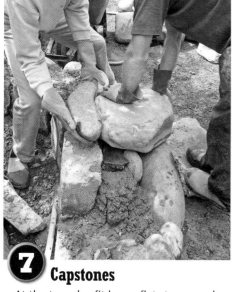

7 Capstones

- At the top, dry-fit large, flat stones and then set them.
- Aim for fairly thin and consistent mortar joints.
- Use a scrap of wood or a jointer to smooth the joints, then wipe away crumbs with a mason's brush. Once the mortar has hardened, wash the stones with a muriatic acid solution to remove haze. Rinse them thoroughly.

Cut-stone Wall

Stones that are at least partially squared off are easier to stack. However, joints on a wall like this are expected to be consistently narrow, so you may need to cut quite a few stones to fit.

Mortared Stone Wall **199**

Faux Dry-stacked Wall

By packing mortar into the center, you can build a stone wall that looks dry-stacked but has the strength of a mortared wall. It's an ideal solution where people will sit on the wall or where you are building with relatively small, squared-off stones.

In a Cold Climate

Where winters are cold enough for the ground to freeze, build the bottom portion of the wall as a true dry-stacked wall, filling in the center with gravel and small stones. When you get to the top foot or so, add mortar between stones, but keep it well back from the face so it doesn't show. This allows the bottom portion of the wall to flex a bit as the ground freezes and thaws. Occasionally you may need to reapply mortar for the capstone.

A reasonably even distribution of large, medium, and small stones give this wall a handmade look that is rich in texture.

The Basic Method

The wall shown here is basically constructed like a dry, freestanding stone wall, but the center is filled with concrete and chunks of stone and concrete. It is built in an area with mild winters, so there is no concrete foundation, only compacted gravel.

The wall is 28 inches deep and 18 inches high, the right height for a bench. If your wall will double as a table for food or drinks, make it about 36 inches high.

1 Lay out & excavate

- Use spray paint, a charged hose (one filled with water), and flour, or stakes and mason's line, to lay out the site.
- For a curved wall, mark one long face, then measure out at several places so the opposite wall curves an equal distance away.
- Remove sod and excavate with a square shovel to a depth of about 6 inches.

2 Gravel base

- Pour compactable gravel into the excavation about 4 inches deep.
- Spread gravel with a rake.
- Tamp with a vibrating plate compactor or a hand tamper.
- Spread a layer of sand or fine gravel about an inch thick.

3 Base stones

- For the bottom course, choose large stones with at least two fairly flat faces that form a right angle.
- Use large, block-shaped stones for corners.
- Set stones on the sand, adjusting and packing sand as needed to make them stable.
- Work to make the front face straight and the top of each stone level.

Stuff to Buy

Compactable gravel
Concrete
Mortar mix
Rebar
Sand
Semidressed stones or
flagstones

Time Commitment

Two days

Tools You'll Need

Chisel
Hammer
Level
Power saw
Rake
Shovel
Tamper
Trowels
Wheelbarrow

Related Topics

Applying mortar, 64–65
Dry-stone garden wall, 196–197
Forming & pouring a footing,
　58–59
Mixing & delivering, 172–173
Mixing mortar, 62–63

4 Cut stones

- Fit stones snugly together, with narrow joints.
- Where bulges keep stones from fitting well together, cut them to fit.
- Here, a hammer and chisel are used to slightly alter a stone.

5 Build corners

- Begin the second course at the corners.
- Use large stones for stability.
- Check the height so you don't set stones higher than you want the wall to be.

6 Add courses

- Continue to dry-lay stones along the perimeter.
- Lay one on top of two, and avoid setting one joint directly above a joint below.
- Outside edges should be straight, but inside edges can be jagged.

7 Add concrete

- As the wall approaches 2 feet tall, prepare a basic concrete mix and pack it into the center of the wall.
- To ensure that the pressure of the wet concrete will not push the stones out of place, allow one layer to set before you add the next.
- Continue filling as you build the wall.

8 Cap the top

- When the concrete has set, place thin, flat shim stones as needed to create a fairly level top.
- Prepare mortar mix, and trowel over the top to create a level base.
- Use a notched trowel to scratch the top of the mortar.

9 Set capstones

- Use thick, flat stones for the top, trimming them as needed so they fit well together and extend an inch or two out from the sides of the wall.
- Use a cardboard template to mark the stones for cutting.
- Trowel more mortar onto the top of the wall and set the capstones in mortar.
- Check with a level. You may need to remove a stone and add more mortar.
- Fill and smooth the joints between stones.

Boulder Retaining Wall

Large dry-stacked boulders make for an impressive and secure retaining wall. The boulders should be stacked both for stability and artful arrangement.

A retaining wall made of boulders is right at home in any setting. Large and flowing crevice plants are at home among massive stones.

How to Do It

1 Mark & dig

- Use spray paint, a charged hose, and flour, or stakes and mason's line, to lay out the wall.
- Dig down with a shovel along the outline.

2 Trench

- Use a skip loader or a scooper to dig a trench for the boulders.
- With practice, you can dig surprisingly accurate trenches.
- Trench to a depth of about a foot, so the boulder looks naturally embedded but most of it shows.

3 Finish trench

- Use shovels to dig out a fairly squared-off trench.
- For very large boulders, you may want to estimate the shape of the excavation so the boulder ends up at the desired angle.

 **Stuff to Buy**

Large boulders

 **Time Commitment**

A weekend

 **Tools You'll Need**

Pry bars
Shovels
Skip loader

 **Related Topics**

Measuring & laying out, 44–45
Transporting heavy stones, 56–57

4 Place boulders

- Pick up a boulder with the forks of the machine and move it to the trench.
- Tilt the forks to slide the boulder into the trench (top).
- Push with the tips of the forks to adjust the boulder's position.

5 Fine-tune

- Even very large boulders can usually be moved slightly with hand tools.
- Use shovels and perhaps pry bars to get the boulders just where you want them.
- To adjust a boulder's angle, have one person (or the machine) pry up while another person shovels dirt or stones underneath.

6 Ends

- Use shorter boulders at an end for a tapering effect.
- Quickly measure a stone using a shovel, then dig the trench to accommodate the boulder.

7 Backfill

- Shovel soil behind the boulders and stomp with your feet to tamp it firm.
- Backfill for each course, then stack further courses only when you are sure the lower boulders are stable.

8 Add courses

- Carefully eyeball the boulders, and perhaps measure them, to select rocks for a good fit.
- Stack them as you would for a dry wall, one on top of two.

9 Finishing touches

- Stand back and examine the arrangement; don't be shy about rearranging—most adjustments take only 15 minutes or so.
- Slide the upper boulders so they batter fairly consistently.
- Fill crevices with packed soil and perhaps crevice plants as well.

Stone Veneer

A plain block or concrete wall can be dressed up with flagstones or faux veneer stones. If the job is done carefully, the result looks very much like a mortared stone wall.

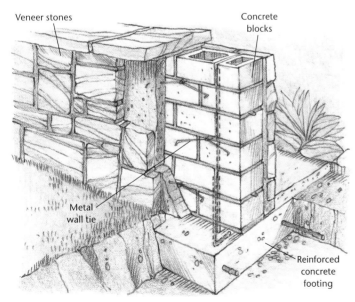

It's relatively easy to achieve straight lines and consistent joints when you choose a lightweight stone veneer.

For a strong, solid wall, use rebar to reinforce both the footing and the blocks, then attach facing stones with plenty of mortar and metal wall ties.

Labels on illustration: Veneer stones · Concrete blocks · Metal wall tie · Reinforced concrete footing

Veneer Options

If you will use natural flagstones, choose stones that are light and thin. The flatter the stones, and the more consistent in thickness, the easier it will be to achieve a wall with an even surface. You can use irregularly shaped stones, as shown here, or stones with squared corners for a more geometric look.

Lightweight faux veneer is the easiest to install. It is thin but gives the impression of large rubble or ashlar. Special pieces that wrap around a corner complete the illusion. Set these stones as you would flagstones.

The wall should be in sound condition. Clean away any oily deposits. If a brick wall is flaking or producing efflorescence (a white powder), correct the problem before you apply face stones.

Work out the placement of veneer stones ahead of time. Do a dry run on a board, as shown on the opposite page, or stack the stones where they will go, as shown here. Don't start mixing mortar and setting stones until you are satisfied with the arrangement.

Facing with Heavy Stones

If the stones are heavy, build as if you were making a new mortared stone wall that just happens to be up against the block wall. Set the bottom row, then allow the mortar to harden before you set higher rows. Have on hand many short lumber scraps to use as shims and supports. Have a helper hold a stone in place while you insert the lumber straps to achieve the desired joint.

Stuff to Buy

Mortar
Thin flagstones or veneer stones

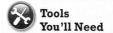

Time Commitment

Two days

Tools You'll Need

Chisel
Grout bag
Hammer
Jointer
Mason's brush
Power saw
Trowel
Wheelbarrow

Related Topics

Applying mortar, 64–65
Cleaning & sealing masonry, 284–285
Cutting bricks, pavers, & stone, 48–51
Mixing mortar, 62–63
Reinforced block wall, 224–225

How to Do It

❶ Dry run

- Lay a sheet of plywood, as wide as the wall is tall, on the ground near the wall.
- Lay stones on the plywood in a dry run as they will appear on the wall.
- Cut the stones to fit as needed.

❷ Mix & apply mortar

- Spread a coat of latex bonding agent onto the wall. In a wheelbarrow, mix a batch of mortar that is stiff but just wet enough to stick to the stones.
- Apply a coat about ½ inch thick to the wall with a straight trowel.
- Cover an area of about 15 square feet.

❸ Bottom row

- Starting at the bottom, press stones into the mortar.
- If the stones do not stick well, moisten their backs with a sponge.
- Where needed, use blocks of wood or small rocks to hold the stones in position.

❹ Set upper stones

- If the stones are light, continue setting them up to the top of the wall.
- If the weight of the upper stones causes lower stones to slide down, wait for the lower mortar to set before you work upward.
- Every so often, remove a stone and check that at least three-quarters of its back is embedded in mortar. If not, back-butter mortar onto the stones or wet the stones.

❺ Fill joints

- After the mortar has hardened, fill the joints with mortar.
- Use a pointed trowel or a mortar bag to slip and press mortar into the joints.
- Once the mortar has started to stiffen so it holds a thumb impression, tool it with a jointing tool or a scrap of wood.

❻ Cap & clean

- At the top of the wall, apply mortar and install large stones that overhang by an inch or two on each side.
- Once the mortar has started to harden, clear away any crumbs with a mason's brush.
- After the mortar has dried, clean smears with a muriatic acid solution.

8 Brick & Block Walls

In this chapter, we concentrate on bricks and blocks. We detail the patterns you can choose, the techniques for mixing and applying mortar, and the different types of decorative joints you can create between bricks. If building an entire wall sounds too daunting, but you're looking for a fun and challenging project, follow the steps on pages 218 through 221 to make a brick mailbox holder and brick planter.

Chapter Contents

Brick Planter

page 221

Stackable Concrete Blocks

page 222

Reinforced Block Wall

page 224

Stuccoing a Wall

page 226

Decorative Blocks Walls

page 228

A Gallery of Beautiful Walls

If you follow directions carefully and take the time to practice "throwing" mortar, you can easily build a short brick wall for your garden. Walls made of concrete block call for similar techniques. Once built, a block wall can be covered with stucco or faced with stone.

Red brick is used here for raised beds, pillars, stairs, and a patio.

This wall has nooks and crannies for cascading plants at three different levels.

A smooth stucco surface, tinted adobe beige, covers concrete-block walls.

The cap of this stucco wall is painted blue, mimicking the gravel below.

These walls are made from decorative concrete blocks, each made to look like seven or eight stones.

Though it looks like an old-world solid stone wall, this is a block wall that has been faced with easy-to-install faux stones.

Molded stucco and tile work like this is a job for the pros.

Brick Bond & Joint Choices

Brick walls may all look alike at a glance, but there are many patterns. The bond you choose, as well as the type of joint, will subtly affect the wall's appearance.

A single-wythe brick wall is topped with flat-laid bricks that overhang to form a corbelled cap.

Brick Bonds

Brick is usually used for a freestanding garden wall rather than for a retaining wall, since bricks cannot be battered (angled back) to hold soil in place. A very low wall or planter can be built with a single wythe, meaning only one horizontal row of bricks laid end to end. But such a wall is not strong. You can even push it over by hand. Double-wythe brick walls are strong enough for most garden purposes. If you need a wall that is taller than 4 feet, consider building with block instead.

On a double-wythe wall, some bricks are turned sideways to tie the wythes together. These bricks are called headers, while the rest of the bricks are called stretchers. Over the centuries, masons have developed patterns known as bonds, which combine headers and stretchers in distinctive ways.

Pro Tip

Most bonds require you to cut bricks. To help you maintain rhythm and concentration as you work, cut a number of bricks ahead of time.

Common bond, also known as American bond, is shown being installed on pages 216–217. It uses headers every fifth course and requires a small amount of extra cutting.

Running bond has no headers. You will need to embed metal reinforcement in the mortar every four or five courses to tie the wythes together. Cut ladder-type reinforcement roughly to fit, as shown at right, or push corrugated wall ties into the mortar every foot or so.

Flemish bond alternates headers and stretchers in each course. You'll need to cut narrow closure bricks at the corners.

English bond alternates courses of headers and stretchers. This pattern also requires you to cut narrow closure bricks at the corners.

Mortar Joints

Striking joints, also called tooling, shapes and compacts the mortar, increasing its strength and its ability to shed water. If you have freezing winters, choose a joint shape that sheds water quickly so ice cannot produce cracks.

Concave joints are the most common, and for good reason. They shed water and do a good job of compacting the mortar. Make concave joints with a standard jointer.

You can produce flush joints by cutting mortar away without striking them. The joints may be pitted, which can be attractive, but they are suitable only for dry, warm climates.

Struck joints require scraping with a trowel tilted upward. The angle creates pleasingly dramatic shadow lines. The joints are compacted and fairly strong, but water can easily collect at the bottom.

Weathered joints are upside-down struck joints. They are watertight and fairly strong.

Raked joints, produced with a joint raker, can cast interesting shadows. They are not suited to wet, cold climates, as water can collect in the grooves. Note, however, that if slightly raked joints are carefully brushed when they are still fairly wet, they will form a good, weather-tight seal, as shown below.

Extruded joints have squeezed-out mortar that has been left alone for a rustic appearance. This actually requires a good deal of skill, because the mortar must be fairly uniform and cannot be reshaped after the bricks are laid. The joints are not very watertight.

Here, a raked joint is brushed so that the mortar is compacted and slightly recessed behind the bricks. This must be done when the mortar is just right—wet enough to work but not so wet that it may smear.

Wide joints like this can be pressed and scraped with a trowel, then lightly brushed to form slight concaves.

On the rear wall of a building, you may find wide joints like these, which lap onto the brick faces. Most people do not find these joints attractive, but they are effective at shedding water.

Mixing & Testing Mortar

Most brick and block walls are held together with mortar. Though mixing mortar is not difficult, it must be done correctly to ensure a lasting result.

Mixing in a Wheelbarrow

Aim to mix as much mortar as you can use in 30 minutes or so. On a hot, dry day, work in the shade or in the early morning or late afternoon so the mortar will not set too quickly. Choose a mixing container and method that will make it easy to get the mortar to the site.

For most residential projects, a wheelbarrow or masonry trough is the best mixing container. Pour an inch or so of water into the container, then add one or two bags of mortar mix. Use a shovel, a mason's hoe, or a garden hoe to scrape the bottom of the container as you mix. Add small amounts of water as you continue to mix, until you get the right consistency.

Mixing in a Bucket

You can mix small amounts of mortar in a 5-gallon bucket. Don't try to do this with a standard 3/8-inch drill, as it will burn out. Instead, rent or buy a heavy-duty 1/2-inch drill and a mixing paddle, as shown to the left. Pour 2 inches of water into the bucket, place the paddle in the bottom, and add half a bag of mortar mix. Pour a bit more water on top. Work the drill in short bursts at first to avoid slopping water out of the bucket. Then run the drill continuously, adding water as needed. Scrape the bottom and sides of the bucket as you mix.

Choosing the Right Mortar

- For building retaining walls or for setting pavers, use Type S mortar, which is high-strength.
- For a modest garden wall, a barbecue, or tuck-pointing, use medium-strength Type N mortar.
- Type M mortar is extremely strong and is used only for serious foundation work, not for the sort of garden structures shown in this book.
- Standard gray mortar can be tinted to many hues, but if you want more vivid color, use white mortar, which is often also used for building glass block walls.

Standard Type S mortar is plenty strong for residential walls and patios. A quick-set mortar is suited mostly for patching. It sets up too fast to be used for a wall.

Coloring Mortar

Use liquid colorants to change the color of the mortar. To maintain an even color throughout a project, keep a careful record of the amounts of mortar mix and colorant. Shake up the bottles thoroughly, or you will end up with sludge at the bottom that is more potent than the thinner color at the top.

Mixing on Plywood

With practice, you can mix a large amount of mortar on a piece of plywood, which can then be transported to the site. Make a pile of mortar mix, or of 2 parts sand to 1 part portland cement. Make a well in the middle and add water, as if adding gravy to mashed potatoes. Working all around from the outside in, scoop the mortar mix over the water, then scrape up. Once most of the dry material is moistened, use chopping motions, then scrape up shovelfuls and turn them over. Splash water as needed over the entire lump and continue mixing. The final mixture will be just stiff enough to form a pile that holds its shape.

Power Mixers

If you have a lot of mortar to mix, save your back by renting an electric or gas power mixer. It's usually easier to add water with a hose rather than with a bucket. Add a few inches of water to the hopper, then pour in one or two bags of mortar mix. Turn on the machine and spray water as it turns. Once the mortar is mixed, tilt the hopper to empty it into a wheelbarrow.

Testing Mortar

Some people say mortar should be the consistency of mayonnaise, while others say toothpaste. Mortar must be wet enough to stick to the bricks or blocks but also firm enough to hold its shape. Scoop up mortar with a trowel or shovel and turn it upside down. It should stick to the tool for a couple of seconds before sliding or dropping off. Most mortar should be just firm enough to hold the shape of a furrow (below).

If you need to fill in small vertical spaces with your fingers and a jointing tool, as shown (right), the mortar needs to be a bit firmer.

Setting Bricks

A professional mason can throw a neat line of mortar at just the right thickness with ease and speed. You will probably not become that fast or proficient, but you can learn to throw mortar well enough to construct a straight wall with neat joints.

Tips for the Unhandy

If you are having a hard time getting the hang of throwing mortar onto a line of bricks, you can still successfully tackle a small project, though it may take four or five times as long as it would take a pro. Here's one method:

If a pointed trowel is difficult to use, try using a margin trowel, as shown at right. Instead of throwing the mortar onto the bricks, use a tapping motion to drop dollops onto them. You won't end up with a smooth line of mortar, so you'll have to go back and shape a line with the trowel.

Work carefully so you don't smear mortar onto the bricks. You may sometimes need to scrape the trowel on the outside corner of the bricks. Use the margin trowel, or switch to a pointed trowel, to furrow the mortar (see step 3 on page 215).

The important thing is that the bricks stick to the mortar. Occasionally lift up on a brick. If it comes up easily, the mortar is not sticking. Try using wetter mortar, or moisten the bricks by spraying them or wiping them with a wet sponge.

Throwing Technique

Masons use the term "throwing" for good reason. Mortar should be firmly dropped onto the bricks. If you attempt to slather instead of throw, the work will proceed very slowly, the mortar will vary in thickness, and you are likely to smear the brick faces. So mix a small batch of mortar and practice for an hour or so until you start to get the knack. Aim for a relaxed, accurate throw that leaves just the right amount of mortar on the bricks.

❶ Mix & test mortar

- Mortar is thick enough if you can cut ridges in it with a mason's trowel and the ridges hold their shape.
- If the mortar appears crumbly, it's too dry.
- If the mortar is too dry or too wet soon after you've mixed it, add more water or dry mix.
- Once it starts to stiffen, after you've been using it for a while, throw it out and mix a new batch.

❷ Throw a line

- To loosen the mortar's grip on the trowel, hold the trowel flat and snap downward quickly to slightly lift the mortar. It should make a smacking sound as it settles back onto the trowel.
- Extend your arm, holding the trowel a few inches above the bricks.
- Rotate the trowel until the mortar starts to slide off, then pull back as you gently throw mortar onto the bricks.
- The process should be quick and smooth, and it should leave a line of mortar 1 to 3 inches thick.

Tools You'll Need

Jointer
Level
Mason's brush
Mason's trowel

Related Topics

Applying mortar, 64–65
Brick bond & joint choices, 210–211
Forming & pouring a footing, 58–59
Mixing mortar, 62–63

3 Furrow

- Turn the trowel upside down and drag its point through the mortar.
- Produce a channel about half the thickness of the mortar line.
- If excess mortar slides off onto the faces of the bricks, slice it off in the same manner as shown in step 6.

4 Butter

- Every brick except the first one in a course needs to have at least one end buttered.
- Hold a brick in one hand and load the trowel with some mortar.
- Scrape the trowel at a 45-degree angle to the brick's end and pull back.
- Shape the mortar this way in all four directions.

5 Place brick

- Set the brick on the mortar bed, about 2 inches from the brick it will abut.
- Slide it into place, pressing slightly so a little mortar squeezes out of all the joints.
- Small mortar gaps can be filled, but if there are gaps greater than an inch, remove the brick, scrape off the mortar, and start again.

6 Slice excess

- Use the trowel like a knife to slice off the squeezed-out mortar.
- Work quickly and gently to avoid smearing the brick faces.

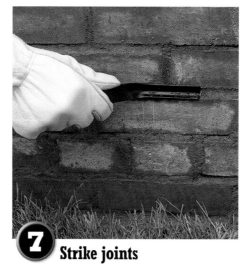

7 Strike joints

- Every 20 minutes or so, depending on the weather, test the joints by pressing with your thumb.
- If a thumbprint holds its shape, it's time to strike.
- Using the jointing technique of your choice, smooth all horizontal joints, then the verticals.
- If a bit of mortar oozes out, don't smear it now. Wait for it to dry.

8 Brush & clean

- Once the mortar starts to get crumbly, go over it lightly with a masonry brush.
- If the mortar smears, wait for it to harden further.
- Clean some smeared mortar with a damp sponge, taking care not to wet the joints, which would weaken them.
- Clean hardened smears with a muriatic acid solution.

Brick Garden Wall

A garden wall can be a centerpiece of a backyard. It takes effort and patience to build one, but you'll be able to point to it with pride for many years to come.

It seems you can never have too much brick. Here, it's used for stairs, a high wall, a low wall, and steppingstones.

Preparing to Build

A mortared brick or block wall must rest atop a solid concrete footing. Form and pour the footing, then wait a week or so for the concrete to cure before you build the wall. While you are waiting for the footing to cure, you can practice throwing mortar and setting bricks.

To quickly measure the bricks for the correct height of the courses, make a story pole (see Step 5 on page 217). Lay a number of bricks with ³⁄₈-inch spaces between them on edge on a flat surface. Then lay a length of 1 × 2 or 1 × 4 next to the bricks and draw marks indicating the centers of each mortar joint. Or you can purchase a ready-made story pole. A standard model has marks every 8 inches to indicate three courses of common bricks, plus the mortar joints.

1 Dry run

- Snap chalk lines on the footing to outline the wall.
- Place bricks on the footing in a dry run, with ³⁄₈-inch dowels between them to represent mortar joints.
- You may need to cut a brick or two at a corner, depending on the bond pattern you have chosen.
- With a pencil, mark the footing for the centers of the joints.

2 Lay first bricks

- Starting at a corner or at the end of a wall, throw a line of mortar for the first three bricks.
- Butter the brick ends (except for the first brick) and set the bricks into place, with the centers of the joints at the pencil marks.
- Check that the bricks are level in both directions.
- Scrape excess mortar and repeat for the second wythe. Also lay bricks for an adjoining wall if you are at a corner.

3 Header course

- Most bond patterns use header courses.
- For the common bond shown here, cut and lay two three-quarter bricks and two one-quarter closure bricks at the corner.

Stuff to Buy

Bricks
Concrete
Dowels
Mortar mix
Rebar

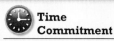

**Time
Commitment**

Several days

**Tools
You'll Need**

Blocks
Jointer
Level
Mason's brush
Mason's line
Mason's trowel
Story pole

**Related
Topics**

4 Build a lead

- Build up the corner or end of a wall, called the lead, seven or eight bricks high.
- Check with a level and a story pole as you go, to see that the lead is plumb, the courses are level, and the joints are consistent in width.
- Also lay a straightedge diagonally on the brick corners to see that the bricks form regular stair steps at the unfinished end.

5 String between leads

- Build a lead at the other end.
- Use a story pole to check that the bricks are the same height on each lead.
- Lay the in-between bricks on the bottom course.
- Hook mason's blocks and stretch a mason's line from one lead to the other at the center of a joint.
- The line should be ⅛ inch from the brick faces and stretched taut.

6 Fill in

- For every second or third course, move the line blocks up and use them as a guide.
- No bricks should touch the line, which would throw the alignment off.
- Before installing the closure brick in the middle, butter it at both ends.
- Slip the closure brick straight down, without sliding it.
- You may need to force more mortar into a joint with a striking tool.

Keeping It Simple

If possible, avoid having to cut bricks to fit in the center of the wall. If the footing is wide enough, you may move the wall over a couple of inches so you can use full-size bricks. Or you may choose to use ½-inch mortar joints instead of the more usual ⅜-inch joints.

Mortar Tips

Every now and then while building a wall, you need to stop stacking and attend to the mortar. Hold a level upright against the wall to make sure the vertical mortar joints are plumb and aligned. Scrape away excess mortar as you go, taking care not to smear the brick faces.

Scrape-and-brush Joint

You may tool the joints using any of the techniques shown on pages 211 and 215. Or try this simpler method, which works especially well with wide ½-inch joints, as shown here. Use a flat jointing tool to gently scrape the joints fairly smooth and to compress the mortar (left). Wait for the mortar to get a bit crumbly (so it won't smear) and sweep it with a masonry brush (right) to make nicely concave joints.

Brick Mailbox

A simple but stately brick pillar topped with cut stone makes an admirable housing for a mailbox and address plaques. A project like this requires care and attention to detail, but it is easier to build than a brick wall.

If your house is set back from the street, an address pillar—this one is also the mailbox holder—can make it easy for visitors to find your home.

How to Do It

A number of outdoor projects—planters, pillars, brick-and-wood fences—involve the construction of a basic upright structure like the one shown on the next three pages. You can incorporate decorative elements as you build. This mailbox is capped with cut stone and has two address blocks in addition to the mailbox.

A specialty masonry supplier can make address blocks for you. Buy a mailbox insert, made for placing in a masonry structure, and have the mailbox on hand. Though you will install the box later, you want to be sure that it will fit.

This project features large used paver bricks, with extra-thick 1/2-inch mortar joints, for a slightly rustic look. You'll notice that the mortar is laid extra thick.

On a project like this, you should plan the exact number of brick courses and determine the course where the mailbox and the address blocks will go.

Not Too Strong

A mailbox, or any structure placed near the side of a street, should be strong enough to stand for many decades but not strong enough to withstand a run-in with an automobile. A brick structure like this is just the right strength. A concrete structure that's reinforced with vertical rebar would be too strong.

1 Pour foundation

- On a flat surface, make a dry run of bricks, with spacers for mortar joints, to determine the size of the foundation. It should be 2 inches wider than the pillar.
- Dig a hole per local codes and build a 2 × 4 form. Check that the form is square.
- Pour concrete and perhaps add rebar or fiber reinforcement.

2 Dry run

- Allow the concrete to set, then remove the forms.
- Place the bottom course of bricks on the foundation. They should come to within an inch of the foundation edges.
- Adjust the brick positions as needed and determine joint thickness.

3 Bottom course

- Mix mortar to the proper consistency, making sure it is stiff enough to hold bricks up.
- Throw a line of mortar on two sides and lay bricks. Then do the other two sides.
- If the foundation is reliably square, follow it. Otherwise, use a carpenter's square to check the corners.

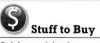
Stuff to Buy
Address blocks
Bricks
Concrete
Mailbox
Mortar mix
Rebar
Stone cap

Time Commitment
Two days

Tools You'll Need
Brick trowel
Carpenter's square
Level
Mason's brush
Mixing paddle
Shovel
Striking tool

Related Topics
Applying mortar, 64–65
Forming & pouring a footing, 58–59
Mixing mortar, 62–63
Setting bricks, 214–215

4 Level & scrape

- Scrape excess mortar on the outside as you go. The interior of the pillar does not need to be scraped.
- Place a level atop the bricks and tap as needed to keep them all level.

5 Build up

- Continue building the wall.
- Use a running bond pattern, as shown, with bricks laid one on top of two.
- Continually check with a straightedge, a level, and a carpenter's square to make sure the courses are straight.

6 Check courses

- Use a story pole to make sure you are maintaining consistently thick mortar joints.
- On the inside, roughly spread the excess mortar against the brick faces.

7 Joint

- Continually check the mortar by pressing gently with your thumb. When it holds an impression, it's time to joint.
- Use the jointing tool of your choice.
- Here, a simple straight jointer is used to smooth and compress the mortar. It will be brushed later.

8 Set address blocks

- At the predetermined height, spread mortar and set the address blocks.
- Center them exactly and check for plumb.

9 Fill inside

- To support the mailbox and provide extra rigidity, fill the inside with concrete blocks or bricks.
- Set them roughly in mortar. There's no need to be exact here.

10 Mailbox platform

- Set blocks or bricks at the right height for supporting the mailbox.
- You may need to roughly cut blocks or bricks, or spread extra-thick mortar, to reach the correct height.

11 Mailbox opening

- Cut bricks as needed to fill in around the mailbox opening.
- The mailbox itself, once installed, will help support the bricks above it.
- For now, use unmortared bricks to hold the mortared bricks in place temporarily.

12 Smooth top

- Because these bricks are rough-hewn, the top was a bit uneven.
- Use a grinder with a masonry bit to knock down the high spots.

13 Stone cap

- Make pencil marks on the bottom of the stone cap indicating the perimeter of the bricks.
- Spread plenty of mortar on top of the pillar and set the cap, using the lines as a guide.
- Tap the cap as needed to make it level in both directions.

14 Finish joints

- When the mortar gets a bit crumbly so it will not smear, sweep it with a masonry brush.
- Here, the brush is used a bit more heavily than usual, since it is actually a part of the jointing process.

15 Add mailbox

- Dry-fit the mailbox to determine how much mortar you need.
- Spread the mortar and slip the box into position.
- Finish the edges with caulk tinted to blend in with the mortar.

Brick Planter

This planter has occasional protruding bricks and openings for crevice plants. You may choose to incorporate cut stones, stacks of tiles, or other decorative elements. The only creative limitation is that the objects should be the same thickness as the bricks.

 Related Topics

Applying mortar, 64–65
Brick mailbox, 218–220
Forming & pouring a footing, 58–59
Mixing mortar, 62–63
Setting bricks, 214–215

How to Do It

1 Pour footing

- Use a dry run of bricks to determine the dimensions of the footing, which should be 2 inches wider than the planter.
- Dig a trench about a foot deep and 8 inches wide, then build a level form on top.
- Mix and pour concrete, then screed it level with a piece of lumber.

2 First course

- Wait a day for the footing to partially cure.
- Snap chalk lines to indicate the perimeter, then check for square.
- Set bricks in a dry run to determine the thickness of the mortar joints.
- Mix and spread Type S mortar (rated for ground contact) and set the first course.

3 Build gaps

- Lay the second course.
- When laying the third course, create planting gaps by omitting bricks.
- In the center of each gap, butter a decorative brick or block on its bottom and set it crosswise.

4 Lay & level

- Continue building courses.
- On a short project, there is no need for a story pole. Just check for level.
- Perhaps add more gaps and decorative bricks as you build.

5 Corbeled cap

- For a corbeled cap, overhang the top course by 1½ inches.
- You will need to cut a small filler brick for each side of the planter.
- Strike and brush the mortar, then wait a day before filling the interior.

6 Fill & plant

- Fill the interior, finishing it with garden or potting soil in the top 6 inches.
- Pack holes with small plants, then fill in the gaps with soil.
- Plant the interior.

Stackable Concrete Blocks

Many concrete block walls are made with all of the blocks set in mortar. An easier method is to simply stack the blocks, then cover the sides with a surface-bonding agent. You can use special interlocking blocks or standard concrete blocks.

This neat and elegant wall was easy to make with interlocking stackable blocks; no mortar was needed.

Choosing Blocks

At masonry yards and through online sources, you can find dry-stack blocks that can be assembled without mortar joints. Many types are available. They are generally shaped so they interlock, and they form a surprisingly strong wall even before you cover them with surface-bonding mortar. Some types have rods running through them horizontally. In many regions, these blocks are considered strong enough to form a foundation for a house. For a low wall, you can simply use standard concrete blocks, which will gain a good deal of strength once you apply the surface mortar.

How to Do It

Depending on how strong the wall needs to be, you may be able to simply stack the blocks and then apply the surface mortar. For added strength, run rebar vertically through the blocks, then fill those cells with "grout," the term used for mortar that is wet enough to pour easily.

❶ First course

- Pour a solid and level concrete footing about 6 inches wider than the blocks.
- Set the blocks in a dry run to determine where you will start.
- Throw a thick layer of mortar on the footing and set the bottom course in it.
- Use a solid-faced block at the end of the wall.

❷ Stack blocks

- Stack succeeding courses in a running bond pattern.
- Every two or three courses, check with a mason's line or a level for straightness.

Stuff to Buy

Cap blocks
Concrete
Concrete blocks
Mortar mix
Rebar

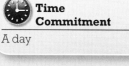

Time Commitment

A day

Tools You'll Need

Brick trowel
Flat trowel
Hoe
Level
Line blocks
Mason's line

Related Topics

Cutting bricks, pavers, & stone, 48–51
Decorative block wall, 228–229
Forming & pouring a footing, 58–59
Reinforced block wall, 224–225
Stuccoing a wall, 226–227

3 Shim

- If a block feels wobbly, go ahead and stack the next course. The weight of the added blocks may solve the problem.
- If it doesn't, remove some blocks and trowel mortar as needed to shim up one or more blocks.
- Or use small shims supplied by the block manufacturer.

4 Cap

- For a square-shaped top, use interlocking caps supplied by the manufacturer.
- Or spread mortar on the top course and lay solid cap blocks.
- For a rounded top, use the technique shown below.

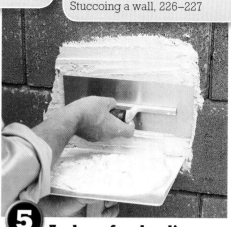

5 Apply surface bonding

- Mix a batch of surface-bonding mortar and place it on a hawk or a piece of plywood.
- Spray the wall with a mist of water and apply surface mortar.
- Work to achieve the stucco texture of your choice, as shown on pages 226–227.

Stacking Standard Blocks

A wall built with standard concrete blocks and no mortar joints will not be as strong as one made with interlocking blocks, but once you apply surface bonding it will be strong enough for a garden wall that is 4 feet tall. Start by forming and pouring a solid concrete footing.

Stack blocks

- Set the first course in a mortar bed.
- Use a level and a mason's line to make sure the blocks are level and straight.
- Stack succeeding courses in a running bond pattern, using line blocks and a line to check every other course.
- Shim the blocks as needed.

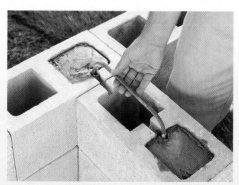

Anchor meeting walls

- To tie two walls together, chip out channels spanning from one block to the next.
- Bend a piece of rebar to fit.
- Fill cells with mortar and set rebar in mortar.
- Do this every other course.

Rounded cap

- For a rounded top, cut and lay wire mesh over the next-to-last course, or fill cells with tightly wadded newspaper.
- Fill the cells of the top course with mortar.
- Add more mortar and use a piece of flexible rubber to form and smooth the top.

Reinforced Block Wall

Building a strong block wall means running rebar up from the footing and through the block cells, then filling some cells with mortar. This does involve extra work, but it's not as complicated or difficult as you may think.

Wall Basics

This wall is in a warm climate, so the footing does not need to go below the frost line. It is also dry, so the blocks can be partway below grade, meaning the footing does not need to be formed to raise the wall above ground. Check with your building department to learn about local footing requirements.

Though it is a small, low wall, the builders went all out making it strong. A vertical rebar runs through every block, and all the blocks are filled with mortar. In effect, the blocks make a form for a nearly solid concrete wall. You may choose to run rebar and pour grout only at every third block or so.

① Prepare footing

- Mark the area to be excavated, using spray paint or a charged (water-filled) hose and flour.
- Dig a trench as required. If needed, build forms to raise the footing above grade.
- Poke some vertical rebar pieces into ground.
- Bend horizontal rebar pieces to follow the trench, and use spray paint to mark the positions of the remaining verticals.

② Pour concrete

- Mix concrete so it is barely pourable.
- Pour it into the formed area to the desired depth.
- Check for level and generally smooth the concrete with a wood or magnesium float.

③ Set blocks

- Allow at least a day for the concrete to partially cure.
- Remove the horizontal rebar. You will reattach it after you lay blocks below it.
- Throw a line of mortar onto the concrete and set the first course of blocks.
- Throw mortar onto the sides of the blocks and set the next course.
- Check for level and tap with a mallet where needed.

④ Cut & face blocks

- Use a grinder or another power tool to cut blocks as needed.
- To prepare for facing the wall with stone, use a flat trowel to apply a layer of mortar.
- Use a scarifying tool (or a piece of 2 × 2 with nails driven through it) to rough up the surface so the next layer of mortar adheres firmly.

⑤ Mortar stones

- Lay veneer stones in a dry run to determine where they will go.
- Cut stones as needed.
- Apply a coat of stiff mortar and press stones into it.

$ Stuff to Buy

Concrete
Concrete blocks
Facing stones
Mortar mix
Rebar

Time Commitment

Two days

Tools You'll Need

Mason's brush
Mixing tools
Rubber mallet
Scarifying tool
Shovel
Trowels

◎ Related Topics

Applying mortar, 64–65
Cutting bricks, pavers, & stone, 48–51
Forming & pouring a footing, 58–59
Mixing mortar, 62–63
Stone veneer, 204–205

6 Fill joints

- This wall features very large joints, so a trowel is used to scoop and press mortar between stones.
- Also use a gloved hand to press the mortar tight.
- Take care not to smear the stones. Wipe away smears quickly.

7 Fill top

- Carefully shovel mortar onto the top of the wall.
- Use a trowel to smooth it, taking care not to smear the stones below.

How the Pros Do It

"On a straight wall, you can usually easily space the vertical rebar correctly so it comes up through the holes in the blocks. On a curved wall, it's harder to measure. However, you can move rebar over an inch or two after the concrete has set. Just hit it at the bottom with a sledgehammer. The concrete will chip a bit, but that won't show once you lay the blocks."

Luis Salazar,
Salazar Custom Concepts

8 Sponge

- Use a large sponge to further smooth the wall's top and joints.
- Keep the sponge damp rather than wet, and rinse it out from time to time.

9 Brush

- Use a mason's brush to clean the stones.
- Dip the brush into water repeatedly so you apply clean water as you brush.

10 Finish

- Allow the mortar to dry, then clean the stones with a mild muriatic acid solution.

Stuccoing a Wall

You can cover a plain or even an ugly block or concrete wall with stucco, thereby transforming it into a mellow, undulating work of art. Stucco can be tinted, or you can paint it after applying it.

Stuccoing is an art that takes some time of time to learn. For the pattern shown here, create raised sections while applying the base coat, then use a thick roller or brush to apply the finish coat.

How to Do It

It will take a few hours of practice to get the hang of stuccoing. Fortunately, the base coat will be covered up. Before applying the finish coat, practice on a vertical piece of plywood or an obscure portion of the wall. That way, when you start applying the final coat, your strokes will produce a consistent-looking surface.

The masonry surface must be clean, and dry, and free of any loose material. If a brick wall is flaking or has produced the dusty white powder called efflorescence, correct the problem before proceeding.

1 First coat

- Coat the wall with latex bonding agent.
- Mix a batch of stucco base-coat mix in a wheelbarrow or trough to a stiff consistency.
- Place a shovelful on a hawk or a piece of plywood.
- Holding the hawk against the wall, scoop some stucco and slather it onto the wall.

2 Spread & scarify

- Press the stucco and spread it about ⅜ inch thick.
- When the stucco starts to stiffen, comb it with a scarifying tool.
- Aim to produce indentations without raising large crumbs.
- To allow the base coat to cure slowly, spray it with water regularly for two or three days.

3 Finish coat

- Mix a batch of finish-coat stucco, slightly wetter than the base coat.
- You may choose to add colorant for integral color.
- Spread the finish coat with a flat trowel, pressing it into the base coat's grooves and smoothing it to ⅜ inch thick.
- Produce the texture of your choice before the stucco starts to stiffen.

Stuff to Buy

Latex bonding agent
Stucco mix

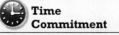

Time Commitment

Two days

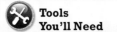

Tools You'll Need

Flat trowel
Mason's hawk
Mixing tools
Scarifying tool
Texture tools

Related Topics

Applying mortar, 64–65
Cleaning & sealing masonry, 284–285
Mixing mortar, 62–63
Stackable concrete blocks, 222–223

Key Techniques

Shape a corner

- At an outside corner, hold a piece of 1 × 4 tightly against the adjoining wall.
- Use a straight trowel to apply stucco up against the 1 × 4.

Control joint

- To control cracking, use a concrete jointer to cut vertical control joints.
- Space the joints about twice as far apart as the wall is high.

Textures

Stucco finishes are as individual as the workers who make them. Practice until you can apply your texture consistently. Start by applying a fairly smooth coat, then use your finishing technique when the stucco is just the right wetness.

For a modest, grainy texture, gently wipe with a grout float. Use a float with a sponge-like surface, not a laminated float. To create a spatter texture, mix a batch of wet stucco in a bucket. Dip a whisk broom into the stucco and flick the mixture at the wall. Once the wall is spattered, you may choose to make a knockdown texture by lightly running a pool trowel over the surface. You can create swirls using a mason's brush or a trowel while the stucco is still wet.

Grainy

Spatter

Brushed swirls   Knockdown   Troweled swirls

Decorative Block Walls

Degree of Difficulty

● Challenging

Decorative concrete blocks can hold back earth, as shown below, or they can be used to make a screen-like wall that lets in dappled light. The grille-block wall on these pages will allow air to circulate through it. You may want to build one to surround a garbage area.

Building a Grille-block Wall

This grille-block wall will have only one wythe, so it needs three kinds of reinforcement. Set the blocks between strong pilasters, set metal reinforcement in the mortar, and add a top cap made of pieces that span the joints between blocks.

None of the blocks can be cut to fit, so you must plan the footing with a determined number of full-size blocks in mind.

1 Footing & rebar

- Dig a trench and build a form for a footing.
- Set blocks in a dry run next to the form, then bend rebar pieces so they will run through the pilaster blocks.
- Pour the footing and make sure it is level.

Stuff to Buy

Cap blocks
Concrete
Concrete blocks
Mortar mix
Pilaster blocks
Rebar

Time Commitment

A couple of days

Tools You'll Need

Jointer
Mason's line
Mason's trowel
Mixing tools
Shovel

Related Topics

Applying mortar, 64–65
Forming & pouring a footing, 58–59
Mixing mortar, 62–63
Setting bricks, 214–215
Stackable concrete blocks, 222–223

❷ Build pilasters

- Cut additional pieces of rebar to the height of the pilasters and tie them with wire.
- Measure carefully to determine the position of the pilasters.
- Throw a bed of mortar onto the footing and set the bottom pilaster block. Check for level.
- Spread mortar onto the top of the block and build up the pilaster.
- Fill the cavity with fairly wet mortar as you go.

❸ Throw & butter mortar

- Snap chalk lines to indicate the outside edges of the blocks.
- Spread mortar ½ inch thick between the lines.
- Butter one side of a decorative block with a layer of mortar ½ inch thick. Furrow the mortar in the middle.

❹ Set first block

- Lower the block onto mortar bed, about 1 inch from the pilaster.
- Slide it over and press the buttered edge against the pilaster.
- Check for level and for alignment with the chalk lines.
- Scrape away excess mortar.

❺ Set bottom course

- Install the next blocks in the same way.
- Work from each end toward the middle.
- To install the closure block, butter both sides generously and slide the block straight down.

❻ Embed reinforcement

- Use mason's line and blocks to check for alignment as you lay additional courses.
- At the top of each course, throw a line of mortar and embed reinforcement in the mortar.
- Two pieces of ⅜-inch rebar were used here, but you can also use ladder-type block reinforcement.

❼ Install wall cap

- When the mortar is stiff enough to hold a thumbprint, strike the joints.
- Set the cap blocks in a bed of mortar.
- Once the mortar is stiff, brush the joints.

9

Water Features

In this chapter, you'll learn how to build a variety of garden fountains and pools. We give you information you need to choose pumps, filters, and liners—from rigid, pre-formed liners to flexible materials that let you customize your garden pond. For fountains, we show you everything from small bubblers that can be tucked into a corner of a yard to fountains that are a garden's focal point.

Chapter Contents

Flexible-liner Pool
page 242

page 242

Pumps & Filters

Inexpensive electrical pumps circulate water quietly and reliably. They can push water up through a fountain or cause it to run over rocks for a waterfall. Filters help maintain a clean, healthy pool by trapping dirt, algae, and fish waste.

Pumps

Have a garden pool salesperson help you choose a pump based on the size of your pool. You can use the same pump to serve more than one pool feature by adding a T fitting to the supply line, as long as the pump is powerful enough to handle the double duty.

Submersible pumps are the most popular choice for garden pools. They sit on the bottom of the pool and are usually quiet and unobtrusive. High-quality submersible pumps have stainless-steel shafts and sealed plastic housings, use no oil, and are quite energy efficient.

- A pump kit (top left) includes a pump, filter, and fountainhead. The one shown here is suitable for a small pool.
- An external pump (top right) moves large amounts of water quickly, making it ideal for a large waterfall.
- The large submersible pump shown (bottom left) is powerful enough to run water through a pool with waterfalls.
- A pump with an attached prefilter (bottom right) has a simple foam filter that helps keep the water clean. You will need to remove and wash or replace the filter from time to time.

Pump kit

External pump

Submersible pump

Pump with prefilter

Filters

Consult a garden pool salesperson for a filter that will work best with your pool. For a large pool with fish, you may choose a mechanical filter that passes water through a box or cylinder filled with activated carbon, foam, or fiber padding.

- A biological filter (left) circulates water through a filtering agent. The filter bed supports a colony of live bacteria that consume ammonia and harmful pathogens and convert them into elements useful for plants and fish. The system depends on a reliable pump that constantly pushes water through the filter.
- An ultraviolet clarifier (right top) uses ultraviolet radiation to rid a pool of virtually all algae, resulting in crystal-clear water. Both submersible and external versions are available.
- A chemical filter (right bottom) uses algicides and other water-cleaning agents to attack impurities. This method is often used in small garden pools with no plants or fish.

Biological filter

Ultraviolet clarifier

Chemical filter

Pebble & Boulder Fountains

For a magical effect, have a pump direct flowing water over pebbles or up through a boulder. A stone fountain has just a few working parts: a bowl, a pump, and tubing that leads to a fountain device, such as a spray nozzle or spout.

Pebble Fountain

A pebble fountain consists of an underground basin topped with a grate covered in decorative stones. A pump in the basin sprays water over the stones. The water then drains through the stones back into the basin.

Use thick wire mesh for the grate. It should overlap the basin by at least 6 inches all around. Purchase a pump, fountain nozzle, and all the pipe and adapters you need.

Dig a hole and fill it with a plastic basin or a liner that's at least 15 inches deep and 18 inches wide. Place the pump at the bottom near the center. Set stones in place and cut pipe to the correct height. Attach the pipe and the nozzle. Cut a hole in the mesh for the fountain, then cut another hole so you can reach in if you need to adjust the pump. Top the access hole with another piece of mesh.

Set stones and adjust the nozzle's height using a brick if needed. Fill the fountain with water, turn the pump on, and adjust the nozzle and pump pressure for the desired coverage. You'll need to refill the basin from time to time.

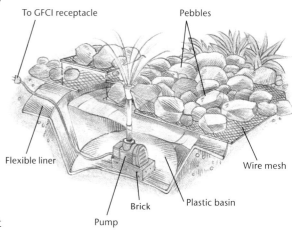

To GFCI receptacle · Pebbles · Flexible liner · Pump · Brick · Plastic basin · Wire mesh

Boulder Fountain

Some stone suppliers sell boulders already drilled for a fountain pipe, or will drill a boulder that you select (drilling a long masonry hole is difficult). Assembly is similar to that of a pebble fountain, except you need to pile concrete blocks into the basin as supports under the boulder. Protect the bottom of the basin by adding liner protection fabric or scraps of liner. If you want the fountain to gurgle and bubble rather than spray, don't install a spray fitting at the end of the pipe. If you want droplets, add a nozzle.

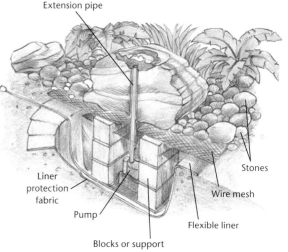

Extension pipe · Liner protection fabric · Pump · Blocks or support · Stones · Wire mesh · Flexible liner

Very Small Fountains

These projects are so small that you don't even need a backyard. You may choose to tuck a small fountain into a corner next to a chair or hammock to add the soothing sight and sound of flowing water to your home.

Container & Bamboo Fountain

This project can be adapted to any kind of watertight container. If your container is not watertight, apply a coat of clear pottery sealer made for water gardens. You can fill it with stones, shells, tiles, glass, or anything else that looks good wet. Bamboo is mostly hollow, so you could make your own pipe and spout by drilling it out. But the best option may be to buy a pre-assembled bamboo fountain at a garden shop, or type "bamboo fountain" into an Internet search engine.

1 Attach pump

- Determine the path that the electrical cord will follow.
- Attach the vinyl tubing to a small submersible pump.
- Place the pump at the bottom of the container, with a few rocks to hold it in place.

2 Add plant

- Choose a plant that grows in water, like this miniature umbrella plant.
- Place the plant in a submersible plant basket, with pebbles on top.
- Place the basket in the bottom of the container and surround it with rocks.

3 Install fountain

- Thread the tubing up through the bamboo and place it on the edge of the container.
- Cut any excess tubing and attach the spout.
- Position the spout so it points toward the rocks you want the water to hit.

4 Decorate & fill

- Add and arrange the rest of the rocks and decorative elements.
- Fill the fountain with water to the desired depth and plug in the pump.
- When the water evaporates, the pump may hum, indicating that you need to add water.

 **Stuff to Buy**

Concrete blocks
Containers
Pebbles, stones
Silicone sealant
Spout, tubing
Submersible pump
Water plants, dish
Wire mesh

 **Time Commitment**

An hour or so

 **Tools You'll Need**

Drill, masonry bit
Level
Shovel
Tin snips

 **Related Topics**

Pumps & filters, 232

Spill Fountain

This is only slightly more challenging than a container fountain. The trick is to bury a plastic container under pebbles so it catches the falling water and recirculates it back into the pot. Choose a pot with a slight texture and a color or glaze that looks good when wet, to emphasize the sheeting effect. If the pot does not have a drainage hole, you will need to bore one just large enough for the plastic tubing to pass through. The plastic container should be at least 3 inches wider than the pot.

1 Set plastic container

• Dig a hole 2 inches wider than the container and deep enough so the rim is at ground level.
• Place the container in the ground and check it for level.
• Tamp the surrounding soil firm.

2 Place the pump

• Place a block in the container to support the pot.
• Slip the tubing onto the fountain spout, then snake it toward the center of the container.
• Lead the pump cord toward the power source.

3 Install wire mesh

• Cut mesh at least 6 inches wider than the container.
• Cut a hole in the center for the vinyl tubing to pass through.
• Bend the cut wire mesh strands back so they do not poke the tubing.

4 Position the pot

• If the pot does not have a drainage hole, bore one for the tubing to pass through.
• Thread the tubing through the hole as you set the pot in place.
• Spread silicone sealant around the tubing and allow a day for it to cure.
• Spread pebbles to cover the mesh, fill the pot with water, and plug in the pump.

Planning a Pool

Plan a pool that fits the scale of your yard, whether it will be a central element or a less dominant feature. Choose a size to accommodate the plants and fish that will live in the pool.

How Deep?

The best depth for a garden pool depends largely on your climate and whether you plan to include fish. Talk with garden pool owners and suppliers in your area to find out what depths are most successful in your climate.

Pools shallower than 18 inches are difficult to stabilize. The water overheats in warm weather and cools quickly as soon as the temperature falls. Plants and fish do not appreciate such rapid fluctuations. On the other hand, pools as deep as 5 feet take a long time to warm up in spring, limiting plant and fish growth.

It is important to maintain a reasonable ratio between pool depth and surface area. As one grows, so should the other. The recommended minimum depths (directly below) apply to standard, modestly sized pools. Make adjustments for larger pools. As a general rule, an 18-inch minimum depth is fine for pools with up to 50 square feet of surface area. For larger pools, increase the depth to at least 24 inches.

To create the best environment for a variety of plants and fish, design your pool with varied depths. Cut out one or more shelves from the side of the pool before installing the liner.

Depending on the size of your pool, your local building department may consider it either a "swimming pool" or an "attractive nuisance." In this case, you will need to obtain permits and have two or more inspections of the excavation and installation. You may be required to install a fence around the pool.

Minimum depth for a pool containing plants or fish — 18"

Minimum depth for a cold-climate pool if you want to overwinter plants — 24"–30"

Minimum depth for raising koi — 36"–48"

How Much Water?

You need to know the gallon capacity of a pool in order to correctly choose a pump, the right amounts of fish and plants, and the filter and treatment system.

If you install a rigid liner, its label will tell you how much water it holds. But if you plan to shape your own pool with a flexible liner, you'll need to pull out the calculator. The illustrations below show the basic calculations. If a pool has a complicated shape, determine the average length, width, and depth and use the appropriate formula. Or divide the pool into simpler shapes, calculate the volume of each, and add them together.

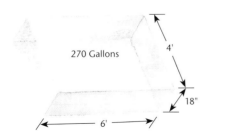
270 Gallons · 4' · 18" · 6'

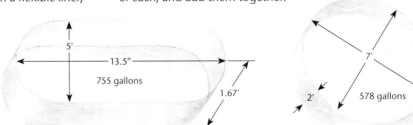
5' · 13.5" · 755 gallons · 1.67'

7' · 2' · 578 gallons

Rectangular: length × width × depth × 7.5,
6' × 4' × 1.5' × 7.5 = 270 gallons
(surface area = 24 square feet)

Oval: length × width × depth × 6.7
13.5' × 5' × 1.67' × 6.7 = 755 gallons
(surface area = 53 square feet)

Circular: length × width × depth × 5.9,
7' × 7' × 2' × 5.9 = 578 gallons
(surface area = 38.5 square feet)

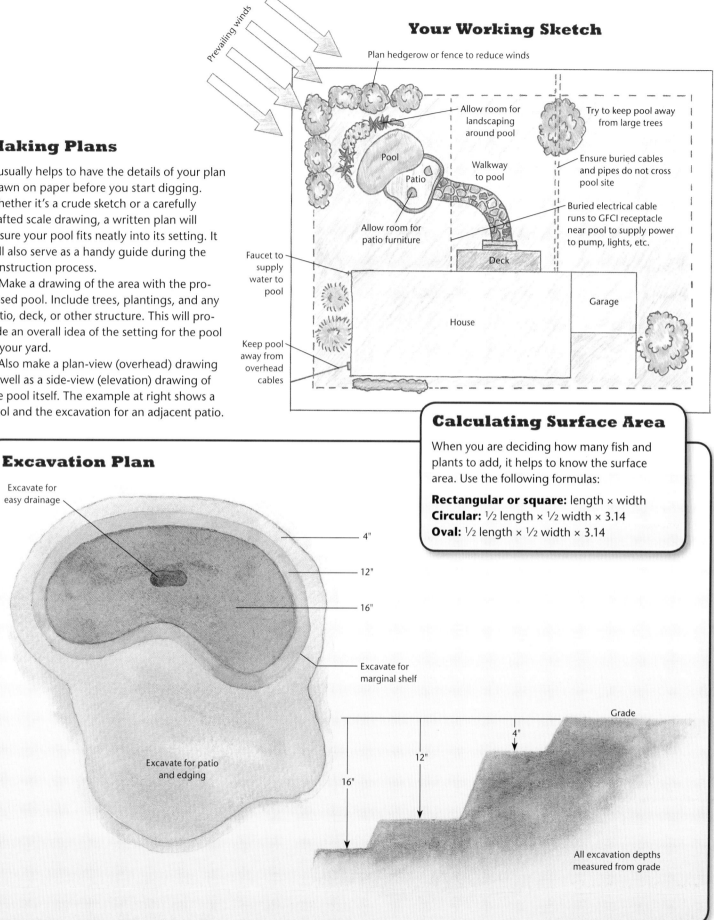

Your Working Sketch

Prevailing winds

Plan hedgerow or fence to reduce winds

Allow room for landscaping around pool

Try to keep pool away from large trees

Pool

Patio

Walkway to pool

Ensure buried cables and pipes do not cross pool site

Allow room for patio furniture

Buried electrical cable runs to GFCI receptacle near pool to supply power to pump, lights, etc.

Faucet to supply water to pool

Deck

Garage

House

Keep pool away from overhead cables

Making Plans

It usually helps to have the details of your plan drawn on paper before you start digging. Whether it's a crude sketch or a carefully crafted scale drawing, a written plan will ensure your pool fits neatly into its setting. It will also serve as a handy guide during the construction process.

Make a drawing of the area with the proposed pool. Include trees, plantings, and any patio, deck, or other structure. This will provide an overall idea of the setting for the pool in your yard.

Also make a plan-view (overhead) drawing as well as a side-view (elevation) drawing of the pool itself. The example at right shows a pool and the excavation for an adjacent patio.

Excavation Plan

Excavate for easy drainage

4"

12"

16"

Excavate for marginal shelf

Excavate for patio and edging

Calculating Surface Area

When you are deciding how many fish and plants to add, it helps to know the surface area. Use the following formulas:

Rectangular or square: length × width
Circular: ½ length × ½ width × 3.14
Oval: ½ length × ½ width × 3.14

Grade

4"

12"

16"

All excavation depths measured from grade

Fountains

Fountains entertain with sound and motion, and they aerate pool water, providing oxygen for plants and fish. Once you've chosen the right fountain materials, installation is usually not difficult.

Spray Fountains for Pools

Even a large, gushing fountain does not use much water. A pump draws water from the pool and feeds it to the fountain, which returns it to the pool to be recycled.

Generally, the pool's diameter should be at least twice the spray's height. Install the fountain jet just above the water level. Be aware that some plants need placid water in order to thrive, so position them well away from the spray. Most fish will avoid the area near a fountain, although the aeration provided by moving water is good for them.

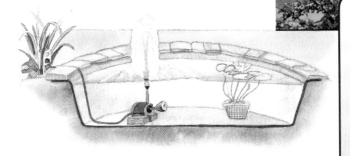

Design Tips

Spray fountains have heads that shoot water upward in patterns ranging from massive columns to delicate and nearly unnoticeable mists. Some general design tips:

- Use a short, heavy column of water in windy spots. Go for height, distance, or drama only where the spray will not blow widely.
- Position a spray fountain against a background that dramatizes the movement of water. A dark background is usually preferable.
- Fine sprays look best when playing against a flat surface, such as a nearby masonry wall.

Spray Patterns

Popular fountain spray heads include various dome shapes, swiveling jets, multi-tiered patterns, and spray rings with adjustable jets. Some pumps come with two or more interchangeable heads. You can also buy heads and pumps separately.

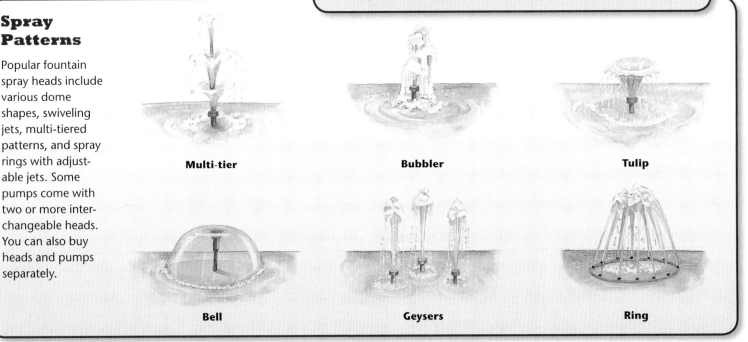

Multi-tier

Bubbler

Tulip

Bell

Geysers

Ring

 Stuff to Buy	Time Commitment	Tools You'll Need	Related Topics
Fountain mask Pump Tubing	A few hours	Drill Level	Anchoring to masonry, 290–291 Pebble & boulder fountains, 233 Pumps & filters, 232

Spill Fountains

Spill fountains emphasize the sound of falling water. The simplest type is a water stream that pours into a pool or container. The stream may pour directly into a pool or travel through a fountain statue. You can also direct water onto spill pans, available at garden supply stores. Water will cascade down from one pan to the next, ending in a pool at the bottom.

To install a wall fountain, as shown on this page, purchase a fountain mask, or drill a hole in just about anything that can attach to a wall. Run the tubing through or behind the wall and have the water spill into a basin below, where you will install the pump.

1 Prepare mask

- Lay the mask facedown on a soft surface.
- Drill a hole at a 45-degree upward angle for hanging the mask (see step 3).
- If the tube will run down the face of the wall, glue corks to the mask to allow space for the tube.
- If no hole exists for the spout, use a glass or masonry bit to drill a hole large enough for the tube fitting.

2 Connect tubing

- Slip an elbow fitting into a short piece of tubing that will emerge from the mask.
- Slip the other end into tubing long enough to reach the pump in the basin or attach the fitting behind or inside the wall.

3 Hang mask

- Drill a 1½-inch-deep hole at a 45-degree upward angle into the brick wall.
- Slide a 3-inch-long dowel into the hole.
- Hang the mask on the wall by sliding it over the other half of the dowel.

4 Connect pump

- Wind the tubing through vines and down the wall, or behind or through the wall, drilling holes as needed.
- Slide the other end of the tubing over a submersible pump's outlet and place it in the basin.
- Fill the basin with water and plug the pump into a GFCI receptacle.

Rigid-liner Pool

The easiest way to build an in-ground pool is with a rigid liner. The liner is not much to look at, but it is easy to cover with edging stones and plants.

How to Do It

Liners come in a variety of shapes and range from 12 to 35 square feet. Most are 18 inches deep. Some models have built-in waterfalls and small streams. A ¼-inch-thick fiberglass or polyethylene liner will last 30 to 50 years. A thinner liner may last only 10 years. A thick liner is especially recommended for an above-grade installation.

Don't start digging until you have the liner on site, so you can accurately mark and dig for the outlines of the pool as well as the various levels. If the liner is heavy, you may choose to make a cardboard or newspaper template of it.

Plants help disguise liner

Edges must be perfectly level

Short, rigid edges can be tricky to conceal

Hole must be carefully backfilled after liner is installed

Edging must have solid base

Level sand base supports liner

Careful excavation and compacted soil create a firm foundation

Keeping It Clean

In many regions, a modest solar pump plus some plants, like floating duckweed, will keep algae in check and the water clean. However, consult the pool dealer. You may need a more powerful pump with a built-in filter, or even a separate filter. In that case, you will need to have a nearby GFCI receptacle to plug into.

1 Trace outline

- Remove any sod and roots from the area.
- Set the liner in place and use a level to mark the outline in the soil.
- Pour flour or sand, or use spray paint, to clearly mark the outlines.

2 Dig

- Dig the hole 2 inches deeper than the liner to accommodate a layer of sand.
- Use a level to check the pool as you work.
- Add sand and set the pool in place.

Stuff to Buy

Edging stones
Plants
Pump with fountain
Rigid liner
Sand

Time Commitment

A full day

Tools You'll Need

Level
Shovel
Stone-cutting tools

Related Topics

Cutting stones, 48–51
Fountains, 238–239
Planning a pool, 236–237
Pumps & filters, 232

3 Level pool

- The pool should be level in all directions.
- Level the pool, then slowly fill it with water.
- As the pool fills, backfill the outside with sand along the perimeter.
- Use soil to create a slope away from the pool's edges.

4 Set edging stones

- Install the pump and perhaps the filter.
- Set large flagstones around the pool.
- Overhang the stones a couple of inches inside the pool.

5 Add plants

- Finish installing the pump and fountain, with the fountain head just above water level.
- Place plants in plant baskets and arrange them in the pool.
- Add nearby plantings that will not drop much debris into the pool.

Solar Pump & Fountain

A small photovoltaic panel powers the submersible pump for this pool. To operate properly, a solar panel must be placed in a sunny, south-facing spot near the pool. This pump comes with a variety of spray heads that generate gentle streams of water, just right for a small pool.

Flexible-liner Pool

If you want a fairly large pool or have a pool shape in mind, use a flexible liner to create the pool of your choosing. The pool shown here has a stacked-stone waterfall that is simple but pleasing.

Underlayment Options

The underlayment material is anything that will protect your liner. If your soil does not contain sharp rocks or large invasive roots, you can use newspaper or old carpeting. For more protection, use an inexpensive liner material.

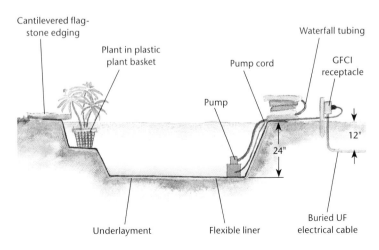

How to Do It

Using a flexible liner may allow you to install a fairly large pool in a tight space, as is the case with this long, narrow pool.

You may need to shop around in order to gather all the materials. For the pool shown on the next four pages, the liner and underlayment came from a pool supplier. The pebbles and flagstones were purchased at a landscaping source, and a home center carried the pump, tubing, electrical supplies, and tools.

The pump needs to be powered by a GFCI electrical receptacle. Plan this before you start digging. If you do not have a nearby receptacle, see page 245 for some tips on installing one.

Cantilevered flag-stone edging
Plant in plastic plant basket
Pump cord
Waterfall tubing
GFCI receptacle
Pump
12"
24"
Underlayment
Flexible liner
Buried UF electrical cable

1 Lay out shape

- Lay a garden hose on the ground in the desired shape of your future pool.
- Check the shape at various times to get a good idea of how the sun and shadows will hit the pool at different times of day, and make adjustments.
- Once you've settled on a shape, mark the ground with spray paint or by sprinkling flour over the hose and then picking it straight up.

 **Stuff to Buy**

Clear plastic tubing
EPDM liner
Flagstones
Pebbles
Plants
Pump with fountain
PVC pipe and fittings
UF cable, box, and fittings
Underlayment

 **Time Commitment**

Two days

 Tools You'll Need

Saber saw

 **Related Topics**

2 Remove organic material

- Remove any plantings or sod inside the pool area.
- If you want to reuse a planting, dig a fairly wide and deep hole around it, place it on a plastic tarp, and keep the roots moist.

3 Dig hole

- Excavate the entire pool area to the minimum depth—here, the marginal shelf that runs along the perimeter.
- Set aside some of the topsoil to be reused to level the edges of the pool later on (step 5).

4 Mark depths

- Arrange pieces of wire or rope to indicate the areas that will be deeper.
- Make sure any shelves will be wide enough for plants.
- Use spray paint or flour to mark the holes, then dig.

5 Level edges

- Mound soil up around the perimeter to make it easier to level.
- Position a straight 2 × 4 atop the mounded soil and check for level in all directions.
- Add or remove soil as needed.

6 Install underlayment

- Use any underlayment material that will keep rocks or roots from cutting the liner.
- If the soil is rocky, dig 2 inches deeper and add a 2-inch layer of sand.
- Spread the underlayment over the area, working to minimize folds.
- Use rocks or soil to keep the underlayment in place.

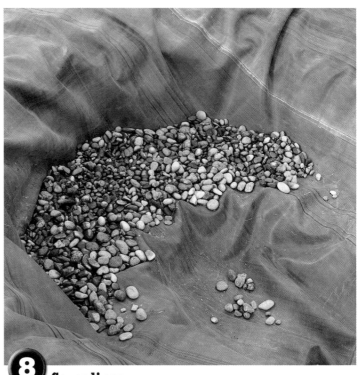

7 Spread liner

- A sturdy EPDM liner is heavy, so work with one or two helpers.
- The liner can stretch once filled with water, but work to follow the contours of the hole to minimize stretching.
- Push the liner into the deepest spot and then work upward.
- Use stones to hold the liner in place.

8 Cover liner

- Spread smooth pebbles over the liner.
- Do this especially in the shallower areas to keep herons or raccoons from poking holes with their talons or claws.
- Run tubing from the pump area in the pool toward the connections (steps 11 and 12).

9 Stack waterfall

- Line the waterfall with the same EPDM liner as the rest of the pool.
- Set large, smooth flagstones on the bottom for a firm base.
- Dry-stack more stones, tilting them slightly toward the pool.
- Create a cave effect in some areas.

10 Test water flow

- Place a hose near where the tubing will be, then turn on the water.
- Make sure water flows into the pool and not backward.
- Adjust the stacked stones to achieve a pleasing waterfall effect.

11 Connect plumbing

- Anchor a short post to provide a firm place for attaching the tubing and fittings.
- Use reducer fittings and perhaps a T if you want to have two water sources.
- Connect the tubing from the pool, then the tubing pieces that run to the waterfall.

12 Prepare pump

- Decide on the exact position of the submersible pump and cut the tubing to length.
- Secure the tubing with a stainless-steel hose clamp.
- Run the pump's cord from the pool toward the electrical receptacle.
- Set the pump in a bed of pebbles.

13 Fill pool

- Run a hose into the pool and turn on the water to fill the pool slowly.
- Wearing rubber boots, stand in the pool and tug on the liner to minimize large, thick wrinkles.
- Particularly unsightly wrinkles can be covered with rocks or plants.

14 Lay stone edging

- Trim several feet of liner at a time, then stack stones so they just barely cover the liner.
- Dry-stack flagstones in two or more layers to cover more of the liner.
- Plug in the pump and add water plants and more pebbles.

Pool Wiring

If a GFCI receptacle is nearby, you can run the cord, or a thick extension, to it. But codes may require you to install new wiring. Be sure to shut off power at the service panel before making any electrical connections, and use wiring methods that are approved by local codes. Unless you are an experienced electrician, either hire a professional or consult *Sunset's You Can Build: Wiring* for complete instructions on planning and running new outdoor electrical service.

   In the photo on the left, UF cable is run through plastic conduit. Connect conduit fittings using the correct primer and cement, and run the conduit 8 inches or more underground, depending on local codes. Firmly plant a post to hold the new watertight electrical box (right). Strip and attach wires to a GFCI receptacle, then install an in-use cover to keep it dry while the pump is plugged in. Connect to power at the other end and restore power.

10

Outdoor Kitchens

In this chapter, we show you how to execute one of the most popular backyard-masonry projects, the built-in barbecue. You'll learn about the appliances that can transform your barbecue area into an outdoor kitchen, the choices you have when it comes to counters, and the shapes you may want to consider. Basic information about the plumbing and wiring required for your outdoor kitchen is also covered.

Chapter Contents

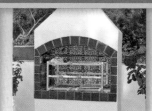

Outdoor Kitchen Features

Today's outdoor kitchens are extensions of the home, with large grills (gas or charcoal), easy-to-clean counters, cabinet space, sinks, refrigerators, and overhead structures. Some people take it even further by adding a wood-burning pizza oven.

Grills & Appliances

Many grills are designed to be set into a counter. For some people, charcoal is the only way to go, but a gas grill is easier to start and to keep clean. You can place a propane tank under the counter to supply gas to your grill. Or, if you do a lot of cooking, run a natural gas line from the house. Buy a sturdy unit with a good warranty, and take it apart to make sure it will be easy to clean.

If you'd like more cooking versatility, consider adding an infrared cooking unit, which directs very high heat at meat to sear it quickly. You can also buy a warming unit with drawers to hold food that has been cooked. And an outdoor sink reduces the number of trips you need to make inside for food prep.

Building in Stages

It's often possible to start small with the idea of adding on later. For instance, start by building a simple attached counter with a barbecue. As you find your appetite whetted, perhaps extend the counter to offer more food-prep space. Later, if space and budget permit, add a pizza oven, an upright oven, or other features.

Manufacturers offer grills with side burners so you can fry, boil, or sauté while you tend to the main dish.

A small refrigerator is a major convenience and completes the functionality of an outdoor kitchen.

Counters & Countertops

When it comes to materials, there are lots of options for the structure. Choose from concrete block, formed and poured concrete, steel or wood studs covered with concrete backerboard, or brick. Once the structure is built, face it with natural stone, faux stone, ceramic tile, stone tile, or stucco. An outdoor counter must be built carefully so that the grill, appliances, and doors will fit.

By installing a door in a counter, you gain access to the cavity inside, where you can store cooking implements, charcoal, or perhaps a propane tank. If you have a sink, you will need to access the plumbing. Purchase cabinet doors from a manufacturer that specializes in outdoor-kitchen products. Stainless steel is the most popular choice, but also consider black powder-coated units, which are a bit easier to keep clean.

Pizza Ovens

A wood-fired pizza oven produces pizza crusts and breads with a distinctively crunchy texture and a slightly smoky flavor. Building one is a major project, however. Typically, you buy an insert made of refractory concrete or special Italian clay. Then you house it in a massive concrete structure, with a roof, to support and insulate the insert. You may be out a cool five grand before you get that first bite of pizza. Still, many people find the taste and the experience of wood baking to be worth the expense and trouble.

GRANITE SLAB

STONE SLAB

DECORATIVE CONCRETE

FLAGSTONE

The Basic Bones

Building a multi-appliance kitchen calls for careful planning and the skills of several trades. Check with your building department to make sure you comply with structural, electrical, and plumbing codes.

Utility Lines

A full-service kitchen may require a gas line, conduit for electrical wiring, water supply pipes, and a drain line. Most people hire pros to dig the trenches, run the lines, and make the hookups to the house. In many areas you can install pipes in trenches 12 inches deep, but your building department may require deeper trenches. Codes may require you to insulate some of the pipes. Check with your utility companies before digging, so you do not damage existing lines.

Four lines

- This trench has ABS drainpipe, black gas pipe, copper cold-water supply (install a tankless water heater inside the cabinet if you want hot water), and PVC conduit for the electrical line.
- Your codes may call for different materials, such as PVC instead of ABS for the drain.
- Have the plan approved by your building department. You will need the trenches, the pipe, and the hookups to the house inspected before you can cover the pipes.

Ready for the pour

- A masonry counter needs to be supported with a strong concrete slab.
- Here, rebar is installed along with the utility lines.
- The rebar is bent up at the perimeter so it can run through the counter's concrete blocks.

Drain line

- Depending on local codes and your planned use for the sink, a drain line may need to be connected to your home's main drain.
- Because the sink will drain only gray water, which is not toxic, you may be able to run the wastewater into a dry well.
- This simple dry well consists of a hole, a large perforated bucket, and stones.
- After inspection, cover with three layers of landscaping fabric or plastic, soil, and sod.

Pouring & finishing the footing

- See pages 58–59 and 170–179 for Steps on forming and pouring a concrete footing or slab.
- Check that the utility lines will end up inside the counter.
- To hold the lines in place while you pour and finish the concrete, anchor them to lumber scraps as shown.

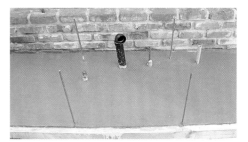

Allow to cure

- In the example shown above, the black drain line and the copper supply line are near the rear of the counter's cavity.
- The gas line is more in the middle, and the vertical rebar pieces are placed where the concrete block will be installed.

Masonry Counters

See pages 222–223 for steps on building a concrete block wall. A counter wall has lots of openings, for the doors, grill, and other appliances. Before you build, make a drawing that shows where each block will go, with exact dimensions for the openings.

Build with blocks

- Allow the concrete footing or slab to cure, then snap layout lines for the counter.
- As you set blocks in concrete, keep careful track of where the doors, grill, and other appliances will go.
- Reinforce the corners with bent rebar, and fill at least some of the cells with mortar.

Angle iron at lintels

- At the lintel (the top of an opening), install angle iron for support.
- If you cannot install the angle iron on top of a block on either side, use a circular saw or grinder with a masonry blade to cut a channel you can slide the lintel into.
- Check the opening to make sure the door or appliance will fit.
- Throw mortar onto the lintel and set blocks in the mortar as needed.

Install electrical boxes

- Conduit may be run inside the counter's cavity or through the cells of the blocks.
- For an electrical box, use a circular saw or a grinder to cut the opening.
- Install the box so it protrudes the thickness of the stones, tile, or other finish material.
- Attach the conduit.
- Use shims to wedge the box tight, then fill in around it with mortar.

Framed Counters

A concrete-block structure makes a very strong counter, but a framed counter will be tough enough for most purposes. Because framing is much lighter than concrete blocks, you can install it on a deck or a thin slab. Check with local codes, as you may be required to use metal studs, which will not catch fire. As you build, periodically check that the doors and appliances will fit into the openings. The frame will be unstable as you build, especially if you are using metal studs. The backerboard will firm it up.

Build with metal studs

- Cut metal studs using tin snips.
- Use channels for the horizontal pieces, and use studs, which fit into the channels, for the verticals.
- At the ends, cut channels so they have "ears," flaps that can be screwed to studs.
- Fasten pieces by driving self-tapping screws made for metal studs.

Add backerboard

- Cut pieces of concrete backerboard to fit.
- In some cases, it's easier to make cuts after the boards are attached.
- Check the structure for square, then attach it with backerboard screws.

Building with wood studs

- As long as the grill or appliances will not be very hot, you can frame it with wood.
- Use pressure-treated wood to prevent rot.
- Continually check for square to make sure the doors and appliances will fit.
- Secure the framing with decking screws.
- Attach backerboard screws with a drill.

Finishing a Counter

Once the lines are roughed in and the counter's structure is built, you can set the countertop, finish the outside of the counter, and install the grill, appliances, and any electrical devices.

Sides & Top

If you choose a granite slab top, have a granite company take measurements and install the top. The company may also install the sink, grill, and other appliances that rest on top. For a tile top, install cross braces every 16 inches or so across the top of the framing or the blocks. Cut and lay two layers of half-inch concrete backerboard, attaching them to the frame and to each other using thinset mortar. The top should overhang the finished sides of the counter by 2 inches or so.

Tiling the sides

- To apply ceramic or stone tile to blocks or backerboard, mix and trowel on thinset mortar.
- Set the tiles in the mortar, using spacers to maintain consistent grout joints.
- Once the mortar has hardened, fill the joints with grout.

Using stone or faux stone

- Faux stone is easier to apply than real stone, because it is light and has special corner pieces.
- Apply mortar to the counter and set the stones in the mortar.
- Use a grinder to cut the stones as needed.
- Fill the joints with mortar.

Stuccoing

- Buy bags of base-coat and finish-coat stucco.
- Apply a base coat to backerboard or block, and use a scarifying tool to etch it with lines.
- Allow the base coat to cure slowly, then apply the finish coat, using the finishing technique of your choice.

Under-counter Connection

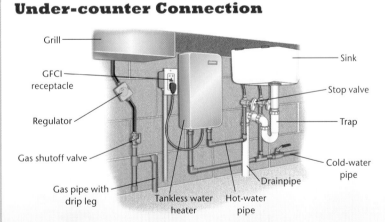

Grill
GFCI receptacle
Regulator
Gas shutoff valve
Gas pipe with drip leg
Tankless water heater
Hot-water pipe
Drainpipe
Sink
Stop valve
Trap
Cold-water pipe

Under-counter hookups may include a small on-demand water heater, which plugs into an electrical receptacle. Here we show a gas line connected to a gas pipe that leads to the house, but you may choose to power your grill with a small propane tank. For the sink, there are connections for the water supply lines and the drain trap.

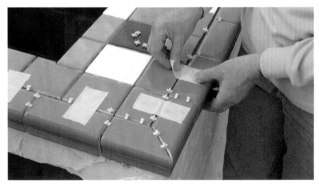

Tiling a top

- Use countertop tiles that are made for outdoor use.
- Cut tiles to fit and lay them in a dry run. Make sure the sink and grill will fit.
- Remove a section of tiles, apply thinset mortar with a notched trowel, and set the tiles in the mortar.
- Use spacers and pieces of tape to hold the tiles in place.
- After the thinset has hardened, fill the joints with grout.

Related Topics

Stone veneer, 204–205
Stuccoing a wall, 226–227
Tiles on concrete, 162–165

Installing Sinks & Grills

Install stop valves for the water, as well as a gas shutoff valve for the gas line, and test to make sure there are no leaks. Make as many plumbing, gas, and electrical hookups as possible before setting the grill and appliances in place. It's easier to work from above than from under the counter. You will need to buy flexible water supply lines, parts for the drain trap, and flexible gas supply lines. Make sure they are long enough. You'll want to caulk carefully around the grill and sink, but be aware that some water is bound to enter the inside of any outdoor cabinet during a strong rainstorm.

Hook up sink lines

- Attach at least some of the sink's trap, as well as the flexible water supply lines.
- Tighten all parts firmly.

Set the sink

- Set the sink in place temporarily and check that the lines will reach.
- Apply a generous amount of caulk to the sink's rim, then set the sink into the opening.
- Tighten the mounting screws and wipe away any excess caulk.

Plumbing hookups

- From below, tighten the nuts at the ends of the supply lines onto the stop valves.
- Open the valves to test for leaks.
- Cut parts as needed and attach the trap pieces.
- Fill the sink with water, then pull the plug and test for leaks

Installing a grill

- Install the flexible gas line, if there is one, onto the grill.
- Temporarily set the grill in place.

Caulk the grill

- Once you are sure of the fit, apply a generous amount of caulk to the grill's flange.
- Connect the gas line to a pipe or to a propane tank.

Attaching doors & appliances.

- Test-fit all doors and appliances.
- Apply caulk to flanges.
- Drive stainless-steel or decking screws through the doors or appliances into the counter.
- If the counter is masonry, use masonry screws.

Winged Counter

This counter has enough cooking power to serve a large group, plus it provides space for a few guests to scoot up to the counter and nosh while talking to the cook. Each wing is at a 45-degree angle to the center counter.

What You Need to Know

An island like this should sit at the center of a patio rather than up against the house, so it can be prominently on display. Here, the materials have been chosen to complement the colors of the patio. The faux stones that cover the sides of counter, and the tiles for the top, are darker than the patio stones, but they are of the same color family.

Check local codes to find out how thick a concrete footing you need. The counter shown is built of 6-inch concrete block, with steel reinforcement every 16 inches. (You could build with steel studs instead, in which case the footing would not need to be massive.) Because the countertop cantilevers 10 inches at the dining area, a substrate made of concrete backerboard would not be strong enough. Instead, this counter's substrate is a formed and poured reinforced concrete slab.

For the sink, run a water supply line from the house. You may choose to add a tankless water heater inside the counter, or just live with cold water only. (Running a hot-water line all the way from the house would not be energy-efficient.) Run a sink drain into the house drain or into a dry well. An electrical line is needed for the receptacle and two lights. You can run a gas line, or hook up to a propane tank inside the cabinet.

Purchase the sink, appliances, and doors ahead of time so you can build the counter walls and the countertop to fit around them.

WINGED COUNTER SUBSTRUCTURE

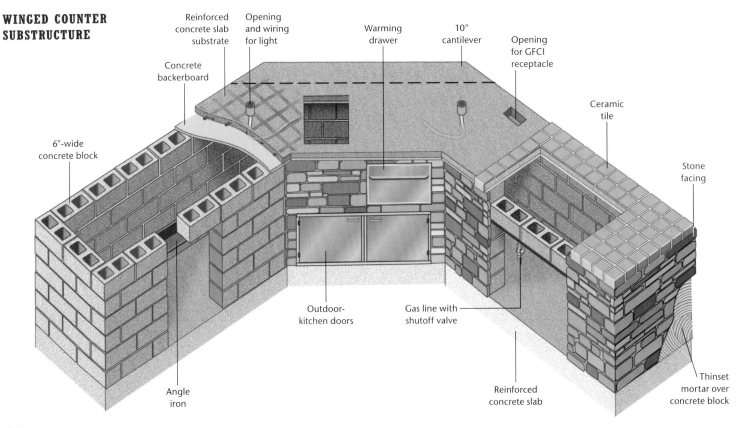

Reinforced concrete slab substrate

Opening and wiring for light

Warming drawer

10" cantilever

Opening for GFCI receptacle

Ceramic tile

Concrete backerboard

Stone facing

6"-wide concrete block

Outdoor-kitchen doors

Gas line with shutoff valve

Angle iron

Reinforced concrete slab

Thinset mortar over concrete block

Stuff to Buy

Concrete and reinforcement for
  the footing
Concrete block, mortar, and
  angle iron
Gas, electrical, and plumbing
  lines and shutoff valves
Sink and plumbing supplies
Stainless-steel grill, side burner,
  and doors

**Time
Commitment**

Several weekends

**Tools
You'll Need**

Cutting tools
Shovels
Trowels

**Related
Topics**

Calculating concrete needs,
  170–171
Finishing a counter, 252–253
Forming & pouring a footing,
  58–59
Reinforced block wall, 224–225
Stone veneer, 204–205
The basic bones, 250–251

How to Do It

ABOUT THE FOOTING

Excavate and frame for a concrete footing
at the same height as the patio. Run the
utility lines, and make sure they poke up at
the most convenient locations. Strengthen
the slab by running rebar through the footing in a grid pattern. Bend the rebar to run
vertically through the blocks. Pour the footing and allow it to cure slowly.

ABOUT THE WALLS

As you build the concrete block walls, set
reinforcement wire every other course. Use
angle irons to support the blocks that span
the doorways. Check that the doors, sink,
and appliances will fit. Fill at least some of
the cells with concrete or mortar. Before
you start on the countertop substrate, add
as many utility valves and connections as
possible.

ABOUT THE COUNTER

Cut pieces of concrete backerboard to fit
so they will overhang the finished counter
by 10 inches on the eating side and by
2 inches everywhere else. Set the backerboard in mortar on top of the counter.
Cut holes for the light fixtures and the
receptacle. Construct a form of 2 × 4s
anchored against the edges of the backerboard. Create openings for the light fixtures
and the receptacle using plastic pipe or
pieces of 1-by lumber. Cut and prop five or
six 2 × 4s below the overhanging section to
hold it in place during the pour. Install steel
reinforcement bar and pour the slab. Wait
several days before removing the props
and tiling the top.

FINISHING

Install faux stones to cover the vertical surfaces, and cover the top with tiles. Hook up
the utilities before you install the doors and
appliances.

Curved Counter with Granite Top

The counter is curved very gently—only 4 inches over a span of 11 feet—but this
slight deviation has a surprising visual impact. While the counter is curved, the countertop is rectangular, so the top overhangs the counter more in some places than in
others. The grill is front and center—where the overhang is most pronounced—
thereby de-emphasizing the difference in shape between counter and top.

   The homeowners who built this structure wanted an uncluttered effect, so they
opted for only one door directly below the grill. This limits usable storage space.
You may choose to add two more doors, one on each side of the grill.

   The only utility line is a gas pipe for the grill and the side burner. If you choose
propane-fired appliances, you would not have to run any utility lines.

CURVED COUNTER SUBSTRUCTURE

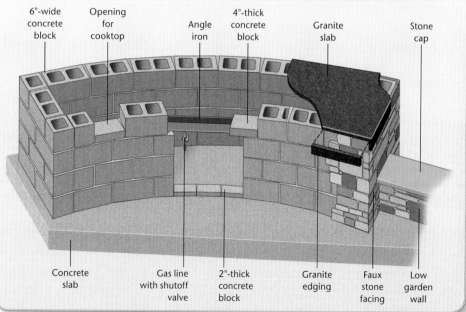

6"-wide concrete block | Opening for cooktop | Angle iron | 4"-thick concrete block | Granite slab | Stone cap

Concrete slab | Gas line with shutoff valve | 2"-thick concrete block | Granite edging | Faux stone facing | Low garden wall

Stackable Churrasco Barbecue

✔ **Degree of Difficulty**
● Moderate

By assembling a kit and covering it with stucco and decorative tiles, you can build a barbecue that is attractive and easy to use. Your rewards will be tender and juicy burgers, chicken, ribs, and other meats.

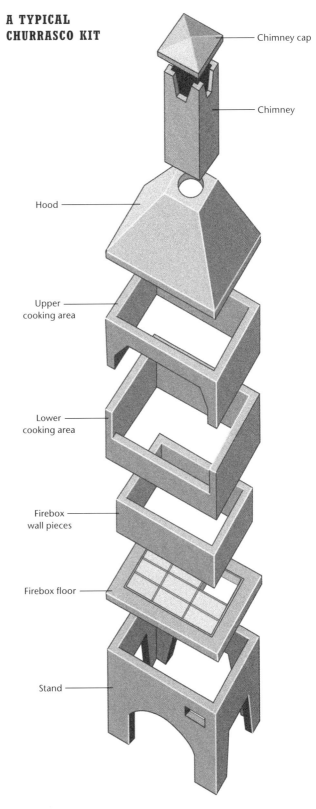

A TYPICAL CHURRASCO KIT

- Chimney cap
- Chimney
- Hood
- Upper cooking area
- Lower cooking area
- Firebox wall pieces
- Firebox floor
- Stand

About the Design

Churrasco barbecue was invented in South America and has gained a loyal following in the United States. It is basically a fireplace with its firebox at a convenient height for cooking. You build a small fire of wood or charcoal under a rotisserie, with two or more spits at graduated heights above the heat. Oven-like walls radiate the heat, cooking the meat on all the spits from all sides at once, thereby sealing in the juices and making the meat exceptionally tender.

You can order a churrasco kit online. It is made of special refractory concrete. The unit weighs about a ton, so first pour a substantial reinforced concrete footing for it to rest on.

Stuff to Buy

Churrasco barbecue kit
Materials for concrete footing
Metal lath
Stucco mix
Tiles

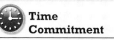

Time Commitment

Several days

Tools You'll Need

Basic masonry and stuccoing tools

Related Topics

Finishing a counter, 252–253
Outdoor kitchen features, 248–249
Stuccoing a wall, 226–227

How to Do It

1 Set firebox floor

- Set each leg of the stand in a dollop of mortar.
- Anchor each leg with an angled bracket and masonry screws.
- Butter the top of the stand with mortar and set the firebox floor in mortar.
- Scrape away any excess mortar.

2 Stack the pieces

- Spread mortar on the lip of the stand and set the lower cooking area piece.
- Check for level in both directions.
- If needed, tap with a rubber mallet to level.
- Continue stacking pieces, setting each in mortar and checking for level.

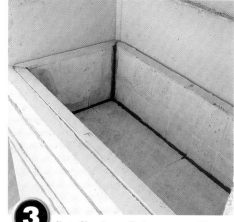

3 Set firebox & inner wall

- Spread refractory mortar along the perimeter of the firebox floor.
- Press the wall pieces into the mortar.
- Apply refractory mortar to fill gaps between wall pieces, and between wall pieces and the floor.

4 Tile upper cooking area

- For decorative purposes, install tiles to the back of the firewall.
- Set the tiles in refractory mortar.
- Also install tiles around the opening.
- Use bullnose tile pieces for a finished look, or regular tiles for a rustic look.

5 Prepare for stucco

- Cut pieces of metal lath.
- Attach them to the sides of the barbecue by drilling holes and driving short masonry screws with washers.
- Cut and install lath carefully so it is no more than ⅜ inch from the surface at any point.

6 Apply stucco

- Cover the tiles with masking tape to protect them.
- Apply base-coat stucco and allow it to cure slowly.
- Apply the finish coat, using the finishing technique of your choice.
- If you want color, mix the finish coat with integral color instead of painting it later, as paint is likely to peel when the barbecue gets hot.

11

Crafty Projects

In this chapter, you'll learn how to use the masonry techniques we showed you on the previous pages to create a variety of smaller-scale projects. Steppingstones are covered, as are techniques for pebble mosaics. If you're ambitious, we show you how to carve a birdbath from a single piece of solid stone. If you just want to get your hands dirty, we offer several planters and pots.

Chapter Contents

Garden Bench
page 272

Marble-like Tabletop
page 274

Concrete Table
page 277

Hypertufa Planters
page 278

Cylindrical Pots
page 280

Pressed Pots
page 281

Pentagonal Steppingstones

Making homemade steppingstones is a fun family project. Your job is to do the serious work of building the form and casting the concrete. The kids get to create the patterns. Suggest that they lay out their patterns first so you can preview, and tweak, the outcomes.

Forming & Decorating

These five-sided steppingstones are about 16 inches wide, but you can easily change the size or shape. Here we use 1 × 2 lumber for the forms, meaning the stones will be 1½ inches thick. You will probably want to add a bit of colorant to the concrete. The form boards are easily cut with a power miter saw, but you can mark them for the angled cuts using an angle square and then cut them with a circular saw or a handsaw.

Choose the decorative elements before you get started. You can leave impressions in the concrete or embed colorful pebbles, beads, and other elements.

Pressing In at the Right Time

If pressing in decorations or imprinting causes the area to become wet and mushy, re-trowel the surface. Wait a few minutes for the concrete to firm up a bit, then try again.

How to Do It

1 Build forms

- For a pentagonal form, cut five 1 × 2s, all the same length, with 72-degree angle cuts at each end.
- Drill pilot holes and drive screws to assemble two sections, one with two pieces and one with three pieces.
- To attach the two sections, drill pilot holes and screw in an eye and a hook at two places, so you can easily disassemble the form.

2 Plan patterns

- Cut pieces of cardboard the same size and shape as the stepping-stones will be.
- Arrange decorative elements on the cardboard so you can easily transfer them to the concrete.
- If you will make impressions, practice to be sure they will be a good size for the stones.

Stuff to Buy

1 x 2s
Acrylic masonry sealer
Cooking oil spray
Glass pebbles
Latex additive
Sand-mix concrete
Screws, eye hooks, eyes

Time Commitment

A few hours

Tools You'll Need

Drill
Magnesium float
Miter saw and box
Paintbrush or mason's brush

Related Topics

Curved steppingstones, 262–263

③ Mix & form

- Make a small batch of sand-mix concrete. Stir in latex additive along with water for extra strength, and add colorant as desired.
- Spray the form with cooking oil so the concrete will not stick.
- Pour concrete into the forms, then trowel over the surface with a magnesium float.

④ Make impressions

- Kids often like to make hand or foot impressions. Encourage them to press straight down, then lift straight up.
- You can also use boots with deep treads, shells, action figures, or anything else that leaves an impression at least 1/8 inch deep.

Carve words or names

- Use the rounded edge of a knife handle, a toothbrush, or another smooth-edged object to make neat-looking letters.
- For a childlike appearance, just scratch letters with a stick.

Leaf imprint

- Use leaves with prominent veins or distinct shapes.
- Press them pretty deep into the concrete to make sure the impression will be visible.
- Peel the leaves away, or allow them to decompose for a week or two.

⑤ Remove molds

- Once the concrete starts to get a bit firm, slice around the edges with a trowel or scraper.
- Undo the hooks.
- Gently pull the forms from the concrete.

⑥ Finish

- Lightly brush the stone with a paintbrush to achieve a uniform finish.
- This will leave a thin film of cement over the decorations, but you can wash it off later.
- Cover the stones with plastic for a couple of days, so they cure slowly, then brush on two or more coats of acrylic sealer.

Curved Steppingstones

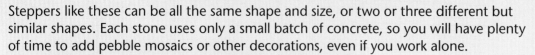
Steppers like these can be all the same shape and size, or two or three different but similar shapes. Each stone uses only a small batch of concrete, so you will have plenty of time to add pebble mosaics or other decorations, even if you work alone.

Planning the Path

While the stones shown on pages 260–261 are mostly for decoration, these are substantial enough to handle foot traffic. Choose a shape and size of stone that will be comfortable to walk on. Plan the route of the path, positioning stones a standard stride apart. To do this, cut out paper templates, lay them on the grass, and try them out.

The steppingstones here have an interlocking shape, even though the stones do not abut. If you want to set stones next to each other, make sure the front curve is the same shape as the rear.

To cut aluminum flashing without creating ripples, score it several times with a utility knife. Then bend it back and forth against a straightedge.

Stabilizing a Steppingstone

If a steppingstone wobbles, ask a helper to tip it up on its edge while you remove a handful of sand at the center of the hole. Smooth the surface and replace the steppingstone. Press down and wiggle the stone from side to side until it seats firmly.

1 Cut the shape

- Sketch the shape on a piece of cardboard.
- The stones shown here are 25 inches by 14 inches.
- Transfer the shape to a piece of plywood and cut it out with a jigsaw.

2 Add sides

- Cut galvanized flashing into two strips 2¾ inches wide and longer than the perimeter of the plywood form.
- To fasten the two strips to the form, drive nails or drill pilot holes and drive screws.
- Cover the inside of the flashing with plastic tape.

3 Apply two sprays

- Spray the plywood with shellac so it won't soak up moisture.
- Spray the interior of the mold—the tape and the plywood—with cooking oil.
- Screw short boards to the ends of the form so you have handles to help remove the form (Step 7).

Stuff to Buy

Cooking oil spray
Nails or screws
Plastic tape
Plywood
Roll of aluminum flashing
Sand-mix concrete
Spray shellac

Time Commitment

Half a day

Tools You'll Need

Brick chisel
Drill
Hammer, mallet
Jigsaw
Scraper
Square shovel
Trowel
Utility knife

Related Topics

Pentagonal steppingstones,
260–261

4 Add concrete & pebbles

- Mix a small batch of sand-mix concrete and pour it into the form.
- Use a trowel to smooth the top of the concrete.
- Dampen pebbles and place them in the concrete, nearly submerging them.

5 Embed pebbles

- Place a piece of plywood over the entire steppingstone and tap with a hammer to further embed the stones.
- Trowel over the entire surface, making sure the pebbles are firmly in place.
- It's OK to cover the pebbles with the concrete's top "cream."

6 Brush

- Wait half an hour or so for the concrete to begin hardening.
- Brush the surface to reveal the pebbles.
- Gently wipe the surface with a damp sponge if the concrete is soft.
- If the concrete is hard, use a wire brush.

7 Unmold

- After another half hour or so, invert the mold and allow the steppingstone to fall out.
- If this doesn't work, tap the plywood with a mallet.
- You might need to run a butter knife along the perimeter to separate the concrete from the plastic tape.

8 Excavate for a stepper

- Place a steppingstone on the lawn where you want it to be.
- Use a hammer and chisel to cut through the sod all along the perimeter of the steppingstone.
- Use your hands or a shovel to remove the sod.

9 Set stone

- Dig away soil about 2 inches deeper than the thickness of the stone.
- Use a board to tamp the soil firm.
- Add a layer of sand and set the stone in it.

Carved Birdbath or Planter

Stone carving may seem like an ancient skill that is beyond your abilities. But with the right tools and some patience, you can carve a boulder into a bowl that will make a fine-looking birdbath or planter.

Here, the narrow end of a rectangular boulder was chosen as the surface to carve, creating a tall, pillar-like birdbath.

Stone Carving for Beginners

Here we show a basic project, a small boulder carved into a basin. You'll find that much of the work can be accomplished with a 4-inch grinder and a variety of cutting and grinding wheels. You'll also need some chisels. You can use basic masonry cold chisels, or you can buy stoneworking chisels, perhaps from an online source.

The type of stone you choose will determine the difficulty of the project. Here we show stonecutter Gray Bragdon of Olympia, Washington, carving a chunk of basalt, which is a very hard stone. He uses diamond blades. If you choose a block of sandstone or limestone for your project, the cutting will be somewhat easier. Depending on the stone, you might be able to use inexpensive black masonry blades instead of diamonds.

❶ Getting started

- Set the boulder on a stable work surface at a comfortable height.
- A wooden table on soil is ideal, as it has a bit of give to prevent the boulder from cracking.
- Draw the outline of the bowl.

❷ First cuts

- Wear long clothing, gloves, and eye protection.
- Position a fan to blow dust away from you.
- Use a 6-inch grinder to make a series of shallow cuts.

❸ Chisel

- Use a narrow chisel to break out the ridges between the cuts.
- You don't have to create a smooth surface, but you should break out all the ridges.

❹ Cut & brush

- Switch to a 4-inch grinder and cut a series of lines again.
- Work carefully, cutting up to the lines but not past them.
- Chisel out the area.

❺ Deep cuts

- Cut more ridges, as deep as possible.
- Be sure the boulder will be at least 1 inch thick at all points.

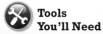

Stuff to Buy	 **Time Commitment**	 **Tools You'll Need**	**Related Topics**
Boulder Butcher's wax Mason's rouge sticks	A day	Cutting wheels Grinder Masonry chisels Polishing wheels Protective eyewear and clothing	Cutting thick stone on a curve, 52–53 Transporting heavy stones, 56–57

6 Mark lip

- At this point, you may choose to change the shape of the bowl slightly.
- Draw a clear line along the perimeter.

7 Glancing cut

- Hold a grinder at an angle and cut along the lines.
- Drag the blade toward the center of the hole, roughly scraping out a bowl.

8 Chisel smooth

- Cut with a variety of chisels to make the bowl as smooth as possible.
- Work carefully, chiseling sideways rather than straight down, to avoid cracking the boulder.

9 Select grinding tools

- Using a variety of grinding tools, ranging from rough to smooth, will make it easier to hollow out a smooth bowl.
- You'll also need a buffer attachment and perhaps mason's rouge, which comes in sticks.

10 Grind

- Using a rough grinding attachment, apply light to medium pressure as you grind out the bowl.
- Take your time; don't try to make it perfect on your first pass.
- Switch to medium-rough attachments and grind again.

11 Apply rouge

- For a very smooth bowl, apply mason's rouge.
- The rouge has fine abrasive particles.

12 Polish

- Use a polishing attachment to rub the rouge.
- Apply rouge and polish again as needed.

13 Wax

- Once you've achieved the desired smoothness, brush or vacuum away all dust.
- Apply several coats of butcher's wax, perhaps thinned with turpentine, to make the bowl watertight.
- Fill the bowl with water.

Pebble Mosaics

Pebbles and other decorative elements, such as mosaic tiles, can be assembled in patterns that resemble an oriental carpet. The work is painstaking and takes all the time you can give it, requiring more patience than skill.

This stone carpet gives definition and boundaries to an outdoor room.

How to Do It

PREP THE SUBSURFACE

The base must be firm and resistant to cracking in your area. A solid concrete slab is ideal. If you live where the ground doesn't freeze, you can install pebbles in mortar on a 3- or 4-inch-thick bed of compacted gravel. Install edging as needed.

CHOOSE & SORT PEBBLES

The pebbles should look good either wet or dry. If you prefer the wet look, coat the surface with acrylic masonry sealer when the job is finished.

A stone yard will carry a wide variety of pebbles, which are sold by weight. You can also find your own along rivers or in fields. Because the stones are small, local officials will probably not mind if you harvest modest amounts from public lands.

You will likely want a large number of small pebbles, plus a smaller number of larger stones that are close to each other in size. You may also want some very large, flat accent stones.

Sort the stones by color in buckets or trays for easy access. Lay some pebbles on a flat surface to see how many of each color you need. You might want to set the pattern on a sheet of plywood first so you can easily transfer the stones to the mortar in the same configuration.

1 Set large pebbles

- Mix mortar and pour it into the area.
- Smooth the mortar about ½ inch below the top of the edging.
- Push each stone into the mortar so two-thirds of it is embedded.

2 Set small pebbles

- Add or scoop out mortar as needed to maintain a consistent height.
- Set the pebbles individually.
- If the pebbles are very small, perhaps sprinkle them onto the surface and press them into the mortar.
- For a textured look, set some pebbles flat and others on edge.

Stuff to Buy

Concrete bonding agent
Decorative pebbles
Edging
Mortar

Time Commitment

About a day

Tools You'll Need

Sponge
Tools for mixing mortar
Trowel

❸ Bed

- Before the mortar starts to harden—within about 15 minutes—set a piece of plywood over the stones and step on the wood.
- Step with enough pressure to press most of the pebbles down a bit.
- Aim for a relatively level surface.

❹ Clean

- When the mortar starts to harden, spray it with a fine mist of water.
- Brush the pebbles or wipe them with a sponge or cloth.
- Cover the area with plastic so it can cure for two or three days.
- Clean away any mortar haze with vinegar or a mild muriatic acid solution.

Pebbles in Pavers

You can also make a pebble pattern when casting steppingstones. Or, to add a mosaic after the stepping-stone is hard, coat it with concrete bonding agent. Cover it with a wet mortar mix about an inch thick and embed the stones in the mortar. Use brushes to clean away the excess mortar.

To cast a pebble mosaic in reverse, build the steppingstone form and spread a layer of sand about ½ inch deep in the bottom. Arrange the stones in a pattern. Mix the mortar and moisten the stones with a fine mist. Carefully pour or place mortar mix into the form, taking care not to dislodge the stones. Allow the paver to harden, then reverse the form and clean the surface.

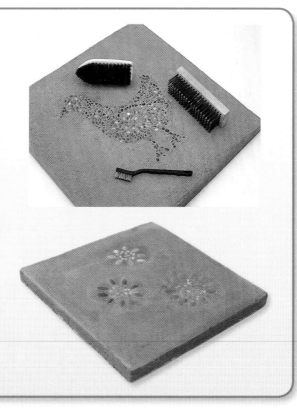

Keep Things Wet

To ensure that the pebbles adhere firmly to the mortar, work when the area is in the shade so the mortar does not dry out. Mix a fairly wet batch of mortar. Keep the pebbles moist or wet before you embed them. Occasionally try to pick one up to test that the pebbles are sticking well.

Free-form Pebbles

A large area can be covered with mosaics, as long as you're willing to put in the time. Work in small sections, but keep the overall pattern in mind. No special skills are needed to do this sort of work, except patience and an eye for artful arrangement.

Before You Begin

Building a pebble mosaic takes more time and more material than you might expect, so start with a small project. With careful planning, it can become part of a larger installation.

For a large project, buy pebbles in bags or bulk from a stone yard. Sort them by color and size and set out some patterns on a piece of plywood to get an idea of how much material you will need.

Start with a firm base that will not crack. "A compacted gravel bed works well, especially in an area without freezing weather. A concrete slab makes an excellent substrate.

The patio mosaic on the left appears to crawl up the side of a rock wall, visually tying the wall to the patio. Using numerous stones of the same size and orientation, as seen on the right, allows you to create patterns and designs that stand out against their free-form backgrounds.

1 Prep base

- If you choose to use a gravel bed, use compactable gravel with stones ¼ inch in diameter or smaller.
- Alternately use a vibrating compactor and spray with a mist of water.
- Spread about one inch of sand to help trace your design.

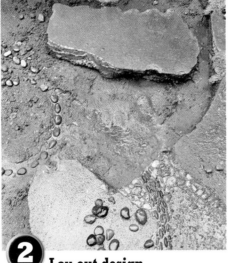

2 Lay out design

- Trace the main features of the design in the sand.
- Temporarily place pebbles along the lines, then stand back to be sure you like the pattern.

3 Apply mortar

- Mix a batch of mortar that is fairly wet—just stiff enough so it does not slump.
- Spread the mortar using a trowel or a gloved hand.
- The top should be about ½ inch below an abutting surface or edging.

 **Stuff to Buy**

Concrete bonding agent
Materials for substrate
Mortar mix
Pebbles

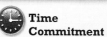 **Time Commitment**

About a day per 6-by-6-foot section

 **Tools You'll Need**

Sponge
Tools for mixing mortar
Trowel
Vibrating compactor

 Related Topics

Applying mortar, 64–65
Edgings, 100–106
Mixing mortar, 62–63
Pebble mosaics, 266–267
Tamping gravel & screeding sand, 108–109

4 Set outline pebbles

- Place the pebbles that establish the design. These are usually on edge.
- Push each stone into the mortar so that at least two-thirds of it is embedded.
- Butt stones closely together.
- Add or subtract mortar as needed to maintain a consistent height.

5 Add fill stones

- Once the design is set, fill in the background area.
- The stones should contrast with the outline pebbles.
- Lay them flat or set them on edge as desired.
- Occasionally try to pick one up to make sure the stones are sticking.

6 Level & bed

- Stop placing stones when you are a few inches from the outside edge of the mortar.
- The excess mortar serves as a dam, which you will chip off in the next step.
- Place plywood over the area and press it down to bed all the stones to the same level.

7 Ensure a clean break

- Unless the pattern is small, you will not finish in a day.
- Once the mortar stiffens, chip off the mortar along an established edge.
- Make sure the next day's pebbles can butt tightly against today's pebbles.

8 Clean

- Use a soft spray from a hose to rinse excess mortar from the surface.
- Use as little water as possible.
- Cover the mosaic with plastic to keep it moist.
- The next day, scrub off any mortar on the surface of the pebbles.
- Wash away any mortar haze by scrubbing with vinegar or a mild muriatic acid solution.

Take It Easy

Repetitive work done in a crouching position can strain your back. Take plenty of stretching breaks, and avoid working on your knees for more than four hours a day. Sitting on a short stool might make the work more comfortable.

Mixing Colored Concrete

The easiest way to enliven the look of concrete is to add pigment, or colorant, while you are mixing it. This is not difficult or expensive, but you must keep careful track of your recipe if you will make multiple batches or if you desire an exact color.

Testing the Color

Concrete lightens as it dries and cures, so you won't know the precise final color until a week or so after you pour it. If you are aiming for an exact shade, take the time to test various recipes, carefully noting the amounts of colorant you use. The test batches will be small, so measure carefully. Any miscalculation will be multiplied when you mix a larger batch.

Getting the Color You Want

At a home center, you can buy liquid concrete pigment, which you simply pour into the concrete mix. The colors are limited to buff, red, black, and charcoal.

WORKING WITH POWDER

You can also buy color as a powder, which you mix with water before adding to the concrete mix. Powder is generally more expensive than liquid pigment, but it produces a more vivid color and a wider variety of hues, including green and blue. If you want consistent color, use one of two methods: You can stir the color into some of the mix water with a whisk, then add the liquid to the concrete mix. Or, if you are using a power mixer, dump the powdered pigment into the mix before adding water. Use the power mixer to blend the dry ingredients, then add the water. If you want streaks of color, mix the concrete with water, then stir in dry pigment.

Mixing tools

- To ensure a smooth, color-consistent mix, buy or rent a half-inch drill with a mixing paddle.
- For a large job, consider renting a mixer with a revolving drum.
- Use clean buckets and a large measuring pail.
- For making small amounts, such as a bag at a time, use household measuring cups to measure the liquid or powdered pigment.

❶ Mix pigment

- Pour liquid or powdered pigment into a measuring container.
- Add it to a fairly large amount of water, but start at the lower end recommended on the concrete-mix label.
- Mix thoroughly, perhaps using a whisk or a power mixer.

Stuff to Buy

Concrete mix
Liquid or powder concrete
pigment

**Time
Commitment**

A few minutes

**Tools
You'll Need**

Buckets and measuring pails
Concrete mixing tools
Mason's hoe
Mixing paddle

**Related
Topics**

Mixing & delivering, 172–173

❷ Add dry mix

- Pour the colored mixture into a large
  bucket or wheelbarrow.
- Add about half of the dry concrete mix.

❸ Make a slurry

- Mix with a power mixer.
- In a minute or less, you will have a slurry
  that looks like gravy.
- Keep mixing, scraping the sides and bottom, until all lumps are gone.

❹ Finish mixing

- Add the rest of the dry mix.
- Power-mix again, holding the tool firmly.

❺ Correct thickness

- Mix for a few minutes, adding small
  amounts of water as needed.
- For most craft projects, the final mix
  should be pretty stiff, like soft clay.

Mixing by Hand

You can achieve fairly consistent color mixing by hand, but it will take more time and
effort. Here, fiber reinforcement is added along with the colorant. Use a shovel or a
mason's hoe to mix, scraping the sides and bottom as you work. Start with a very dry
mix, then slowly add more water.

Garden Bench

This garden bench is spacious enough for two people to share comfortably. It was acid-stained after it was built, but you can tint the concrete when you mix it.

Building a Three-part Bench

This bench is built in three parts—two legs plus a slab seat. The seat has two recesses underneath that slip over rebar stubs protruding upward from the legs. The top's edges are ragged, to mimic the look of rough-hewn stone. The legs have rippled edges, which you can create by slipping short pieces of metal roofing into the form.

1 Cut roofing

- Use a circular saw to cut two pieces of corrugated metal roofing, each 6 inches wide.
- Set the roofing on saw horses and use a jig made of plywood as a saw guide.
- Cut with a metal-cutting blade, or a plywood-cutting blade attached backward.
- Wear protective clothing and eyewear.

2 Build the leg form

- On a piece of melamine-coated particleboard, draw a cut-off triangle, 16 inches high, 15 inches wide at the base, and 7 inches wide at the top.
- Cut pieces to follow along the lines, as shown, and attach them with screws to each other and to the bottom board.
- Drill a 1/2-inch hole in the middle of the top.
- Cut metal roofing pieces to fit, then slide them into place.

3 Concrete for legs

- Spray the inside of the form with cooking oil.
- Mix an 80-pound bag of concrete mix, with two handfuls of portland cement added, and fill the form halfway.
- Slip a 6-inch-long piece of rebar through the hole, so it protrudes 5/8 inch above the concrete.
- Finish filling the form and then smooth the concrete with a trowel.

$ Stuff to Buy

Acid stain
Concrete mix
Corrugated metal roofing
Form-release oil
Melamine-coated particleboard
Pipe caps
Portland cement
Potter's clay
Reinforcement bar

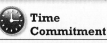
Time Commitment

A weekend

Tools You'll Need

Brushes
Circular saw
Drill
Flour sifter
Potter's cutting tool
Trowels

Related Topics

Acid staining, 148–149
Mixing colored concrete, 270–271

4 Unmold & cut clay

- After a day or two, disassemble the form and remove the leg.
- Cut pieces for the seat form, 15 inches wide, 48 inches long, and 3½ inches wide.
- Slice off pieces of clay with a wire cutter.

5 Mold seat form

- Screw the sides to a melamine base and to each other at the corners.
- Press clay against the sides.
- To form an edge that looks like stone, press a broken brick against the clay all around.
- Use a potter's cutting tool to carve a rounded edge along the base so the seat will not have sharp edges.

6 Prep the form

- Spray the clay and form bottom with cooking oil.
- You may choose to sift drifts of white cement over the bottom to create a Milky Way look on the top of the seat.

7 Fill seat form

- Prepare a batch of concrete mix, reinforced with extra portland cement.
- Add concrete a handful at a time, until it is ½ inch thick.
- With a hammer, beat on the form from underneath until bubbles rise and a water glaze covers the surface.

8 Finish filling

- Continue filling the form with concrete, tapping occasionally.
- When the form is filled, lay three pieces of rebar lengthwise on the concrete, so they are 1 inch from the ends, and press down into the middle of the concrete's thickness.
- Smooth the surface with a trowel.
- To create recesses for the rebar pieces on the legs, press pipe caps into the concrete.

9 Finish the seat

- Cover the seat and allow it to cure for two days.
- Fill any holes with a paste of cement, pigment, and water.
- Allow the concrete to cure for two weeks, then apply acid stain.

Marble-like Tabletop

It's surprisingly easy to mold a concrete slab with the rich texture of marble. The marbling effect is actually the result of imperfections that occur naturally when you press concrete against a form.

How to Do It

To create a marbled look, press stiff tinted sand-mix concrete against a mold, one handful at a time. This produces a series of gaps and veins, which you will fill later with a cement slurry that is tinted the same color or a contrasting one. (Even if you use the same pigment, the colors will come out different because the moisture and aggregate content of the patch differs from that of the main batch.) This creates a subtle marble effect.

This technique works only if you cast upside down or inside out in a mold. You can use marbleized concrete for flowerpots or basins, fireplace surrounds, and a host of other decorative purposes.

1 Build the form

- Make a straightforward rectangular form by screwing together 2½-inch-wide strips of melamine-coated particleboard onto a melamine base.
- To make the edges thicker than the middle, screw 1-inch-wide spacers to the top edge of each sidepiece (see Step 8).

2 Make a screed

- Build a screed guide that you will use to hollow out the center of the table.
- Cut one piece 6 inches longer than the table's width, plus another that's 8 inches shorter.
- Screw the two pieces together so the shorter piece drops down 1½ inches below the longer piece.

3 Add reinforcement

- Cut ladder-type metal reinforcement pieces so they will be 1 inch shorter than the tabletop at all sides.
- Remove the reinforcement pieces and set them aside to be placed later.

Stuff to Buy

Concrete colorant
Concrete sealer
Form-release oil
Melamine-coated particleboard
Plywood
Polypropylene fiber concrete
  reinforcement
Portland cement
Sand-mix concrete

Time Commitment

A day

Tools You'll Need

Drill
Grinder with stone polisher
Mason's brush
Saw
Trowels
Wire brush

Related Topics

Mixing colored concrete,
270–271

4 Oil the form

- Spray a thin layer of form-release oil or cooking oil over the entire form.
- Wipe away any puddles.

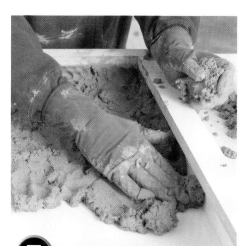

5 Press concrete into mold

- Prepare a very stiff batch of sand-mix concrete.
- One handful at a time, pat the mixture into the mold.
- Press all the way up the sides but only ¾ inch deep in the center.

6 Add reinforcement

- Place crisscrossed reinforcement onto the concrete, keeping it 1 inch from all edges.
- Mix a handful of polypropylene fibers into the remaining concrete.
- Press in another ¾-inch layer of concrete.

7 Screed

- Use the screed guide from Step 2 to smooth the center of the table.
- Also work to create crisp 90-degree angles along the thick edges.

8 Remove the mold

- Remove the screws holding the mold together.
- With a helper, slide the tabletop just far enough off your worktable so you can grip it.
- Pivot the piece up.
- When it's balanced on one edge, have one person slide four pairs of short 2 × 4s onto the table as spacer blocks.
- Lower the tabletop onto the blocks.

⑨ Marbleize

- Where you see light-colored lines, only a thin layer of cement covers gaps.
- Use a wire brush to remove this layer and expose the gaps.
- Sweep away crumbs with a brush.

⑩ First slurry coat

- Mix a slurry of portland cement, latex fortifier, and pigment.
- The slurry should have the consistency of yogurt.
- Use a wide taping knife or a flat trowel to squeegee the slurry into most of the gaps.

⑪ Second slurry coat

- After an hour, the first coat will dry and shrink.
- Mix a second slurry batch and squeegee it as well.
- Mist the tabletop with water and cover it with plastic.

⑫ Polish

- Work in an area that's OK to get wet.
- Keeping the surface damp, use a stone polisher with a 200-grit wheel to smooth the surface.
- Repeat with progressively finer polishers —400-grit, 800, and so on.

⑬ Finish

- Once you achieve the desired smoothness, use a hand sander to ease the corners.
- Allow the table to cure for about two days.
- Apply penetrating sealer, followed by a topical sealer.

Concrete Table

This project uses some elements of the bench on page 272 to create a taller table. It ends up about 33 inches tall—just right for a work surface or a serving table.

Stuff to Buy

Concrete colorant
Concrete sealer
Form-release oil
Melamine-coated particleboard
Polypropylene fiber concrete
  reinforcement
Portland cement
Sand-mix concrete

Related Topics

Acid staining, 148–149
Mixing colored concrete,
  270–271

How to Do It

This full-day project uses the same legs as those for the garden bench, but it stacks them two high. A length of pipe runs through the middle of each leg section and up into recesses in the tabletop. The top is formed right side up, with tinted concrete and decorative leaf impressions.

1 Leg form

- Build a leg form like the one on page 272, but drill 5/8-inch holes in the top and bottom.
- Cut a 1/2-inch plastic pipe to fit between the holes, and use a dowel to hold it in place.
- Also build a simple open box, with 3½-inch-wide sides, to serve as a mold for the tabletop.

2 Reinforced concrete

- Mix a stiff batch of tinted concrete, reinforced with polypropylene fibers.
- Pour it into the mold.
- Cut four pieces of rebar, about 3 inches shorter than the table, and tap them into the center of the top's thickness.
- Smooth the surface with a magnesium float or a trowel.
- Use pipe caps to create recesses for the pipe (see Step 8 on page 273).

3 Decorate & finish

- When the surface water is gone, mist the veined side of leaves, then dust with a mixture of pigment and cement.
- Press the leaves, pigment side down, onto the concrete.
- Smooth the edges so the leaves adhere, then trowel over them.
- Cover the top with plastic and allow it to cure slowly, for three days or so.
- Remove the edge forms.

Hypertufa Planters

Combine peat moss, sand, and portland cement to produce hypertufa (also called tufa), a material that's easy to form into containers and sculptures that look like natural rock. In time, it may develop a crust of moss or lichen, which will only add to its appeal.

Sifted Peat Moss

The peat moss should not have noticeable woody chunks. To avoid them, either buy bags of more expensive sphagnum peat moss or hand-sift all the chunks out of less expensive peat moss.

The great thing about working with hypertufa is that you can create a pot in the exact proportions you desire.

How to Do It

MIXING

There is no exact recipe for hypertufa, but it usually uses portland cement, sand, and peat moss in various combinations. To make the tufa lighter, you can substitute perlite for some of the sand. To ensure against cracking, especially in an area with freezing winters, add a small handful of fiber reinforcement. You can add concrete pigment to change the color. If you want vivid color, use white cement instead of gray.

FORMING

Because rustic appearance is part of the charm, you can use just about anything to help form hypertufa. Shown here is a simple pair of cardboard boxes. You can also use a plastic pot or pail, or any container you don't mind getting dirty. If you make the mixture stiff, you can even mold pots or sculptures free-form.

Hypertufa Recipe

The basic recipe for hypertufa is 2 parts sand, 2 parts sifted peat moss, and 1 to 1½ parts cement. You can also add concrete reinforcement fibers to prevent cracking. Mix the dry ingredients in a trough or wheelbarrow, using a hoe, shovel, or garden trowel. Slowly add water (perhaps mixed with colorant) until the mixture is moist but still firm enough to form into clumps.

Using a Box

❶ Make forms

- The inner box should be smaller so all the walls and the floor are at least 1 inch thick.
- Here, a piece of wood is inserted because the outer box is too long.
- For drainage, cut a hole in the boxes and tape a short length of pipe in place.

❷ Form

- Spray the form with cooking oil.
- Pack the bottom firmly with 1½ inches or so of tufa.
- Set the inner box in place and fill it with sand.
- Pack the walls with tufa, tamping as you go.
- Cover the project and allow it to cure for several days. Then remove the forms and shape it.

 Stuff to Buy

Concrete pigment
Cooking oil spray
Fiber reinforcement
Perlite
Sand
Sphagnum peat moss

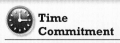 **Time Commitment**

Several days, including curing

 **Tools You'll Need**

Hoe or garden trowel
Kitchen implements for shaping
Masonry and carpentry tools
Mason's trough

 Related Topics

Molding Around a Bowl

1 Prep the bowl

- To protect the bowl, wrap it with plastic.
- You could spray it with cooking oil, but it will stain.
- Place the bowl on a sturdy surface.

2 Form the pot

- Mix a batch of tufa stiff enough to hold its shape.
- Form palm-size slabs and pat them onto the bowl, starting at the rim and working up.
- Make the walls about 1 inch thick.

3 Drain hole

- Shape the bottom of the planter so it is concave; this will eliminate wobbling.
- Poke a drain hole if you want one.

4 Remove the mold

- Cover the pot and allow it to cure for several days.
- Remove the mold.

Shaping

Smooth

- Use a wire brush, rasp, or sure-form tool to generally smooth the surface.
- If you want a rougher surface, scrape with a notched trowel or another toothed tool.

Carve

- Carve details with just about any tool, such as a knife, stick, or trowel.
- Though you are after a rustic look, aim to make the design as symmetrical as possible.
- Work carefully, as the tufa is still fragile.
- Cover the project again for a week or so, then uncover it and wait two weeks before using it.

Cylindrical Pots

Here, metal flashing is used to create hypertufa cylinders, which can be carved easily into fanciful designs. A cylinder is stronger than a bowl shape, so with this design you can unmold and start carving the tufa after just a few hours.

Greening a Pot

To hasten the growth of moss or algae on a planter, coat it with pulverized moss mixed with either buttermilk or beer and sugar.

How to Do It

1 Make forms

- With a circular saw, cut melamine-coated particleboard to make a base.
- Drill a hole and insert a dowel for the drain hole.
- Cut two lengths of flashing to go around the base, plus a few inches.
- Fit one piece of flashing around the base, tie it with string and tape, and screw it to the base.
- Make the other form at least 2 inches narrower.

2 Fill with tufa

- Pack tufa into the bottom, about 1½ inches thick.
- Insert the smaller form and check that it's centered.
- In small batches, fill and tamp the walls.

3 Carve

- After a few hours, remove the outside form.
- Carve your design using a knife, nail, trowel, or any other tool.
- Cover the project and allow it to cure for several days.
- Uncover the project and remove the inside form.

Pressed Pots

To give your creations a more sophisticated appearance, follow the hypertufa recipe on page 278, but eliminate the peat moss. A pot made only with cement and sand will have smooth sides and look surprisingly professional.

A Natural Sand Color

Because the cement never gets wet enough to form a paste, you don't need to add pigment, as the sand color predominates. You may want to look for tan or yellowish sand to create a distinctive look.

How to Do It

1 Prep the mold

- If the plastic pot flexes, embed it in sand.
- Here, part of the base is filled with clay. The remaining sections are for forming attractive feet.
- For drainage, drill a hole in the pot and insert a dowel.

2 Press in the tufa

- Spray the pot with cooking oil.
- Mix tufa using 2 parts sand, 1 part cement, and a large pinch of reinforcement fibers.
- Press, then pound, handfuls against the pot using a round rock.
- Make the walls at least 1 inch thick.

3 Remove the mold

- Cover the pot and allow it to cure for several days.
- Invert the bowl and remove the dowel for the drain hole.
- Tap with a mallet to free the pot.

4 Smooth

- If the top edge is ragged, smooth it with a rasp and a sanding sponge.
- Use scrapers or the sponge to smooth the inside.
- Cover the project and allow it to cure for a couple of weeks.

Help Section

In this chapter, we show you how to perform routine masonry repairs and maintenance, so you can fix something before it needs to be replaced. Techniques for safely cleaning masonry are covered, as are the ways to repair cracks in concrete and repoint worn-out mortar. You'll even learn how to remove a broken brick or block to make a damaged wall look as good as new.

Chapter Contents

Cleaning & Sealing Masonry

Concrete, brick, and block are porous, so stains can be difficult to clean. Prevent stains by covering masonry with a sealer. When a staining substance does spill, try to deal with it right away, before it has a chance to set.

Masonry cleaners include heavy-duty degreasers and etchers, which contain a mild acid solution. Read instructions carefully and protect yourself with long clothing, eyewear, and gloves.

Cleaning

There are three or four escalating strategies for cleaning concrete, brick, or block. First, apply a detergent solution and scrub with a stiff-bristle brush. Rinse the area well and allow the surface to dry. If the spot or discoloration remains, try pressure-washing it (below left), or scrub it with a product made for cleaning masonry. If that doesn't solve the problem, try scrubbing with an acid solution (below right).

WIRE-BRUSH CLEANING

If you need to clean a very specific spot, wire brushing may be the solution. A hand wire brush can be effective, but a drill equipped with an attachment is easier to use and control. Brush a small area first to make sure you are not creating unattractive scratches.

PRESSURE WASHING

A rented pressure washer offers plenty of power, but an inexpensive model purchased at a home center might supply all the pressure you need. Work carefully to avoid marring the surface. A nozzle that directs a single stream can dent a brick or block surface, so use a fan nozzle instead.

ACID CLEANING

Muriatic acid, sold at many hardware stores and home centers, can damage clothing and cause serious skin irritation, and the fumes can make you sick. Work in a well-ventilated area. Wear long clothing and heavy-duty rubber gloves. If you are working on a slab, wear kneepads to keep your knees dry. If you do spill acid on yourself, rinse the area repeatedly with clean water.

Mix a solution of 5 parts water to 1 part muriatic acid. Always add acid to water, never water to acid. Carefully pour or wipe the solution onto the surface and scrub with a brush. A light bubbling indicates the acid is working. Once the bubbling stops, rinse the area thoroughly. If a mild solution does not do the trick, use progressively stronger solutions.

Sealing

Wait until concrete or mortar cures fully—usually a week or two—before applying a sealer. Consult a local patio expert or paint dealer to find the most durable product for the surface. A basic clear acrylic sealer made for masonry is usually best.

Apply sealer using a paintbrush, a paint roller, or a pump sprayer. If the sealer soaks in immediately, another coat is needed. The second coat should stay shiny wet for at least a few seconds. If it does not, apply a third coat.

IMPORTANT: Do not seal a brick wall if your house has double-brick construction, which is usually the case in older homes. For more information about this, see page 292.

If a wall tends to get slightly damp, waterproofing paint can solve the problem. Do not apply it if the wall gets very damp. Apply the first coat with a stiff masonry brush, working it into the surface. Apply the second coat with a paintbrush or roller.

Treating Efflorescence

1 Identify

- A powdery white substance called efflorescence often forms when masonry stays moist for long periods.
- Take steps to keep the surface dry.

2 Scrape

- Use a wire brush to remove most of the efflorescence.
- You may need to use a scraper if the powder is thick.

3 Clean

- Scrub with a muriatic acid solution or a masonry cleaner.
- Wait several months to be sure the efflorescence will not return. Then apply a sealer.

Repairing Concrete

Before attempting to repair concrete, determine whether the damage is structural or merely cosmetic. With most structural problems, the best solution is to demolish the slab and start again. But if a slab is basically stable, almost any damage can be corrected.

Evaluating Concrete Problems

You can usually diagnose concrete damage, whether minor or severe, by examining the surface carefully.

If only a specific area of a slab is cracked or suffers from crazing or spalling, cut around the area and apply a patch. Cracks and chipped corners can also be repaired.

If the problem affects the entire slab and is not structural, consider the solutions shown in chapter 5 (pages 144–165). You may apply a top coat, or cover the surface with stain or epoxy paint. Or consider covering the slab with tiles, pavers, or stones.

Anchoring with Masonry Screws

If damage to a step is deeper than 3 inches, drill pilot holes in the step and partially drive in several masonry screws to improve the bond. Make sure the screws will not protrude outside the patch.

Crazing

- A web of hairline cracks is called crazing.
- As long as the slab is firm, the problem is not serious. But it can grow worse, especially in an area with freezing winters.
- Apply sealer or resurface the slab.

Undermined support

- If you can see that the substrate has been eroded or otherwise compromised, the slab is in danger of failing.
- Consult a pro, who might recommend that you shore up the substrate or demolish the slab and pour a new one.

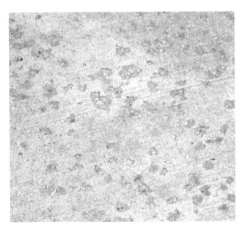

Popouts & spalling

- Small holes scattered throughout a slab are called popouts.
- Flaking of the surface is called spalling or scaling.
- Seal or resurface the slab to keep the problem from growing worse.

Uneven sections

- If one section is higher than another, the slab itself may be strong but the substrate may have shifted.
- You can simply live with the condition, or hire a pro to raise the lower section using a process called mudjacking.

Large cracks

- A series of large cracks usually means the slab needs to be replaced.
- Over time, the problem will worsen.

Repairing Cracks

To repair a crack, use patching cement reinforced with vinyl or latex. It costs more, but it resists cracking.

Caulk a small crack

- Purchase concrete repair caulk, which is stronger and longer-lasting than standard caulk.
- Clean out all debris and scrub away oily stains.
- Apply caulk and smooth it with a scraper or your finger.
- You might need to reapply it every year or two.

1 Key the crack

- Use a hammer and a cold chisel to chisel the crack at an angle, so the bottom of the crack is wider than the top.
- Remove all debris, scrape with a wire brush, and wash away any oily stains.
- Coat the crack with latex concrete-bonding agent.

2 Fill in

- Mix a small batch of concrete patching compound.
- Using a pointed trowel, stuff the compound into the crack as tightly as possible.
- Scrape the surface so the patch is at the same height as the slab.
- When the compound starts to stiffen, gently wipe it with a brush.

Chipped Step

If a corner chips in one piece, you might be able to set the piece back in place with polyurethane glue. Or coat the surfaces with concrete bonding agent, then apply a small amount of concrete patch to the stair and press the chip back into place. Use duct tape to hold the chip firm while the patch sets.

1 Cut around the damage

- Use a grinder or a circular saw equipped with a masonry blade to cut around the damaged area.
- Angle the blade to key the cut, meaning the bottom will be wider than the top.
- Clean away all debris with a wire brush and clean away any oily stains.

2 Form & patch

- Build a simple form with plywood or boards that are held in place with a heavy block or stone.
- Spray the inside of the boards with cooking oil to keep concrete from sticking.
- Apply concrete bonding agent and fill the hole with patching concrete.
- Trowel the surface; remove the board as soon as the patch stiffens. Use a brush to blend the patch with the surrounding concrete.

Small chip

- If the chip is small, make an even simpler form using two pieces of wood and duct tape.
- Follow the instructions for a larger patch to fill and smooth the repair.

Patching a Damaged Section

If the patched area will be highly visible, take the time to get the patch's color close to that of the existing concrete. Spread a thin layer of patching material in an unobtrusive spot or on a piece of plywood, then wait a day or two for it to cure. Add a bit of colorant to achieve a less obvious patch.

Read instructions on the patching compound to make sure the patch will be neither too thick nor too thin. Most compounds can be applied as thin as 1/8 inch and as thick as 1/2 inch.

1 Cut

- Draw a geometric shape around the damaged area.
- Use a grinder or a circular saw with a masonry blade to cut lines about 1/2 inch deep.
- Chisel out the area inside the cut lines.

2 Apply bonding agent

- Use a wire brush to remove all loose matter, then scrub with cleaner.
- Coat the area with latex concrete-bonding agent.

3 Apply patch

- Mix a batch of concrete patch so it is just liquid enough to pour.
- Use a trowel to press the patch into the area.

4 Smooth

- Use a magnesium or wood float to smooth the surface level with the surrounding concrete.
- Use a brush or a steel trowel to finish the surface so it matches the surrounding surface's texture.

Leaky Basements

A basement can become wet or damp for several reasons.

- If it is generally damp, the air is humid and moisture in the air can condense on cool surfaces, such as a concrete floor, pipes, or ducts. Check that the clothes dryer is efficiently venting moisture to the outside. Try turning on a dehumidifier or installing an exhaust fan.
- If water enters the basement, especially after rain, you have a more serious problem. Water is likely collecting next to the foundation wall, building up pressure until it is strong enough to force its way through small cracks.

SOLUTIONS

The first remedy is to divert rainwater from the house. Make sure the yard is sloped away from the house so water does not pool next to the house. Plants beside the house may encourage water to pool there, so you might need to move them.

If you have window wells, see that they are clean of debris and have good drainage. The surrounding yard should slope away from the wells. Use downspout extenders to move the water farther from the house (facing page, bottom left). If that doesn't solve the problem, the solution might be to apply a plug from inside the basement (facing page, far right).

Repair Products

In addition to standard concrete patching materials, you can buy an epoxy floor patch kit. Mix the two parts and apply. In addition, some newer dry-mix concrete patching materials combine hydraulic cement with polymers and very fine aggregate, for an extra-strong patch. These products usually come in gray but are also available in white and can be tinted with standard concrete colorants.

Some products can be feathered at the edges, so you don't have to cut an 1/8-inch-deep hole in the concrete. Some can even be applied with a paintbrush, and some can be sanded smooth after application.

Seepage or Condensation?

① Tape foil

- To check whether moisture is seeping through the wall or is simply the result of humid air, tape a piece of aluminum foil to an area that gets wet.
- Press firmly on the tape so water cannot seep in.

② Inspect the area

- After three days, remove the foil.
- If the room side is wet, you have damp basement air, so dehumidify the air.
- If the wall side is wet, you have seepage, so keep water away from the house.

Keeping Water Away

Downspout extender

- Buy a flexible or solid downspout extender that fits your downspout. The most common sizes are 2 × 3 inches and 3 × 4 inches.
- Attach the extender to the end of the downspout and extend it away from the house to an area where water will flow away.

Another option

- A roll-up extender stretches outward only when it fills with water, for a less obtrusive appearance.
- Some types have a grid of holes so they act like a sprinkler.

Plug a Leak

If a basement wall leaks from a specific crack or hole during rainstorms, try patching the crack from inside. Use hydraulic cement, made for patching basement walls.

Run water from a hose near the house and watch the crack to find just where the water is coming from. Turn off the water. Use a hammer and chisel or a rented electric chipping tool to widen and key the crack.

Turn on the water. When the water starts dribbling through the crack, mix hydraulic cement with water to a putty-like consistency. Work quickly, as you'll have only a few minutes before the cement starts to harden. Roll the cement into a snake and push it firmly into the crack with your thumb. Start at the bottom and work up. If the patch succeeds, the leak will stop. If the leak moves higher, you might need to widen the crack there and fill it as well. If the patch does not succeed, chisel it out and try again.

Anchoring to Masonry

A variety of products allow you to secure brackets, ledgers, or post anchors to concrete, brick, or block. If you are pouring new concrete, you can set an anchor while the concrete is wet. But many firm anchors are installed in hardened masonry.

Setting a J-Bolt

About J-bolts

- J-bolts designed to be anchored in concrete come in several sizes.
- Usually, at least 5 inches of the bolt is sunk into the concrete.

1 Pour & insert

- Pour the concrete, then strike and smooth it as desired.
- Insert the J-bolt into the concrete.
- Make sure the threads stick out far enough for your purposes.

2 Add a post anchor

- Allow the concrete to harden.
- Install a post anchor or other attachment hardware.
- Many anchors are adjustable so that you can move them over an inch or two.

Anchoring Cement

Here, anchoring cement is being used to secure a brace to a concrete patio. The brace is one of two that will keep a wooden bench in place. The steps are to drill the holes about twice the diameter of the screws, then vacuum out the dust. Fill the holes with cement, position the brace, and push in the screws. Wait for the cement to expand and set completely (about an hour) before you attach the other part of the brace to the bench.

Using Masonry Screws

Choose screws

- Masonry screws come in various diameters and lengths.
- When you buy them, also buy a masonry bit of the correct size.
- A hex-head screw is easier to drive firmly than a Phillips-head screw.

Drill & drive

- Drill the hole about ¼ inch deeper than the screw will reach.
- Drive the screw into the hole.

Other Fasteners

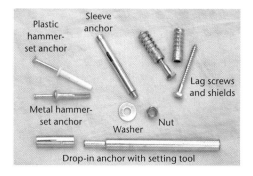

Plastic hammer-set anchor · Sleeve anchor · Lag screws and shields · Metal hammer-set anchor · Washer · Nut · Drop-in anchor with setting tool

Many products anchor to brick, block, or concrete.

- Lag screws and shields take time to install but are very strong. See Steps below for installation instructions.
- To install a sleeve anchor, drill a hole, insert the anchor, and screw in the threaded rod. As you tighten the nut onto the rod, the anchor expands to grip the masonry.
- Hammer-set anchors are the quickest to install. Drill a hole, insert the anchor, and pound it in with a hammer. Metal hammer-set anchors are stronger than plastic ones.
- To use a drop-in anchor, insert it into a hole, then tap it with a special setting tool that causes it to expand and become firm. Now you can screw a bolt into the anchor.

Injectable Epoxy

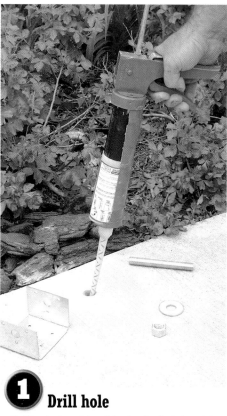

1 Drill hole

- Drill a hole with a bit that's slightly wider than the bolt to be anchored.
- Vacuum out the hole.
- Squirt fastening epoxy into the hole.

2 Set rod

- Immediately insert a threaded rod to the desired depth.
- Leave the assembly undisturbed for a day so the epoxy can dry.
- Slip on a washer and tighten a nut.

Working with Lag Shields

1 Drill hole

- Using a masonry bit sized for your masonry screws, drill a hole slightly deeper than the shield's length.
- Work slowly and take breaks to avoid overheating the bit and the drill.
- On a tough concrete surface, use a hammer drill.

2 Add shield

- Use a vacuum, a screw or a bent wire, to remove most of the dust from the hole.
- Press the shield into the hole.
- Tap it with a hammer if you need to.

3 Add bolt

- Push against the wall as you screw in the bolt (here we show an eye bolt).
- The shield will expand and grip the wall as you screw in the bolt.
- If the shield pulls out, remove it, drill a bit deeper, and try again.

Repointing Brick Walls

Decades of weather exposure will cause mortar joints to become porous. As a result, cracks and gaps appear, and they will get worse in time. The solution is a process called repointing or tuckpointing.

Special Measures for Older Homes

Most brick homes built before World War II feature double- or triple-brick construction. In these cases, two or three wythes of bricks were used because the bricks provided the structural support for the house.

It is very important that these sorts of walls be able to breathe. Moisture, which inevitably forms inside of a wall because of condensation, must be able to "exhale" through the mortar. Otherwise, moisture in a wall will seep through the bricks and cause serious damage.

So if you have an older home, be sure your repointing mortar contains lime. Limed mortar will breathe, while the more common cementitious mortar will not. Even professional repointers sometimes neglect this crucial detail, and the results can be disastrous.

If you have a newer home, the bricks are simply a single wythe of veneer, and the house's actual structure is made of wood studs. This type of wall has weep holes near the bottom that allow moisture to escape. It's fine to use standard cementitious mortar on this type of wall; just don't plug the weep holes.

A masonry supply store might have mortar color samples, which can help you choose a new mortar that blends in with the old.

How to Do It

Repointing a small area does not take special skill, but if you have a large area to cover, consider hiring a pro. Experienced repointers grind out joints quickly, and they have scaffolding that enables them to reach high areas.

Test that you have the right color before repointing. A masonry supply store will have a fairly wide choice of premixed colors.

If none of the samples quite match, consider mixing your own color using powdered colorant. Keep careful track of the recipe so you can repeat it with each batch.

For a small area, you can chip out the old mortar with a narrow cold chisel and a hammer, or a raking tool. But a grinder does a better and faster job.

1 Grind joints

- Equip a grinder with a masonry blade.
- Wear long clothing, gloves, and protective eyewear, as chips will fly.
- Get into a comfortable position and grind carefully to avoid damaging the bricks.

2 Clean joints

- Use a hand raking tool to finish cleaning out the mortar.
- At corners and edges, use a narrow cold chisel and a hammer to remove the last bits.

3 Check depth

- Make sure you have removed mortar to a depth of at least $1/2$ inch at all points.
- The raking tool shown here has a built-in depth gauge.

4 Repoint

- Mix a batch of mortar stiff enough to stick to a trowel. If the new mortar is too thin, it will flake off in time.
- Load a dollop of mortar onto a hawk or a flat trowel and press it against the wall, just below the joint.
- Use a repointing tool to scrape mortar into the joint, pressing firmly.
- Fill horizontals first, then verticals.

5 Strike or brush

- If surrounding joints are tooled, smooth the joints using a striking tool (see pages 211 and 215).
- If surrounding joints bulge slightly outward, simply brush the new mortar to match.

Striking Tips

With practice, you can produce joints that nearly match those already on the wall. Practice with a striking tool until you are proficient. Press firmly to eliminate any air bubbles. When applying mortar to a vertical joint, scrape from the top down.

Chimney Repairs

Masonry chimneys and fireplaces are notorious trouble spots. Have yours inspected annually by an expert to make sure it is safe. A buildup of creosote on the inside of a chimney must be cleaned, or it could cause a chimney fire. If a chimney is blocked, building a fire could fill the house with smoke.

On the outside, the upper part of a chimney is exposed to the weather and hard to reach. As a result, mortar and brick problems are common. Check the joints and repoint them as needed. If the bricks themselves are flaking or cracking, call in a mason to determine whether you can simply seal them or if you'll need to rebuild the chimney.

At the top of a chimney, it's often a good idea to install a metal cap, which keeps critters and most rainwater out. Installing one is easy, as long as you measure carefully and get one that fits.

Where the chimney meets the roof, you'll usually find a complicated arrangement of metal flashing, which includes multiple pieces of step flashing along the sides, with specially shaped flashing pieces at the top and bottom. Some of these pieces are bent at the top and inserted into mortar joints. If you have flashing problems, you probably need to call in a roofer, because it's difficult to install this stuff correctly. However, if you notice that flashing has come loose, or if caulking has gaps, you can apply repair caulk.

Replacing Bricks & Blocks

If only a few bricks or blocks are damaged, they can be replaced. However, if the wall has general damage, you're better off replacing the wall or covering it with stucco.

Working with Bricks

Take a brick to a masonry supply source to find a replacement that nearly matches in color and size. Also buy mortar that matches the existing mortar.

1 Cut around

- Use a grinder equipped with a masonry blade to cut deeply into the horizontal joints above and below the brick.
- Cut carefully to avoid damaging surrounding bricks.
- Drill holes every 2 inches or so through the mortar all around the brick.

2 Chip out

- Use a hand sledge or a mason's hammer and a cold chisel to break the brick, then chip it away.
- Chisel out all the old mortar.
- Use a wire brush to clear all debris, and wipe the area with a wet cloth.

3 Replace brick

- Apply a thick bed of mortar to the bottom of the brick.
- Wet the brick and butter its top and sides with mortar.
- Set the brick on a trowel and slip it straight into the opening.
- Scrape away squeezed-out mortar and press to fill any gaps.
- Strike the joint to match the surrounding area.

Working with Blocks

1 Drill holes

- Drill a series of holes throughout the damaged block.
- Where you encounter a solid web of hairline cracks, drill only an inch deep.

2 Chip away

- Use a grinder to cut mortar around the block.
- With a hammer and a cold chisel, break the block's face.
- Save webs if you can, but it's okay if a web crumbles.
- Cut a replacement block in half lengthwise (see page 113).

3 Prep the opening

- Tap debris into the cavity so holes are nearly filled.
- Set two ¼-inch-thick shims in the bottom of the opening.
- Test-fit the new block face and further cut the opening or the face as needed.

4 Set block face

- Mix a batch of stiff mortar.
- Dampen the new block face and the opening in the wall.
- Spread a thick layer of mortar onto the bottom and sides of the opening.
- Lightly butter the bottom and sides of the face and heavily butter the top.
- Press the face into place, taking care not to push too far.
- Allow the mortar to stiffen, then remove the shims and fill in any gaps.

Stucco Repair

Occasional cracks and holes in stucco should be repaired soon so they won't grow. If problems affect an entire wall, call in a pro to assess whether you need to rebuild the wall.

Choosing Materials

Small cracks can be filled with caulk and then painted. For large cracks and holes up to about 6 inches wide, use a stucco-patching compound.

For even larger holes, apply two or three coats of stucco. The first one or two coats form the base. Scarify, or scratch, the base coat so the finish coat will adhere firmly. For the first coat(s), buy a bag of stucco base-coat mix. For the final coat, purchase a stucco finish mix of the desired color, or apply white stucco and paint it later. Spend some time practicing finishing techniques so the patch will blend in with its surroundings.

Fill a Crack

Narrow cracks in masonry can be repaired with stucco caulk. Clean the area with a wire brush, then apply the caulk. Use a trowel, your finger, or a brush to wipe the caulk so it blends. After the caulk dries, paint it.

Repairing a Hole

1 Prep the hole

- Remove all loose stucco with a hammer and a cold chisel.
- Scrub the area with a wire brush.

2 Patch

- Mix a batch of stucco patch.
- Apply it with a trowel.
- If the hole is deep, apply the patch mix in two or three coats, scratching the bottom coats with a nail so the next coats will adhere.

3 Texture

- Before the top coat sets, trowel it fairly even with the surrounding surface.
- Use a whisk broom, trowel, or other tool to match the surrounding texture (see pages 226–227).

Glossary

A

adobe Clay bricks made into blocks. Originally, adobe was dried in the sun. Modern adobe is typically fired in a kiln and may be reinforced with asphalt.

ashlar Stones cut into rectangular units; used for building walls with a geometric appearance.

B

batter The way a retaining wall leans back toward the soil it retains, to add greater strength.

bleed water Moisture that rises to the surface of concrete as it is being worked. Bleed water should be allowed to dry before the concrete is worked further.

bolster A device, made of wire or of a small concrete block with wire, used to hold rebar at the correct height.

brick A paving unit made from clay that has been molded and fired in a kiln.

buttering Smearing mortar with a trowel onto one or more edges of a brick or other masonry unit just prior to setting it in place. Tiles may be "back buttered," meaning that mortar is troweled onto their backs.

C

concrete A mixture of water, sand, gravel or crushed stone, and portland cement.

concrete block A wall unit formed of high-strength concrete, usually with two or three hollow cells.

concrete pavers Paving units formed from high-strength concrete; available in a variety of sizes and shapes.

control joint A shallow line that is meant to contain stress cracks and is scribed in a concrete slab.

course In a masonry wall, one horizontal row.

curing The process by which concrete or mortar achieves maximum strength in the weeks after being installed. The slower the curing process, the stronger the final product will be.

D

dry-mix concrete Bags, usually 60 or 80 lb., containing all the dry ingredients of concrete; add water and mix in a wheelbarrow or trough.

E

edging The process of rounding the edge of a concrete slab to make it less likely to chip when bumped.

efflorescence A whitish discoloration on brick that typically occurs when moisture causes minerals to bleed to the surface.

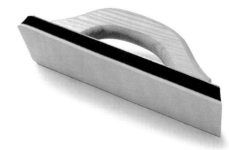

finishing The third and final step (after screeding and floating) in smoothing concrete; usually done with either a steel trowel or a broom.

floating The intermediate stage of smoothing wet concrete (see screeding and finishing), usually using a bullfloat, a darby, or a magnesium float. Floating causes bleed water to rise to the surface.

footing A concrete base used for the support of structures. A wall requires a long footing that is wider than the wall. To avoid frost heave in cold climates, a footing should extend below the frost line.

frost line The maximum depth at which soil freezes during winter. This measurement is determined by local building codes.

header A wall brick or block that is positioned perpendicular to the stretchers so that its short end, rather than its longer side, is visible when the wall is completed.

isolation joint The junction where a concrete slab is mechanically separated from an abutting surface, usually with a fibrous isolation joint material. This inhibits cracks from forming when the slab heaves or expands and contracts differently than the abutting surface.

mortar A mixture of portland cement, sand, water, and sometimes lime, used to join masonry units.

paver Any regularly sized unit used to form the finished surface of a patio. The most common pavers are paving bricks, concrete pavers, and cut stones.

plumb The condition of being perfectly vertical, in other words, exactly 90 degrees from level.

portland cement A mixture of lime, silica, alumina, and iron that has been fired and then crushed into a fine powder. The result is a powerful adhesive used in mortar and concrete.

ready-mixed concrete Concrete delivered wet in a truck, ready to pour.

reinforcing bar (rebar) Lengths of steel pole used to strengthen concrete. Rebar is typically set in the middle of the concrete's thickness, and the pieces are tied together with wire.

reinforcing wire or mesh Steel wire welded into a grid, commonly with 6-inch squares; stucco lath is a denser mesh that should be used for smaller projects.

repointing Also called tuckpointing. Refinishing mortar joints that have begun to decay.

rowlock A cap brick (used to finish the top of a wall) laid on edge and perpendicular to the wall.

sailor On a patio, an edging brick set standing upright with its face outward.

screeding The first step in smoothing wet concrete, typically by moving a straight board across the top form boards. Screeding also refers to smoothing a sand bed prior to installing pavers. In that case, a special screeding guide is used. The guide is composed of two pieces of lumber attached so as to screed the sand at a height that is one paver thickness below the edging. In another type of installation, lengths of pipe are used as screed guides.

soldier An edging brick set upright with the edge facing out.

story pole A tool used to quickly check that bricks in a wall are at the correct height. It consists of a board marked at regular intervals; each mark indicates the center of a mortar joint between bricks.

stretcher A wall brick or block laid lengthwise. In a typical wall, most bricks or blocks are stretchers.

stucco A particularly hard form of mortar, often made with white portland cement.

surface bonding agent A stucco-like material applied to the face of concrete blocks that have been stacked, rather than mortared, in place.

tuckpointing (See repointing.)

weep hole A hole, near the bottom of a mortared retaining wall or a house wall, through which collected moisture can seep out. Never plug weep holes, or you could damage the wall.

wythe In a masonry wall, the width of one brick or block board across the top form.

Resources & Credits

Acknowledgments

We'd like to thank the professionals and companies who helped us with this book:

A-1 Contractors
www.a1contractorsinc.com

Aitken & Associates
www.aitkenlandscapes.com

Jeffrey Bale Garden Design
www.jeffreygardens.com

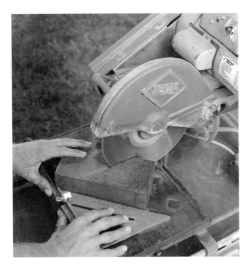

Blue Sky Design
www.blueskydesignsinc.com

Gray Bragdon
The Studio at Stone Haven
Olympia, WA

The Care of Trees
www.thecareoftrees.com

Chalet Landscape Company
www.chaletnursery.com

McNear Brick & Block
www.mcnear.com

Joseph Salerno Designs
www.josephsalernodesigns.com/

Resources

Advanced Pavement Technology
www.advancedpavement.com

Allan Block
www.allanblock.com

GardenMolds
www.gardenmolds.com

Keystone Retaining Wall Systems
www.keystonewalls.com

Modello Designs
www.modelloconcrete.com

Oly-Ola Edgings
www.olyola.com

Original Color Chips
www.originalcolorchips.com

Portland Cement Association
www.cement.org

Robinson Brick
www.robinsonbrick.com

SoCal Custom Concrete
www.socalcustomconcrete.com/

Soil Retention Systems, Inc.
www.soilretention.com

Sonoma Cast Stone
www.sonomastone.com

Photo Credits

T = *top*, B = *bottom*, L = *left*, R = *right*, M = *middle*

All photos by Steve Cory unless noted below.

Courtesy *Advance Pavement Technology:* 128–129 all; Courtesy Aitkin and Associates: 61TL, 61BL, 225BR; Courtesy Allan Block: 222TL, 226TL; Courtesy Amerimax: 289BL; Courtesy Blue Sky Designs: 13 all, 56BR, 74 all, 84TL, 84TR, 138BL, 152TL, 182BL, 182BM, 182BR, 226TL; Marion Brenner: 15T, 67BR, 72T, 72BM, 72BR, 94TL, 208BL, 242–245 all; Karen Bussolini: 22B, 86BR, 94B; *Wayne Cable:* 42BL, 42, BR,

43BL, 43BR, 64TM, 64BMR, 67TL, 152BM, 152BR, 153 all, 162 bottom row, 163TR, 163TM, 164BL, 164BR, 165 all; *David Cavagnarro:* 66BL; Peter Christiansen: 14BL; Courtesy Dacor: 248BL; Janet Davis: 136TR; R. Todd Davis: 29MR; Sergio De Paula: 249BL, 250TL, 250TM, 250BR, 256–257 all; Alan & Linda Detrick: 10 all, 15B, 28 all, 35TR, 54TL, 55TR, 86T, 86TM, 89TL, 89TR, 100TL, 104T, 116TL, 122TR, 158TR, 190 all, 191B, 198TL, 209BR; Andrew Drake: 208TL; Courtesy DRYLOK: 285TR, 285 bottom row; Catriona Tudor: 194TR, 199BR, 209MR; Cheryl Fenton: 18TM, 18TR, 40, 41, 101 bottom row; *Scott Fitzgerrell:* 40 (4), 41 (4), 43BL; Roger Foley: 32BL, 136TM, 248T; Frank Gaglione: 14BM, 14BL, 15BL, 15B, 16 (2), 17BL, 19T, 20 all except BL, 22T, 24B, 25TM, 25TR inset, 40 (3), 40 (4), 42–43 (21), 45TM, 45TR, 45BL, 45BM, 46BL, 46BR, 47 top row, 48 all except TR, 49 all except TL, 51TM, 51TR, 51BL, 51BM, 56TL, 56TM, 64TL, 67TM, 67BL, 72BL, 73 all, 74BR, 75 all,

80BM, 80BR, 87 top row, 88 all, 96TR, 97BM, 98BL, 98BR, 101 top row, 102 bottom row, 103 all, 105–107 all, 108 bottom row, 110 all except TR, 111–114 all, 115TL, 115BL, 115BM, 116R, 117 all, 118TL, 118TR, 120 all, 127 all, 130BL, 130BR, 132BL, 132BM, 137TR, 141 all, 146BL, 156TM, 156TR, 157BM, 157BR, 168BR, 180BM, 180BR, 181TM, 181TR, 181BL, 181BM, 183 all, 184MR, 184BL, 184BR, 185TL, 185TR, 193BR, 197 top row, 205 all, 214BM, 214BR, 215–216 all, 217 top row, 222BL, 222BR, 223 all, 226 all except T, 227 all, 228BR, 229all, 249TR, 249M, 249BR, 245T, 255T, 259T, 266BL, 266BR, 266TL, 266TR, 270BL, 270BR, 271 top row, 271BL, 274–276 all, 287 (3), 288 all; J. S. Sira/Garden Picture Library: 233TL; Courtesy Garden Molds: 81T (4); John Granen: 249MR; Dave Toht/Greenleaf Publishing: 60TR, 134 bottom row, 135 all, 227BR, 251–253 all, 264–265 all, 289TL, 289TM, 289BM; Steven Gunther: 162TR; *Pamela Harper: 85TL, 202TL; Philip Harvey: 25TR, 41TR; Saxon Holt: 9 all, 14T, 21BL, 22B, 24T, 25BL, 26BR, 55TL, 67TR, 82BL, 87BR, 124TL, 127TL, 140TL, 140BL, 191T, 208T, 210T, 238TR;* Courtesy *Jeffrey Bale:* 268TL, 268TR; Courtesy Keystone Retaining Wall Systems: 192TL, 193 top row, 193BL; Dennis Krukowski: 95B; *Chuck Kuhn:* 33BL, 33BR, 115BL, 115BM, 124 all except TL, 125 all, 146 all except BL, 168TL, 169T (4), 171BL, 175 all, 177TL, 177TM, 177BR, 180TL, 186 bottom row, 187 all, 194BR, 195 all, 200 bottom row, 201 all, 262–263 all, 267M, 267B, 272–273 all, 277–282 all; A. M. Leonard: 46BM, 98TL; Janet Loughrey: 208BR; *Allan Mandell:* 64BMR, 65BR, 67BR, 82T, 83TR, 97BR, 126BL, 198 bottom row, 199 top row, 199BL, 204R, 266TL, 268 bottom row, 269 all; *Charles Mann:* 82TL, 138TR, 236TR; Courtesy *Marvel:* 248BR; Courtesy *Modello*

Designs: 150–151 all; Courtesy Mucktruck: 56BL; Courtesy Mutual Materials: 132TR; Courtesy Oly-Ola Edgings: 96BR, 100BR; Courtesy Original Color Chips Company: 147 all; Jerry Pavia: 11 all, 35L, 58TR, 67BL, 70BL, 86BL, 107TR, 134T, 138BM, 196T, 204TL, 209L, 209TR, 211BL, 216TL; Norman A. Plate: 85TR, 130T, 131 all, 133TR, 133 bottom row, 232 all, 234 all, 240–241 all; Courtesy Portland Cement Association: 171TR, 173BL, 286TL; Courtesy Robinson Brick: 15BR, 20BL; Susan A. Roth: 70, 95T, 137B; *Mark Rutherford:* 41TM, 41TR, 172TR; Loren Santow: 12, 19L, 64TM, 79 all, 173TR, 174 bottom row, 176 all, 177TR, 177BL, 178–179 all; Courtesy *SoCal Custom Concrete:* 148–149 all; Courtesy SoilRetention.com: 90–91 all; Courtesy Sonoma Cast Stone: 19B; *Thomas J. Story:* 23T, 76–77 all, 99 top row, 235 all, 238–239 all; *Dan Stultz:* 30TR, 56TR, 67TL, 81 bottom row, 107TL, 163 bottom row, 168BR, 197 bottom row, 221 all, 227BL, 227BM, 251BL, 251BM, 284 all except TL, 260–261 all, 271BR, 287TL, 287 bottom row, 289BR, 290BL, 290BR, 291TM, 291TR, 292–295 all; *Michael S. Thompson:* 27TR, 89B; *Tim Street-Porter:* 126TL; *Spencer Toy:* 16M, 17BM, 17BR, 96TL; *Jessie Walker:* 80TR; *Russ Widstrand:* 8, 17TR, 21TR, 26T, 36, 55TL, 71TL, 174TR, 181BR; *Michael Winokur:* 80BL, 286TR; *Karen Witynski:* 29TR

Illustration Credits

T = *top*, B = *bottom*, L = *left*, R = *right*, M = *middle*

Anthony Davis: 136M, 136, 136BR, 192TR; Tracy La Rue Hohn: 236–238 all, 240T, 242BL; Jim Kopp Illustration, Inc: 171L; Greg Maxson: 100BL, 100BM, 128T, 179TL; *Bill Oetinger: 27B (4),* 29 all, 30–32 all, 34 all, 44, 46 all, 58–59 all, 82 all, 117L (8), 140TR, 168ML, 170 all, 173BR, 175BR, 179BR, 194L, 198TR, 210–211 all; *Rik Olson: 83 all, 104 all,* 138–139 all, 196 all, 204BL, 233 all; Ian Worpole: 252BL, 254B, 255B, 256R

Index

You Can Build...
Do-it-yourself • Pro-level results
Step-by-step instructions

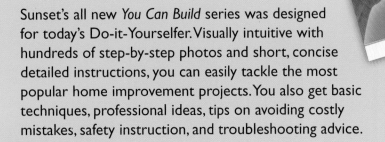

Sunset's all new *You Can Build* series was designed for today's Do-it-Yourselfer. Visually intuitive with hundreds of step-by-step photos and short, concise detailed instructions, you can easily tackle the most popular home improvement projects. You also get basic techniques, professional ideas, tips on avoiding costly mistakes, safety instruction, and troubleshooting advice.